JIG AND FIXTURE DESIGN

JIG AND FIXTURE

DESIGN

A TREATISE COVERING THE PRINCI-
PLES OF JIG AND FIXTURE DESIGN,
THE IMPORTANT CONSTRUCTIONAL
DETAILS, AND MANY DIFFERENT
TYPES OF WORK-HOLDING DEVICES

EDITED BY
FRANKLIN D. JONES

FOURTH EDITION
1960 PRINTING

PUBLISHERS OF MACHINERY
& MACHINERY'S HANDBOOK

The
INDUSTRIAL
PRESS

93 WORTH STREET   NEW YORK 13, N. Y.

Distributors for the British Empire
MACHINERY PUBLISHING CO., NATIONAL HOUSE
WEST STREET, BRIGHTON 1, ENGLAND

Library of Congress Catalog Card Number 55-7771
PRINTED IN THE UNITED STATES OF AMERICA

CONTENTS

and sliding bushings used as locating means. Adjustable
locating points. Special types of adjustable stops. Locating
from finished holes. Locating by keyways in the work. Common defects in jig design.

Types of clamps. Hook-bolts. Screw tightening devices.
Swinging leaves. Wedge or taper gib. Eccentric clamping
arrangements. Applications to jig design. Conclusion.

Drill jig having automatic locating devices. Cam-operated
clamping slide on drill jig. Jig for drilling ring. Indexing jig
operated by hand-lever and foot-treadle. Jig having lever-
and spring-operated clamping members. Drill jig for fork
links. Drill jig for machining half holes. Jigs having rockers
upon which it is turned over. Drill jig designed for rapid
indexing. Indexing jig provided with work-locating device.
Indexing jigs mounted on trunnions. Multiple drill jig for
yoke ends. A vise drilling jig. Jig for drilling deep holes in
studs. Jig for straight and angular drilling. Quick-operating
drill jig. Drill jig equipped with milling attachment. Jig for
cross-drilling pistons. Jig for facing bosses in pistons. Universal jigs. Jig attachments for drilling in vises. Multiple
drilling jig of reversible type. Jig for drilling power press
dial plates. Duplex clamping arrangement on drill jig.

Boring jig of simple design. Adjustable boring jigs. Boring
jig supported on work. Jigs for supporting bar on one side of
hole only. When holes are not parallel. Jigs for multiple
boring. Boring jig designs. Four-part boring jig. Alignment
of jig when holes are at an angle. Using work to guide
boring-bar. Combination drill and boring jigs.

Detachable jaws for vise. Fixture for milling to given
length. Duplex fixture. Adjustable fixture for angular work.
Fixture arranged for lateral and angular adjustment. Lever-
operated fixture for milling oil-groove in bushing. Indexing
milling fixture for roller separator. Indexing fixture for
milling clutches. Radial milling fixtures. Radial fixture for
rough-milling slot. Pivoted type of radial fixture. Radial

fixture for gear-cutting operation. Radial fixture having hand- and power-operated feed. Profile milling fixture for recoil cylinder liner. Duplex fixture for routing oil-grooves. Planing fixtures. Planing fixtures for lathe carriage casting. Gang-planing fixtures. Radial planing fixture.

Important points in design. Adjustable fixture for holding castings of different diameters. Adjustable fixture for special bevel-gear blanks. Adjustable fixture with means of maintaining accuracy. Adjustable fixtures for the vertical boring mill. Fixture with adjustable driver and soft internal jaws. Adjustable fixture for a cast-iron bracket. Adjustable fixture for a bronze worm-gear sector.

Important points in the application of the floating principle. Piston drill jig with floating clamps. Drill jig for a rough collar. Drill jig with floating bushings and locating vees. Milling fixture with floating clamps and locator. Locating device with floating pressure compensator. Chucking fixture with floating clamps and taper locating plug. Two-jaw chuck arranged with a floating jaw. Piston chuck having floating clamping features. Chuck jaws with floating locating points. Floating clamping ring on grinding fixture.

Three-point locating and clamping devices. Three-point support for flywheel fixture. Three-point fixture for a pot casting. Two methods of obtaining a three-point support on a hub casting. Fixture having three clamping jaws and three locating pads. Double three-point locating device.

Points pertaining to upkeep. Drill jig for a receiver forging. Drilling and reaming jig. Indexing fixture for a clutch gear. Fixture with inserted jaws. Bevel-gear fixture with adjustable features. Fixture for a hub casting.

CHAPTER XV

Tests for warpage or distortion and vibration. Welded jigs
and fixtures cost less than the cast type. Arc-welded jig is
light and strong. Establishing standards for welded construction. Materials used. Assembling, welding, and annealing.
Sand-blasting and painting. Standard shapes for welded jigs
and fixtures. Jigs and fixtures can be changed to suit changes
in product. Examples showing flexibility of design.

CHAPTER XVI

How cylinders are loaded simultaneously. Locating the cylinders automatically. Jig designed to shift the cylinder blocks
transversely. Operation of the dumping table. Milling ends
of crankshaft bearings. Fixture for cylinder boring machine.
Jig that clamps from the bottom. Jig that automatically
raises, locates, and clamps cylinder heads.

CHAPTER XVII

What are universal drill jigs? Speed of operation with uni-
versal drill jigs. Interchangeability of universal drill jigs.
Tool and design costs saved by using universal drill jigs.
Savings in time-study cost. Where are universal drill jigs
used to best advantage? Design practice as applied to universal jigs. The location of the work in universal drill jigs.
Locating work concentrically. When chip clearance is required. Case I — Concentric internal location from top plate.
Case II — Concentric internal location from adapter. Case
III — Concentric external location from top plate. Case IV
— Concentric external location from adapter. Radial location in universal jigs. Radial location from top plate. Radial
location from the adapter. Coolant reservoir. Tools for making top plates. Simple drill plate. Dividing-head fixture.

CHAPTER XVIII

Advantages of plastic jigs. Production of plastic drill jigs.
Examples of plastic jig construction. Experiments with
different materials.

CHAPTER XIX

Self-centralizing devices for jigs. Simple clamp for accurately locating fixtures on a machine table. Jig for drilling and counterboring unevenly spaced holes. Adjustable bushing plate for casting variations. Toggle-action drill jig to clamp casting at four points. Work-holding fixtures for special lathe operations. Chucks for holding work-pieces by threaded portions. Vise with hydraulic jaw for clamping irregular-shaped castings. Jig designed for rapid drilling. Indexing fixture for milling thrust-type washers. Drill chuck adapted as work-holding device. Quick-acting milling fixture. Fixture for holding small parts in series. Fixture jaws combining downward pull with closing action.

CHAPTER I

PRINCIPLES OF JIG DESIGN

Jigs and fixtures may be defined as devices used in the manu-facture of duplicate parts of machines and intended to make possible interchangeable work at a reduced cost, as compared with the cost of producing each machine detail individually. Jigs and fixtures serve the purpose of holding and properly locating a piece of work while machined, and are provided with necessary appliances for guiding, supporting, setting, and gaging the tools in such a manner that all the work produced in the same jig or fixture will be alike in all respects, even with the employment of unskilled labor. When using the expression "alike," it implies, of course, simply that the pieces will be near enough alike for the purposes for which the work being machined is intended. Thus, for certain classes of work, wider limits of variation will be permissible without affecting the proper use of the piece machined, while in other cases the limits of variation will be so small as to make the expression "perfectly alike" literally true.

Objects of Jigs and Fixtures. — The main object of using jigs and fixtures is the reduction of the cost of machines or machine details made in great numbers. This reduction of cost is obtained in consequence of the increased rapidity with which the machines may be built and the employment of cheaper labor, which is possible when using tools for interchangeable manufacturing. Another object, not less important, is the accuracy with which the work can be produced, making it possible to assemble the pieces produced in jigs without any great amount of fitting in the assembling department, thus also effecting a great saving in this respect. The use of jigs and fixtures practically does away with the fitting, as this expression was understood in the old-time shop; it eliminates cut-and-try methods, and does

away with so-called "patch-work" in the production of machinery. It makes it possible to have all the machines built in the
shop according to the drawings, a thing which is rather difficult
to do if each individual machine in a large lot is built without
reference to the other machines in the same lot.

The interchangeability obtained by the use of jigs and fixtures
makes it also an easy matter to quickly replace broken or worn-
out parts without great additional cost and trouble. When
machines are built on the individual plan, it is necessary to fit
the part replacing the broken or worn-out piece, in place, involving considerable extra expense, not to mention the delay and the
difficulties occasioned thereby.

As mentioned, jigs and fixtures permit the employment of
practically unskilled labor. There are many operations in the
building of a machine, which, if each machine were built individually, without the use of special tools, would require the work
of expert machinists and toolmakers. Special tools, in the form
of jigs and fixtures, permit equally good, or, in some cases, even
better results to be obtained by a much cheaper class of labor,
provided the jigs and fixtures are properly designed and correctly made. Another possibility for saving, particularly in the
case of drill and boring jigs provided with guide bushings in the
same plane, is met with in the fact that such jigs are adapted to
be used in multiple-spindle drills, thereby still more increasing
the rapidity with which the work may be produced. In shops
where a great many duplicate parts are made, containing a
number of drilled holes, multiple-spindle drills of complicated
design, which may be rather expensive as regards first cost, are
really cheaper, by far, than ordinary simple drill presses.

Another advantage which has been gained by the use of jigs
and fixtures, and which should not be lost sight of in the enu-
meration of the points in favor of building machinery by the use
of special tools, is that the details of a machine that has been
provided with a complete equipment of accurate and durable
jigs and fixtures can all be finished simultaneously in different
departments of a large factory, without inconvenience, thus making it possible to assemble the machine at once after receiving

the parts from the different departments; and there is no need of waiting for the completion of one part into which another is required to fit, before making this latter part. This gain in time means a great deal in manufacturing, and was entirely impossible under the old-time system of machine building, when each part had to be made in the order in which it went to the finished machine, and each consecutive part had to be lined up with each one of the previously made and assembled details. Brackets, bearings, etc., had to be drilled in place, often with ratchet drills, which is a slow and always inconvenient operation.

Difference between Jigs and Fixtures. — To exactly define the word "jig," as considered apart from the word "fixture," is difficult, as the difference between a jig and a fixture is oftentimes not very easy to decide. The word jig is frequently, although incorrectly, applied to any kind of a work-holding appliance used in the building of machinery, the same as, in some shops, the word fixture is applied to all kinds of special tools. As a general rule, however, a jig is a special tool, which, while it holds the work, or is held onto the work, also contains guides for the respective tools to be used; whereas a fixture is only holding the work while the cutting tools are performing the operation on the piece, without containing any special arrangements for guiding these tools. The fixture, therefore, must, itself, be securely held or fixed to the machine on which the operation is performed; hence the name. A fixture, however, may sometimes be provided with a number of gages and stops, although it does not contain any special devices for the guiding of the tools.

The definition given, in a general way, would therefore classify jigs as special tools used particularly in drilling and boring operations, while fixtures, in particular, would be those special tools used on milling machines, and, in some cases, on planers, shapers, and slotting machines. Special tools used on the lathe may be either of the nature of jigs or fixtures, and sometimes the special tool is actually a combination of both, in which case the term drilling fixture, boring fixture, etc., is suitable.

Fundamental Principles of Jig Design. — Before entering upon a discussion of the minor details of the design of jigs and fixtures, the fundamental principles of jig and fixture design will be briefly outlined. Whenever a jig is made for a component part of a machine, it is almost always required that a corresponding jig be made up for the place on the machine, or other part, where the first-mentioned detail is to be attached. It is, of course, absolutely necessary that these two jigs be perfectly alike as to the location of guides and gage points. In order to have the holes and guides in the two jigs in alignment, it is advisable, and almost always cheaper and quicker, to transfer the holes or the gage points from the first jig made to the other. In many instances, it is possible to use the same jig for both parts. Cases where the one or the other of these principles is applicable will be shown in the following chapters in the detailed descriptions of drill and boring jigs.

There are some cases where it is not advisable to make two jigs, one for each of the two parts which are to fit together. It may be impossible to properly locate the jig on one of the parts to be drilled, or, if the jig were made, it may be so complicated that it would not be economical. Under such conditions the component part itself may be used as a jig, and the respective holes in this part used as guides for the tools when machining the machine details into which it fits. Guide bushings for the drills and boring bars may then be placed in the holes in the component part itself. In many cases, drilling and boring operations are also done, to great advantage, by using the brackets and bearings already assembled and fastened to the machine body as guides.

One of the most important questions to be decided before making a jig is the amount of money which can be expended on a special tool for the operation required. In many cases, it is possible to get a highly efficient tool by making it more complicated and more expensive, whereas a less efficient tool may be produced at very small expense. To decide which of these two types of jigs and fixtures should be designed in each individual case depends entirely upon the circumstances. There should be a careful comparison of the present cost of carrying out a certain operation, the expected cost of carrying out the same operation with an efficient tool, and the cost of building that tool itself. Unless this is done, it is likely that the shop is burdened with a great number of special tools and fixtures which, while they may be very useful for the production of the parts for which they are intended, actually involve a loss. It is readily seen how uneconomical it would be to make an expensive jig and fixture for a machine or a part of a machine that would only have to be duplicated a few times. In some cases, of course, there may be a gain in using special devices in order to get extremely good and accurate results.

Locating Points. — The most important requirements in the design of jigs are that good facilities be provided for locating the work, and that the piece to be machined may be easily inserted and quickly taken out of the jig, so that no time is wasted in placing the work in position on the machine performing the work. In some cases, a longer time is required for locating and clamping the piece to be worked upon than is required for the actual machine operation itself. In all such cases the machine performing the work is actually idle the greater part of the time, and, added to the loss of the operator's time, is the increased expense for machine cost incurred by such a condition. For this reason, the locating and clamping of the work in place quickly and accurately should be carefully studied by the designer before any attempt is made to design the tool. In choosing the locating surface or points of the piece or part, consideration must be given to the facilities for locating the corresponding part of the machine in a similar manner. It is highly important that this be done, as otherwise, although the jigs may be alike, as far as their guiding appliances are concerned, there may be no facility for locating the corresponding part in the same manner as the one already drilled, and while the holes drilled may coincide, other surfaces, also required to coincide, may be considerably out of line. One of the main principles of location, therefore, is that two component parts of the machine should be located from corresponding points and surfaces.

If possible, special arrangements should be made in the design of the jig so that it is impossible to insert the piece in any but

the correct way. Mistakes are often made on this account
in shops where a great deal of cheap help is used, pieces being
placed in jigs upside down, or in some way other than the correct one, and work that has been previously machined at the
expenditure of a great deal of time is entirely spoiled. Therefore, whenever possible, a jig should be made "fool-proof."

When the work to be machined varies in shape and size, as,
for instance, in the case of rough castings, it is necessary to have
at least some of the locating points adjustable and placed so
that they can be easily reached for adjustment, but, at the same
time, so fastened that they are, to a certain extent, positive. In
the following chapters different kinds of adjustable locating
points will be described in detail.

Clamping Devices. — The strapping or clamping arrangements
should be as simple as possible, without sacrificing effectiveness,
and the strength of the clamps should be such as to not only hold
the piece firmly in place, but also to take the strain of the cutting
tools without springing or "giving." When designing the jig,
the direction in which the strain of the tool or cutters acts upon
the work should always be considered, and the clamps so placed
that they will have the highest degree of strength to resist the
pressure of the cut.

The main principles in the application of clamps to a jig or
fixture are that they should be convenient for the operator,
quickly operated, and, when detached from the work, still connected with the jig or fixture itself, so as to prevent the operator from losing them. Many a time, looking for lost straps,
clamps, screws, etc., causes more delay in shops than the extra
cost incurred in designing a jig or fixture somewhat more complicated, in order to make the binding arrangement an integral
part of the fixture itself. Great complication in the clamping
arrangements, however, is not advisable. Usually clamping
arrangements of this kind work well when the fixture is new, but,
as the various parts become worn, complicated arrangements
are more likely to get out of order, and the extra cost incurred in
repairing often outweighs the temporary gain in quickness of
operation.

The judgment of the designer is, in every case, the most important point in the design of jigs and fixtures. Definite rules for all cases cannot be given. General principles can be studied, but the efficiency of the individual tool will depend entirely upon the judgment of the tool designer in applying the general principles of tool design to the case in hand.

When designing the jig or fixture, the locating and bearing points for the work and the location of the clamps must also be so selected that there is as little liability as possible of springing the piece or jig, or both, out of shape, when applying the clamps. The springing of either the one or the other part will cause incorrect results, as the work surfaces will be out of alignment with the holes drilled or the faces milled. The clamps or straps should therefore, as far as possible, be so placed that they are exactly opposite some bearing point or surface on the work.

Weight of Jigs. — The designer must use his judgment in regard to the amount of metal put into the jig or fixture. It is desirable to make these tools as light as possible, in order that they may be easily handled, be of smaller size, and cost less in regard to the amount of material used for their making, but, at the same time, it is poor economy to sacrifice any of the rigidity and stiffness of the tool, as this is one of the main considerations in obtaining efficient results. On large-sized jigs and fixtures, it is possible to core out the metal in a number of places, without decreasing, in the least, the strength of the jig itself. The corners of jigs and fixtures should always be well rounded, and all burrs and sharp edges filed off, so as to make them convenient and pleasant for handling. Smaller jigs should also be made with handles in proper places, so that they may be held in position while working, as in the case of drilling jigs, and also for convenience in moving the jig about.

Jigs Provided with Feet. — Ordinary drill jigs should always be provided with feet or legs on all sides which are opposite the holes for the bushings, so that the jig can be placed level on the table of the machine. These feet also greatly facilitate the making of the jig, making it easier to lay out and plane the different finished surfaces. On the sides of the jig where no feet are required, if the body is made from a casting, it is of advantage to have small projecting lugs for bearing surfaces when laying out and planing. While jigs are most commonly provided with four feet on each side, in some cases it is sufficient to provide the tool with only three feet, but care should be taken in either case that all bushings and places where pressure will be applied to the tool are placed *inside* of the geometrical figure obtained by connecting, by lines, the points of location for the feet.

While it may seem that three feet are preferable to use, because the jig will then always obtain a bearing on all the three feet, which it would not with four feet, if the table of the machine were not absolutely plane, it is not quite safe to use the smaller number of supports, because a chip or some other object is liable to come under one foot and throw the jig and the piece out of line, without this being noticed by the operator. If the same thing happens to a jig with four feet, it will rock and invariably cause the operator to notice the defect. If the table is out of true, this defect, too, will be noticed for the same reason.

Jig feet are generally cast solid with the jig frame. When the jig frame is made from machine steel, and sometimes in the case of cast-iron jigs, detachable feet are used.

Materials for Jigs. — Opinions differ as to the relative merits of cast iron and steel as materials from which to construct the jig and fixture bodies. The decision on this point should depend to a great extent upon the usage to which the fixture is to be put and the character of the work which it is to handle. For small and medium sized work, such as typewriter, sewing machine, gun, adding machine, cash register, phonograph, and similar parts, the steel jig offers decided advantages, but for larger work, such as that encountered in automobile, engine, and machine tool fixtures, the cast-iron jig is undoubtedly the cheaper and more advisable to use. The steel jig should be left soft in order that at any future time additional holes may be added, or the existing bushings changed as required. With a cast-iron jig this adding of bushings is a difficult matter, as the frame is usually bossed and "spot finished" at the point where the bushings are located, and it is very difficult to build up on the jig frame in order to locate or change the bushings. When designing the jig, these points should be remembered and provision made for them, where possible.

General Remarks on Jig Design. — One mistake, quite frequently made, is that of giving too little clearance between the piece to be machined and the walls or sides of the jig used for it. Plenty of clearance should always be allowed, particularly when rough castings are being drilled or machined in the jigs; besides, those surfaces in the jig which do not actually bear upon the work do not always come exactly to the dimensions indicated on the drawing, particularly in a cast-iron jig, and allowance ought to be made for such differences.

In regard to the locating points, it ought to be remarked that, in all instances, these should be visible to the operator when placing the work in position, so that he may be enabled to see that the work really is in its right place. At times the construction of the piece to be worked upon may prevent a full view of the locating points. In such a case a cored or drilled hole in the jig, near the locating seat, will enable a view of same, so that the operator may either see that the work rests upon the locating point, or so that he can place a feeler or thickness gage between the work and the locating surface, to make sure that he has the work in its correct position. Another point that should not be overlooked is that jigs and fixtures should be designed with a view of making them easily cleaned from the chips, and provision should also be made so that the chips, as far as possible, may fall out of the jig and not accumulate on or about the locating points, where they are liable to throw the work out of its correct position and consequently spoil the piece.

The principles so far referred to have all been in relation to the holding of the work in the jig, and the general design of the jig for producing accurate work. Provisions, however, should also be made for clamping the jig or fixture to the table of the machine, in cases where it is necessary to have the tool fixed while in operation. Small drilling jigs are not clamped to the table, but boring jigs and milling and planing fixtures invariably must be firmly secured to the machine on which they are used.

Plain lugs, projecting out in the same plane as the bottom of the jig, or lugs with a slot in them to fit the body of T-bolts, are the common means for clamping fixtures to the table. For boring jigs, it is unnecessary to provide more than three such clamping points, as a greater number is likely to cause some springing action in the fixture. A slight springing effect is almost unavoidable, no matter how strong and heavy the jig is, but, by properly applying the clamps, it is possible to confine this springing within commercial limits.

Jigs should always be tested before they are used, so as to make sure that the guiding provisions are placed in the right relation to the locating points and in proper relation to each other.

Summary of Principles of Jig Design. — Summarizing the principles referred to, the following rules may be given as the main points to be considered in the designing of jigs and fixtures:

1. Before planning the design of a tool, compare the cost of production of the work with present tools with the expected cost of production, using the tool to be made, and see that the cost of building is not in excess of expected gain.

2. Before laying out the jig or fixture, decide upon the locating points and outline a clamping arrangement.

3. Make all clamping and binding devices as quick-acting as possible.

4. In selecting locating points, see that two component parts of a machine can be located from corresponding points and surfaces.

5. Make the jig "fool-proof"; that is, arrange it so that the work cannot be inserted except in the correct way.

6. For rough castings, make some of the locating points adjustable.

7. Locate clamps so that they will be in the best position to resist the pressure of the cutting tool when at work.

8. Make, if possible, all clamps integral parts of the jig or fixture.

9. Avoid complicated clamping arrangements, which are liable to wear or get out of order.

10. Place all clamps as nearly as possible opposite some bearing point of the work, to avoid springing.

11. Core out all unnecessary metal, making the tools as light as possible, consistent with rigidity and stiffness.

12. Round all corners.

13. Provide handles wherever these will make the handling of the jig more convenient.

14. Provide feet, preferably four, opposite all surfaces containing guide bushings in drilling and boring jigs.

15. Place all bushings inside of the geometrical figure formed by connecting the points of location of the feet.

16. Provide abundant clearance, particularly for rough castings.

17. Make, if possible, all locating points visible to the operator when placing the work in position.

18. Provide holes or escapes for the chips.

19. Provide clamping lugs, located so as to prevent spring· ing of the fixture, on all tools which must be held to the table of the machine while in use, and tongues for the slots in the tables in all milling and planing fixtures.

20. Before using in the shop, for commercial purposes, test all jigs as soon as made.

Types of Jigs. — The two principal classes of jigs are drill jigs and boring jigs. Fixtures may be grouped as milling, planing, and splining fixtures, although there are a number of special fixtures which could not be classified under any special head.

Drill jigs are intended exclusively for drilling, reaming, tapping, and facing. Whenever these four operations are required on a piece of work, it is, as a rule, possible to provide the necessary arrangements for performing all these operations in one and the same jig. Sometimes separate jigs are made for each one of these operations, but it is doubtless more convenient and cheaper to have one jig do for all, as the design of the jig will not be much more complicated. Although it may be possible to make a distinction between a number of different types of drill jigs, it is almost impossible to define and to get proper names for the various classes, owing to the great variety of shapes of the work to be drilled. There are, however, two general types that are most commonly used, the difference between them being very marked. These types may be classified as *open jigs* and *closed jigs*, or *box jigs*. Sometimes the open jigs are called *clamping jigs*. The open jigs usually have all the drill bushings in the same plane, parallel with one another, and are not provided with loose or removable walls or leaves, thereby making it possible to insert the piece to be drilled without any manipulation of the parts of the jig. These jigs are often of such a construction that they are applied to the work to be drilled, the jig being placed on the work, rather than the work being placed in the jig. The jig may be held to the work by straps, bolts, or clamps, but in many cases the jig fits into or over some finished part of the work and in this way the jig is located and held in position.

The closed drill jigs, or box jigs, frequently resemble some form of a box and are intended for pieces where the holes are to be drilled at various angles to one another. As a rule, the piece to be drilled can be inserted in the jig only after one or more leaves or covers have been swung out of the way. Sometimes it is necessary to remove a loose wall, which is held by bolts and dowel pins, in order to locate the piece in the jig. The work in the closed drill jig may be held in place by set-screws, screw bushings, straps, or hook-bolts.

The combination drilling and boring jig is another type of closed jig designed to serve both for drilling and boring operations. Before designing a combination drill and boring jig, the relation between, and number of, the drilled and bored holes must be taken into consideration, and also the size of the piece to be machined. In case there is a great number of holes, it may be of advantage to have two or even more jigs for the same piece, because it makes it easier to design and make the jig, and very likely will give a better result. The holes drilled or bored in the first jig may be used as a means for locating the piece in the jigs used later on. Combination drill and boring jigs are not very well adapted for pieces of large size.

Open Jigs. — Open jigs of the simpler forms are simply plates provided with bushed holes which are located to correspond with the required locations for the drilled holes. While holes are sometimes drilled by first laying out the holes directly upon the work, it is quite evident that this method of drilling would not be efficient if a large number of duplicate parts had to be drilled accurately, as there is likely to be more or less variation in the location of the holes, and considerable loss of time. In the first place, a certain amount of time is required for laying out these holes preparatory to drilling. The operator,

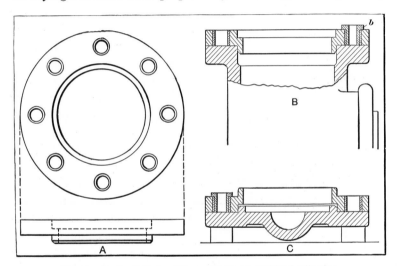

Fig. 1. Jig for Cylinder Flange and Head, and its Application

when starting the drill, must also be careful to make it cut concentric with the scribed circle, which requires extra time, and there will necessarily be more or less variation. To overcome these objections, jigs are almost universally used for holding the work and guiding the drill, when drilling duplicate parts, especially when quite a large number of duplicate pieces must be drilled.

The ring-shaped jig shown at *A* in Fig. 1 is used for drilling the stud bolt holes in a cylinder flange and also for drilling the cylinder head, which is bolted to the cylinder. The position of

the jig when the cylinder flange is being drilled is shown at
B. An annular projection on the jig fits closely in the cylinder
counterbore, as the illustration shows, to locate the jig concentric
with the bore. As the holes in the cylinder are to be tapped or
threaded for studs, a "tap drill," which is smaller in diameter
than the bolt body, is used and the drill is guided by a removable bushing *b* of the proper size. Jigs of this type are often
held in position by inserting an accurately fitting plug through
the jig and into the first hole drilled, which prevents the jig
from turning with relation to the cylinder, when drilling the
other holes. When the jig is used for drilling the head, the

opposite side is placed
next to the work, as
shown at *C*. This side
has a circular recess or
counterbore, which fits
the projection on the
head to properly locate
the jig. As the holes in
the head must be slightly
larger in diameter than
the studs, another sized
drill and a guide bushing
of corresponding size are
used. The cylinder is, of
course, bored and the

Fig. 2. Drill Jig of the Box Type

head turned before the drilling is done.

Jigs of the open class, as well as those of other types, are
made in a great variety of shapes, and, when in use, they are
either applied to the work or the latter is placed in the jig.
When the work is quite large, the jig is frequently placed on it,
whereas small parts are more often held in the jig, which is so
designed that the work can be clamped in the proper position.
The form of any jig depends, to a great extent, on the shape of
the work for which it is intended and also on the location of
the holes to be drilled. As the number of differently shaped
pieces which go to make up even a single machine is often very

great, and as most parts require more or less drilling, jigs are made in an almost endless variety of sizes and forms. When all the holes to be drilled in a certain part are parallel, and especially if they are all in the same plane, a very simple form of jig can ordinarily be used.

Box Jigs. — A great many machine parts must be drilled on different sides and frequently castings or forgings are very irregular in shape, so that a jig which is made somewhat in

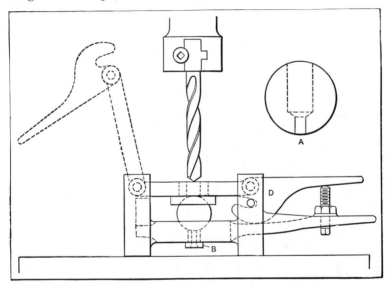

Fig. 3. Box Jig for Drilling Ball shown enlarged at *A*

the form of a box, and encloses the work, is very essential, as it enables the guide bushings to be placed on all sides and also makes it comparatively easy to locate and securely clamp the part in the proper position for drilling. This type of jig, which, because of its form, is known as a closed or "box jig," is used very extensively.

A box jig of simple design is shown in Fig. 2. This particular jig is used for drilling four small holes in a part (not shown) which is located with reference to the guide bushings *B* by a central pin *A* attached to the jig body. This pin enters a hole in the work, which is finished in another machine in connection with a previous operation. After the work is inserted in the jig, it is clamped by closing the cover C, which is hinged at one end and has a cam-shaped clamping latch D at the other, that engages a pin E in the jig body. The four holes are drilled by passing the drill through the guide bushings B in the cover.

Another jig of the same kind, but designed for drilling a hole having two diameters through the center of a steel ball,

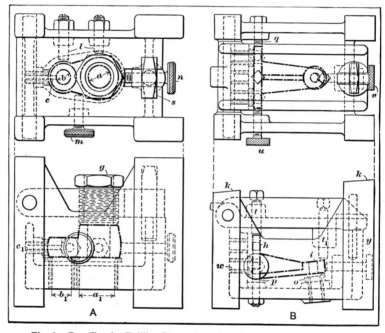

Fig. 4. Box Jigs for Drilling Parts shown by Heavy Dot-and-dash Lines

is shown in Fig. 3. The work, which is shown enlarged at A, is inserted while the cover is thrown back as indicated by the dotted lines. The cover is then closed and tightened by the cam-latch D, and the large part of the hole is drilled with the jig in the position shown. The jig is then turned over and a smaller drill of the correct size is fed through guide bushing B on the opposite side. The depth of the large hole could be gaged for each ball drilled, by feeding the drill spindle down to a certain position as shown by graduation or other marks, but if the spindle has an adjustable stop, this should be used. The work is located in line with the two guide bushings by spherical seats formed in the jig body and in the upper bushing, as shown. As the work can be inserted and removed quickly, a large number of balls, which, practically speaking, are duplicates, can be drilled in a comparatively short time by using a jig of this type.

A box jig that differs somewhat in construction from the design just referred to is illustrated at *A* in Fig. 4, which shows

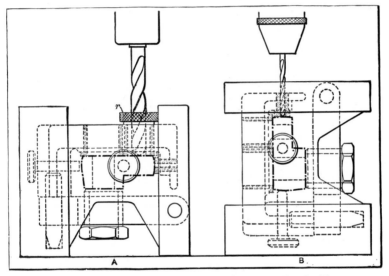

Fig. 5. Jig shown at *A*, Fig. 4, in Two Different Drilling Positions

a side and top view. The work, in this case, is a small casting the form of which is indicated by the heavy dot-and-dash lines. This casting is drilled at *a*, *b*, and *c*, and the two larger holes *a* and *b* are finished by reaming. The hinged cover of this jig is opened for inserting the work by unscrewing the T-shaped clamping screw *s* one-quarter of a turn, which brings the head in line with a slot in the cover. The casting is clamped by tightening this screw, which forces an adjustable screw bushing *g* down against the work. By having this bushing adjustable, it can be set to give the right pressure, and, if the height of the castings should vary, the position of the clamping bushing could easily be changed.

The work is properly located by the inner ends of the three guide bushings a_1, b_1, and c_1, and also by the locating screws l against which the casting is held by knurled thumb-screws m and n. When the holes a and b are being drilled, the jig is placed with the cover side down, as shown at A in Fig. 5, and the drill is guided by removable bushings, one of which is shown at r. When the drilling is completed, the drill bushings are replaced by reamer bushings and each hole is finished by reaming. The small hole c, Fig. 4, is drilled in the end of the casting by simply placing the jig on end as shown at B, Fig. 5. Box jigs which have to be placed in more than one position for drilling the different holes are usually provided with feet or extensions, as shown, which are accurately finished to align the guide bushings properly with the drill. These feet extend beyond any clamping screws, bolts, or bushings which may protrude from the sides of the jigs, and provide a solid support. When inserting work in a jig, care should be taken to remove all chips which might have fallen upon those surfaces against which the work is clamped and which determine its location.

Still another jig of the box type, which is quite similar to the one shown at A, Fig. 4, but is arranged differently, owing to the shape of the work and location of the holes, is shown at B in the same illustration. The work has three holes in the base h, and a hole at i which is at an angle of 5 degrees with the base. The three holes are drilled with the jig standing on the opposite end y, and the angular hole is drilled while the jig rests on the four feet k, the ends of which are at such an angle with the jig body that the guide bushing for hole i is properly aligned with the drill. The casting is located in this jig by the inner ends of the two guide bushings w and the bushing o and also by two locating screws p and a side locating screw q. Adjustable screws t and t_1 in the cover hold the casting down, and it is held laterally by the two knurled thumb-screws u and v. If an attempt were made to drill this particular part without a jig (as would be done if only a few castings were needed) it would have to be set with considerable care, provided the angle between hole i and those in the base had to be at all accurate, and it would be rather difficult to drill a number of these castings and have them all duplicates. By the use of a jig, however, designed for drilling this particular casting, the relative positions of the holes in any number of parts are practically the same and the work can be done much more quickly than would be possible if it were held to the drill-press table by ordinary clamping appliances. Various designs of jigs will be described in Chapter VII.

Details of Jig Design. — The general principles of the design and use of jigs have been explained. The details of jig design will now be considered. Generally speaking, the most important parts of a jig are the guide bushings for the drills and other tools, the clamping devices, and the locating points, against which the work is placed to insure an accurate position in the jig. The guides for the cutting tools in a drill jig take the form of concentric steel bushings, which are placed in the jig body in proper positions.

The drill bushings are generally made of tool steel, hardened and lapped, and, where convenient, should be ground inside and out. They should also be long enough to support the drill on each side regardless of the fluting, and they should be so located that the lower end of the bushings will stop about the same distance above the work as the diameter of the drill, so that chips will clear the bushings readily. Where holes are drilled on the side of a convex or a concave surface, the end of the bushing must be cut on a bevel and come closer to the part being drilled, to insure the drill having adequate support while starting into the work. The bushings should have heads of sufficient diameter. Long bushings should be relieved by increasing the hole diameter at the upper end. The lower end of the bushing should have its edges rounded, in order to permit some of the chips being shed from the drill easily, instead of all of them being forced up through the bushing. It is also good practice to cut a groove under the head for clearance for the wheel when grinding the bushing on the outside. A complete treatise covering dimensions and design is given in the chapter on "Jig Bushings."

In order to hold the work rigidly in the jig, so that it may be held against the locating points while the cutting tools operate upon the work, jigs and fixtures are provided with clamping devices. Sometimes a clamping device serves the purpose of holding the jig to the work, in a case where the work is a very large piece and the jig is attached to the work in some suitable way. The purpose of the clamping device, however, remains the same, namely, that of preventing any shifting of the guiding bushings while the operation on the work is performed. The clamping device should always be an integral part of the jig body in order to prevent its getting lost. Different types of clamping devices are shown and described in the chapter on "Jig Clamping Devices."

The locating points may consist of screws, pins, finished pads, bosses, ends of bushings, seats, or lugs cast solid with the jig body, etc. The various types used are described in detail in the chapter on "Locating Points and Adjustable Stops."

CHAPTER II

DESIGN OF OPEN DRILL JIGS

To give any rational rules or methods for the design of drill jigs would be almost impossible, as almost every jig must be designed in a somewhat different way from every other jig, to suit and conform to the requirements of the work. All that can be done is to lay down the principles. The main principles for jigs as well as fixtures were treated at length in Chapter I. It is proposed in the present chapter to dwell more in detail on the carrying out of the actual work of designing jigs.

Jig Drawings. — Before making any attempt to put the layout of the jig on paper, the designer should carefully consider what the jig will be required to do, the limits of accuracy, etc., and to form, in his imagination, a certain idea of the kind of a jig that would be suitable for the purpose. In doing so, if a model or sample of the work to be made is at hand, it will be found to be a great help to study the actual model. If the drawing, as is most often the case, is the only thing that is at hand, then the outline of the work should be drawn in red (or other colored) ink on the drawing paper, on which the jig is subsequently to be laid out, and the jig built up, so to speak, around this outline. The designing of the jig will be greatly simplified by doing this, as the relation between the work and the jig will always be plainly before the designer, and it will be more easily decided where the locating points and clamping arrangements may be properly placed. When drawing and projecting the different views of the jig on the paper, the red outline of the work will not in any way interfere, and when the jig is made from the drawing, the red lines are simply ignored, except to the extent to which the outline of the pieces may help the toolmaker to understand the drawing and the purpose of certain locating points and clamping devices.

If possible, the jig should be drawn full size, as it is a great deal easier to obtain the correct proportions when so doing. Of course, in many cases, it will be impossible to draw the jigs full size. In such cases the only thing to do is to draw them to the largest possible regular scale. Every jig draftsman should be supplied with a set of blueprints containing dimensions of standard screws, bolts, nuts, thumb-screws, washers, wing-nuts, sliding points, drills, counterbores, reamers, bushings, etc.; in short, with blueprints giving dimensions of all parts that are used in the construction of jigs, and which are, or can be, standardized. It should be required of every designer and draftsman that he use these standards to the largest possible extent, so as to bring the cost of jigs down to as low a figure as possible.

It is highly desirable, for the obtaining of best results, that, before starting cn the drawing, the draftsman who is to lay out the jig should consult the foreman who is actually going to use the jig. Oftentimes this man will be able to supply the best idea for the making of the jig or tool. The combined experience of the draftsman and the foreman will generally produce a much better tool than could either of them alone.

As a jig drawing, in most cases, is only used once, or at most only a very few times, it is not advisable to make a tracing or blueprint from the drawing, but, as a rule, the pencil drawing itself may be used to advantage. If, however, it is given out in the shop directly as it comes from the drawing-board, it is likely to become soiled, so that, after a while, it would be impossible to make out the meaning of the views shown on it. For this reason jig drawings should be made on heavy paper, preferably of brown color, which is not as quickly soiled as white paper; and in order to prevent the drawing from being torn, it should be mounted on strawboard, and held down along the edges by thin wooden strips, nailed to the board. It is also desirable to cover the drawings with a thin coat of shellac before they are sent out into the shop. When this is done, dirt and black spots may be washed off directly; and the shellac itself may be washed off by wood alcohol, when the drawing is returned to the draft-ing-room. The drawing, after having been cleaned, is then detached from the strawboard, which may be used over and over again. The drawing is, of course, filed away according to the drafting-room system. The most advantageous sizes for jig drawings for from medium to heavy work are about as follows:

1. Full-size sheet, 40 × 27½ inches.
2. Half-size sheet, 27½ × 20 inches.
3. Quarter-size sheet, 20 × 13¾ inches.
4. Eighth-size sheet, 13¾ × 10 inches.

Of course, these sizes will vary in different shops, and in many cases, particularly when the tool-designing department and the regular drafting-room are combined as one drafting department, the jig drawings should be of the same regular sizes as the ordinary machine drawings.

It is common practice in a great many shops to make no detailed drawings of jigs, but simply to draw a sufficient number of views and sections, and to dimension the different parts directly on the assembly drawings. In cases where the jig drawings are complicated, and where they are covered with a large number of dimensions which make it hard to read the drawing and to see the outlines of the jig body itself, it has proved a great help to trace the outlines of the jig body, and of such portions as are made of cast iron, on tracing paper, omitting all loose parts, and simply putting on the necessary dimensions for making the patterns. A blueprint is then made from this paper tracing, and is sent to the patternmaker, who will find the drawing less of a puzzle, and who will need to spend far less time to understand how the pattern actually looks. It is, however, good policy to detail jig drawings completely, the same as other machine details.

When jigs are made for pieces of work which require a great many operations to be carried out with the same jig, and where a great number of different bushings, different sizes of drills, reamers, counterbores, etc., are used, a special operation sheet should be provided, which should be delivered to the man using the jig, together with the jig itself. This enables him to use the jig to best advantage. On this sheet should be marked the order in which the various operations are to be performed and the

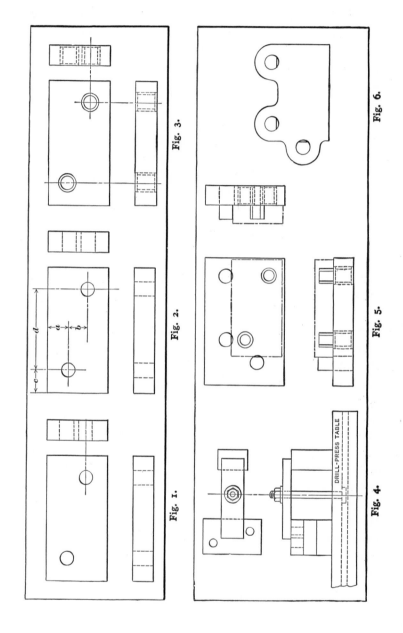

Fig. 1.

Fig. 2.

Fig. 3.

Fig. 4.

Fig. 5.

Fig. 6.

tools and bushings which are to be used. The bushings should be numbered or marked in some way so as to facilitate the selection of the correct bushing for the particular tool with which it is used. If this system is put in force and used for simpler classes of jigs also, the operator will need few or no instructions from the foreman, outside of this operation sheet.

Designing Open Jigs. — The present chapter will be devoted to explaining and illustrating the application of the principles previously outlined, to the simplest and most common design of drill jig — the open jig. Assume that the drill jig is to be designed for a piece of work, as shown in Fig. 1. Consideration must first be given to the size of the piece, to the finish given to the piece previous to the drilling operation, the accuracy required as regards the relation of one hole to the other, and in regard to the surfaces of the piece itself. The number of duplicate pieces to be drilled must also be considered, and, in some cases, the material.

The simplest kind of drill jig that could be used for the case taken as an example would be the one illustrated in Fig. 2, which simply consists of a flat plate of uniform thickness of the same outline as the piece to be drilled, and provided with holes for guiding the drill. Such a jig would be termed a jig-plate. For small pieces, the jig-plate would be made of machine steel and casehardened, or from tool steel and hardened. For larger work, a machine-steel plate can also be used, but in order to avoid the difficulties which naturally would arise from hardening a large plate, the holes are simply bored larger than the required size of drill, and are provided with lining bushings to guide the drill, as shown in Fig. 3. It would not be necessary, however, to have the jig-plate made from steel, for large work, as a cast-iron plate provided with tool steel or machine-steel guiding bushings would answer the purpose just as well, and be much cheaper. The thickness of the jig-plate varies according to the size of the holes to be drilled and the size of the plate itself.

The holes in the jig in Fig. 2 and in the bushings in the jig in Fig. 3 are made the same size as the hole to be drilled in the work, with proper clearance for the cutting tools. If the size and location of the holes to be drilled are not very important as regards accuracy, it is sufficient to simply drill through the work with a full-sized drill guided by the jig-plate, but when a nice, smooth, standard-sized hole is required, the holes in the work must be reamed. The hole is first spotted by a spotting drill, which is of exactly the same size as the reamer used for finishing, and which nicely fits the hole in the jig-plate or bushing. Then a so-called reamer drill, which is 0.010 inch, or less, smaller in diameter than the reamer, is put through, leaving only a slight amount of stock for the reamer to remove, thereby obtaining a very satisfactory hole. Sometimes a separate loose bushing is used for each one of these operations, but this is expensive and also unnecessary, as the method described gives equally good results.

By using the rose reaming method very good results will also be obtained. In this case two loose bushings besides the lining bushing will be used. These bushings are described and tabulated in a following chapter. The drill preceding the rose chucking reamer is $\frac{1}{16}$ inch smaller than the size of the hole. This drill is first put through the work, a loose drill bushing made of steel being used for guiding the drill. Then the rose chucking reamer is employed, using, if the hole in the jig be large, a loose bushing made of cast iron.

When dimensioning the jig on the drawing, dimensions should always be given from two finished surfaces of the jig to the center of the holes, or at least to the more important ones. In regard to the holes, it is not sufficient to give only the right angle dimensions, a, b, c, and d, etc., Fig. 2, but the radii between the various holes must also be given. If there are more than two holes, the radii should always be given between the nearest holes and also between the holes that bear a certain relation to one another, as, for instance, between centers of shafts carrying meshing gears, sprockets, etc. This will prove a great help to the toolmaker. In the case under consideration, the dimensions ought to be given from two finished sides of the work to the centers of the holes, and also the dimension between the centers of the holes to be drilled.

When using a simple jig, made as outlined in Figs. 2 and 3, this jig is simply laid down flat on the work and held against it by a C-clamp, a wooden clamp, or, if convenient, held right on the drill-press table by means of a strap or clamp, as shown in Fig. 4. Here two pieces of the work are shown beneath the jig-plate, both being drilled at one time.

Improving the Simple Form of Jig. — The first improvement that could be made on the jig shown in Fig. 3 would be the placing of locating points in the jig-plate in the form of pins, as shown in Fig. 5, in which the dotted lines represent the outline of the work. The plate need not necessarily have the shape shown in

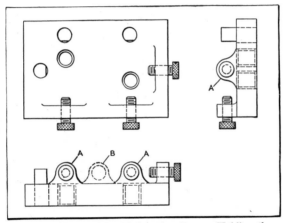

Fig. 7. Simple Jig with Locating Screws Holding the Work in Place

Fig. 5, but may have the appearance shown in Fig. 6, according to the conditions.

The adding of the locating points will, of course, increase the cost of the jig, but the amount of time saved in using the jig will undoubtedly make up for the added expense of the jig, provided a fair number of pieces is to be drilled; besides a great advantage is gained in that the holes will always be located in the same relation to the two sides resting against the locating pins on all the pieces drilled. The locating pins are flattened off to a depth of $\frac{1}{16}$ inch from the outside circumference, and dimensions should be given from the flat to the center of the pin

holes and to the center of the nearest or the most important of
the holes to be drilled in the jig. The same strapping or clamping arrangements for the jig and work, as mentioned for the
simpler form of jig, may be employed.

Improving the Jig by Adding Locating Screws. — The next
step toward improving the jig under consideration would be to
provide the jig with locating screws, as shown in Fig. 7. By
the addition of these, the locating arrangements of the jig become complete, and the piece of work will be prevented from
shifting or moving sideways. These locating screws are placed
so that the clamping points come as nearly opposite to some
bearing points on the work as possible. In order to provide for
locating set-screws in our present jig, three lugs or projections
A are added which hold the set-screws. If possible the set-screw
lugs should not reach above the surface of the work, which
should rest on the drill-press table when drilling the holes.

The present case illustrates the difficulty of giving exact rules
for jig design. Two set-screws are used on the long side of the
work, but in a case like this, where the piece is comparatively
short and stiff, one lug and set-screw, as indicated by the dotted
lines at *B* in Fig. 7, would be fully sufficient. The strain of the
set-screw placed right between the two locating pins will not be
great enough to spring the piece out of shape. When the work
is long and narrow, two set-screws are required on the long side,
but, in the case illustrated, two lugs would be considered a waste-
ful design.

Providing Clamps and Feet for the Jig. — The means by which
the work has been clamped or strapped to the jig when drilling
in the drill press (see Fig. 4) have not been integral parts of the
jig in the simple types shown. If clamping arrangements that
are integral parts of the jig are to be added, the next improvement would be to add four legs in order to raise the jig-plate
enough above the surface of the drill-press table to get the required space for such clamping arrangements. The completed
jig of the best design for rapid manipulation and duplicate work
would then have the appearance shown in Fig. 8. The jig here
is provided with a handle cast integral with the jig body, and

with a clamping strap which can be pulled back for removing and inserting the work. Instead of having the legs solid with the jig, as shown in Fig. 8, loose legs, screwed in place, are sometimes used, as shown in Fig. 9.

These legs are round and provided with a shoulder A, preventing them from screwing into the jig-plate. A headless screw or pin through the edge of the circumference of the threads at the top prevents the studs from becoming loose. These loose legs are usually made of machine steel or tool steel, the bottom end

Standard Jig Feet

	A	B	C	A	B	C
	3/8	3/16	1/8	13/16	13/32	7/32
	7/16	7/32	9/64	3/4	3/8	1/4
	1/2	1/4	5/32	7/8	7/16	9/32
	9/16	9/32	11/64	1	1/2	5/16
	5/8	5/16	3/16	....	....	....

Screws for Jig Feet

	A	B	C	D	A	B	C	D
	0.160	1/8	0.110	9/32	0.299	7/32	0.192	7/16
	0.191	9/64	0.123	5/16	0.343	1/4	0.219	15/32
	0.213	5/32	0.137	11/32	0.386	9/32	0.246	1/2
	0.233	11/64	0.150	3/8	0.426	5/16	0.273	17/32
	0.256	3/16	0.164	13/32	.....	....	.....	....

being hardened and then ground and lapped, so that all four legs are of the same length. It is the practice of many toolmakers not to thread the legs into the jig body, but simply to provide a plain surface on the end of the leg, which enters into the jig-plate, and is driven into place. This is much easier, and there is no reason why, for almost all kinds of work, jigs provided with legs attached in this manner should not be equally durable.

Jig feet are also made of the form shown in the accompanying table, where a separate screw is used for holding the jig feet to the jig body.

When jigs are made of machine or tool steel, and feet are

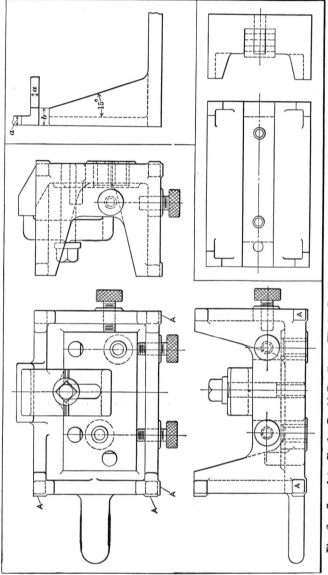

Fig. 8. Complete Jig for Rapid Duplicate Work; Design of Legs for Cast-iron Jig Bodies; and Form of Jig that may be Used for Drilling a Number of Pieces Simultaneously

required, the only way to provide them is to insert loose feet. In the case of cast-iron jigs, however, solid legs cast in place are preferable. The solid legs cast in place generally have the appearance shown in the upper right-hand corner of Fig. 8. The two webs of the leg form a right angle, which, for all practical purposes, makes the leg fully as strong as if it were solid. The leg is tapered 15 degrees, as a rule, as shown in the engraving, but this may be varied according to conditions. The thickness of the leg varies according to the size of the jig, the weight of the work, and the pressure of the cutting tools, and depends also upon the length of the leg. The length b on top is generally made one and one-half times a. As an indication of the size of the legs required, it may be said that for smaller jigs, up to jigs with a face area of 6 square inches, the dimension a may be made from $\frac{5}{16}$ to $\frac{3}{8}$ inch; for medium-sized jigs, $\frac{1}{2}$ to $\frac{5}{8}$ inch; for larger-sized jigs, $\frac{3}{4}$ to $1\frac{1}{2}$ inch; but, of course, these dimensions are simply indications of the required dimensions. As to the length of the legs, the governing condition, evidently, is that they must be long enough to reach below the lowest part of the work and the clamping arrangement, as clearly indicated in the design in Fig. 8.

If a jig is to be used in a multiple-spindle drill, it should be designed a great deal stronger than it is ordinarily designed when used for drilling one hole at a time. This is especially true if there is a large number of holes to drill simultaneously. It is evident that the pressure upon the jig in a multiple-spindle drill is as many times greater than the pressure in a ccmmon drill press as the number of drills in operation at once.

Referring again to Fig. 8, attention should be called to the small lugs A on the sides of the jig body which are cast in place for laying out and planing purposes. The handle should be made about 4 inches long, which permits a fairly good grip by the hand. The design of the jig shown is simple, and fills all requirements necessary for producing work quickly and accurately; at the same time, it is strongly and rigidly designed. Locating points of a different kind from those shown can, of course, be used; and the requirements may be such that adjustable locating points, as described in a following chapter, may be required. A more quick-acting, but, at the same time, a far more complicated clamping arrangement might be used, but the question is whether the added increase in the rapidity of manipulation offsets the expense thus incurred.

A question which the designer should always ask himself is: Can more than one piece be drilled at one time? In the present case, the locating pins can be made longer, or, if there is a locating wall, it can be made higher, the legs of the jig can be made longer, and the screw holding the clamp can also be increased in length. If the pieces of work are thick enough, set-screws for

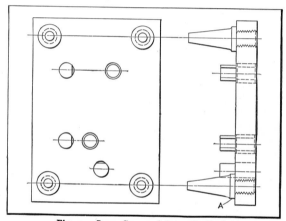

Fig. 9. Legs Screwed into Jig Body

holding the work against the locating pins can be placed in a vertical line, or if the pieces are narrow, they can be placed diagonally, so as to gain space. If the pieces are very thin, the locating might be a more difficult proposition. If they are made of a uniform width, they may simply be put in the slot in the bottom of the jig, as shown in the lower right-hand corner of Fig. 8, or if a jig on the principles of the one shown to the left is used, they might be located sideways by a wedge, as shown in Fig. 10. A couple of lugs A would then be added to hold the wedge in place and take the thrust. In both cases the pieces must be pushed up in place endways by hand. If the pieces are not of exactly uniform size and it is desired to drill a number at a time, they must be pushed up against the locating pins by hand from two sides, and the clamping strap must be depended upon to clamp them down against the pressure of the cut, and at the same time prevent them from moving side or endways. If the accuracy of the location of the holes is important, but one piece at a time should be drilled.

Examples of Open Drill Jigs. — A typical example of an open drill jig, very similar to the one just developed and explained, is shown in Fig. 11. The work is located against the three locating pins A, and held in place against these pins by the three set-screws B. The three straps C hold the work securely against

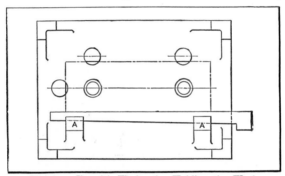

Fig. 10. Jig with Wedge for Holding the Work

the finished pad, in the bottom of the jig. These clamps are so placed that when the work has been drilled and the clamp screws loosened, the clamps will swing around a quarter of a turn, allowing the work to be lifted directly from the jig and a new piece of work inserted; then the clamps are again turned around into the clamping position, and the screws tightened. These straps are integral parts of the jig; at the same time, they are quickly and easily manipulated, and do not interfere with the rapid removal and insertion of the work. The strength and rigidity of the feet in proportion to the jig should be noted, this strength being obtained by giving proper shape to the feet, without using an unnecessary quantity of metal.

The jig in Fig. 11 is also designed to accommodate the component part of the work when it is to be drilled. When this is done, the work is held on the back side of the jig, shown in Fig. 12.

This side is also provided with feet, and has a finished pad against which the work is held. The locating pins extend clear through the central portion of the jig body, and, consequently, will locate the component part of the work in exactly the same position as the piece of work drilled on the front side of the jig. The same clamping straps are used, the screws being simply put in from the opposite side into the same tapped holes as are used when clamping on the front side of the jig. The four holes *D* are guide holes for drilling the screw holes in the work, these being drilled the body size of the bolt in one part, and the tap drill size

Fig. 11. Example of Open Drill Jig. View showing Front Side

in the component part. The lining bushing in the holes *D* serves as a drill bushing for drilling the body size holes. The loose bushing *E*, Fig. 11, is used when drilling the tap holes in the component part, the inside diameter of this bushing being the tap drill size, and the outside diameter a good fit in the lining bushing. The two holes *F*, Fig. 12, are provided with drill bushings and serve as guides when drilling the dowel pin holes, which are drilled below size, leaving about 0.010 inch, and are reamed out after the two component parts of the work are put together. The two holes shown in the middle of the jig in Fig. 11, which are provided with lining bushings, and also with loose bushings, as shown inserted in Fig. 12, may be used for drilling and reaming the bearing holes for the shafts passing through the work. In this particular case, however, they are used only for rough-drilling the holes, to allow the boring-bars to pass through when finishing the work by boring in a special boring jig, after the two parts of the work have been screwed together.

The large bushings shown beside the jig in Fig. 11 are the loose bushings shown in place in Fig. 12. It will be noted that the bushings are provided with dogs for easy removal, as explained in a following chapter. As the central portion of the

Fig. 12. Rear View of Drill Jig shown in Fig. 11

jig body is rather thin, it will be seen from Fig. 12 that the bosses for the central holes project outside of the jig body in order to give a long enough bearing to the bushings. This, of course, can be done only when such a projection does not interfere with the work. The bosses, in this particular case, also serve another purpose. They make the jig "fool-proof," because the pieces drilled on the side of the jig shown in Fig. 11 cannot be put on the side shown in Fig. 12, the bosses preventing the piece from being placed in position in the jig.

Attention should be called to the simplicity of the design of this jig. It simply consists of a cast-iron plate, with finished seats, and feet projecting far enough to reach below the work when drilling, three dowel pins, set-screws for bringing the work up against the dowel pins, three clamps, and the necessary bushings. The heads of all the set-screws and bolts should, if possible, be made the same size, so that the same wrench may be used for tightening and unscrewing all of them. It can also be plainly seen from the halftones that there are no unnecessarily finished surfaces on the jig, a matter which is highly important in economical production of tools.

Another example of an open drill jig, similar in design to the one just described, is shown in Fig. 13. The work to be drilled

Fig. 13. Drill Jig Used for Drilling Work shown to the Right

in this jig is shown at A and B at the right-hand side of the jig. In this case, the work is located from the half-circular ends. The pieces A and B are component parts and, when finished, are screwed together. The piece A is located against three dowel pins, and pushed against them by set-screws C, and held in position by three clamping straps, as shown in Fig. 14. In this case, the straps are provided with oblong slots as indicated, and when the clamp screws are loosened the clamps are simply pulled backward, permitting the insertion and removal of the work without interference. It would improve this clamping arrangement to place a stiff helical spring around the screws under each strap, so that the straps would be prevented from falling down to the bottom of the jig when the work was removed. At the same time this would prevent the straps from swiveling around the screws when not clamped.

In Fig. 15, the part *B* in Fig. 13 is shown clamped in position for drilling, the opposite side of the jig being used for this purpose. In jig design of this kind it is necessary to provide some means so that the parts *A* and *B* will be placed each on the correct side of the jig, or, as mentioned, the jig should be made "fool-proof." In the present case, the parts cannot be exchanged and placed on the wrong side, because the cover or guard *B* cannot be held by the three straps shown in Fig. 14, as the screws

Fig. 14. Drill Jig shown in Fig. 13 with Work in Place

for the straps are not long enough. On the other hand, the piece *A* could not be placed on the side shown in Fig. 15, because the long bolt and strap used for clamping on this side would interfere with the work.

It may appear to be a fault in design that three straps are used to fasten the piece *A* in place, and only one is employed for holding piece *B*. This difference in clamping arrangement, however, is due to the different number and the different sizes of holes to be drilled in the different pieces. The holes in the piece *A* are larger and the number of holes is greater, and a heavier clamping arrangement is, therefore, required, inasmuch as the thrust on the former is correspondingly greater, the multiple-spindle drill being used for drilling the holes. If each hole were drilled and reamed individually, the design of the jig could have been comparatively lighter.

In the design shown, the locating of each piece individually in any but the right way is also taken care of. The piece *A*, which is shown in place in the jig, Fig. 14, could not be swung around into another position, because the strap and screw at *E* would interfere. For the same reason, the cover or guard *B* could not be located except in the right way. As shown in Fig.

Fig. 15.   Rear View of Drill Jig shown in Fig. 13, with Cover to be Drilled in Place

15, the strap and screw would have to be detached from the jig in order to get the cover in place, if it were turned around. The locating pins for the work pass clear through the body of the jig, and are used for locating both pieces. The pieces are located diagonally in the jig, because, by doing so, it is possible to make the outside dimensions of the jig smaller. In this particular case the parts are located on the machine to which they belong, in a diagonal direction, so that the additional advantage is gained of being able to use the same dimensions for locating the jig holes as are used on the drawing for the machine details themselves. This also tends to eliminate mistakes in making the jigs.

Sometimes, when more or less complicated mechanisms are

composed of several parts fitted together and working in relation
to each other, as, for instance, friction clutches, one jig may be
made to serve for drilling all the individual parts, by the addition
of a few extra parts applied to the jig when different details of
the work are being drilled. In Figs. 16, 17, and 18, such a case
is illustrated. The pieces A, B, and C, in Fig. 16, are component
parts of a friction clutch, and the jig in which these parts are
being drilled is shown in the same figure, to the left. Suppose
now that the friction expansion ring A is to be drilled. The jig
is bored out to fit the ring before it is split and when it is only

Fig. 16. Drill Jig for Parts of Friction Clutches shown at the Right

rough-turned, leaving a certain number of thousandths of an
inch for finishing. The piece is located, as shown in Fig. 17,
against the steel block D entering into the groove in the ring, and
is then held by three hook-bolts, which simply are swung around
when the ring is inserted or removed. The hook-bolts are
tightened by nuts on the back side of the jig. Three holes
marked E in Fig. 17 are drilled simultaneously in the multiple-
spindle drill, and the fourth hole F (see Fig. 16) is drilled by
turning the jig on the side. The steel block D, Fig. 17, is hardened, and has a hole to guide the drill when passing through into
the other side of the slot in the ring. The block is held in place
by two screws and two dowel pins.

3 J

When drilling the holes in the lugs in the friction sleeve *B*, Fig. 16, the block *D* and the hook-bolts are removed. It may be mentioned here, although it is a small matter, that these parts should be tied together when removed, and there should be a specified place where all the parts belonging to a particular jig should be kept when not in use. The friction sleeve *B* fits over the collar *G*, Fig. 18. This collar is an extra piece, belonging to the jig, and used only when drilling the friction sleeve; it should be marked with instructions for what purpose it is used. The collar *G* fits over the projecting finished part *H* in

Fig. 17.   Drill Jig shown in Fig. 16, with One of the Pieces in Place

the center of the jig, and is located in its right position by the keyways shown. The keyway in the friction sleeve *B*, which must be cut and placed in the right relation to the projecting lugs before the piece can be drilled, locates the sleeve on the collar *G*, which is provided with a corresponding keyway. A flange on the collar *G*, as shown more plainly at *L* in Fig. 18, locates the friction sleeve at the right distance from the bottom of the jig, so that the holes will have a proper location sideways. Two collars, *G* and *L*, are used for the same piece *B*, this being necessary because the holes *M* and *M* in the projecting lugs shown in Fig. 16 are not placed in the same relation to the sides of the friction sleeve. The collars are marked to avoid mistakes, and corresponding marks on the jig provided so as to assure proper location. The friction sleeve is clamped in place by a strap which, in this case, does not form an integral part of the jig. This arrangement, however, is cheaper than it would have been to carry up two small projections on two sides of the jig and employ a swinging leaf and an eye-bolt, or some arrangement of this kind. Besides, the strap is rather large, and could not easily get lost. The jig necessarily has a number of loose parts, on account of being designed to accommodate different details of the friction clutch.

The friction disks C, in Fig. 16, when drilled, fit directly over the projecting finished part H of the jig, and are located on this

Fig. 18. Drill Jig shown in Fig. 16 used for Drilling Friction Sleeve

projection by a square key. The work is brought up against the bottom of the jig and held in this position by the strap shown in Fig. 18 for holding the friction sleeve. The bushings of different sizes shown in Fig. 18 are used for drilling the different sized holes in the different parts.

In all the various types of drill jigs described, the thrust of the cutting tools is taken by the clamping arrangement. In many cases, however, no actual clamping arrangements are used, but the work itself takes the thrust of the cutting tools, and the locating means are depended upon to hold the piece or jig in the right position when performing the drilling operation.

It may be well to add that loose bushings ought to be marked with the size and kind of cutting tool for which they are intended; and the corresponding place in the jig body where they are to be used should be marked so that the right bushing can easily be placed in the right position.

A few more examples of open drill jig designs of various types may prove instructive. In Fig. 19 are shown two views of a jig for drilling two holes through the rim of a handwheel. To the left is shown the jig itself and to the right the jig with the hand-

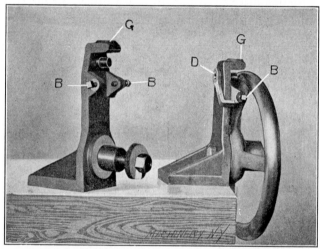

Fig. 19. Drill Jig for Holes in Rim of Handwheel

wheel mounted in place, ready for drilling. As shown, the handwheel is located on a stud through its bore, and clamped to the jig by passing a bolt through the stud, this bolt being provided with a split washer on the end. The split washer permits the easy removal of the handwheel when drilled, and the putting in place of another handwheel without loss of time. The handwheel is located by two set-screws B passing through two lugs projecting on each side of a spoke in the handwheel, the set-screws B holding the handwheel in position, while being drilled, by clamping against the sides of the spoke. The jig is fastened on the edge of the drill-press table, in a manner similar to that indicated in the illustration, so that the table does not interfere with the wheel. The vertical hole, with the drill guided by bushing G, is now drilled in all the handwheels, this hole being drilled into a lug in the spoke held by the two set-screws B. When this hole is drilled, the jig is moved over to a horizontal drilling machine, and the hole D is drilled in all the handwheels, the jig being clamped to the table of this machine in a manner similar to that on the drill press.

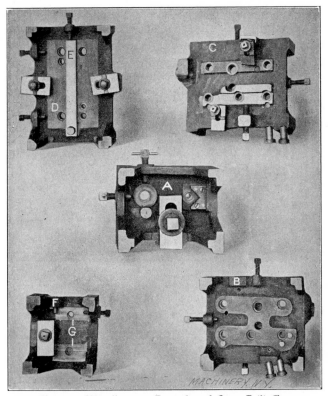

Fig. 20. Miscellaneous Examples of Open Drill Jigs

In Fig. 20, at A, an open drill jig of a type similar to those shown in Figs. 11 and 13, is shown. This jig, however, is provided with a V-block locating arrangement. An objectionable feature of this jig is that the one clamping strap is placed in the center of the piece to be drilled. Should this piece be slender, it may cause it to bend as there is no bearing surface under the work, at the place where the clamp is located, for taking the thrust of the clamping pressure.

At B and C in the same illustration are shown the front and back views of a drill jig, where the front side B is used for drilling a small piece located and held in the jig as usual; and the back side C, which is not provided with feet, is located and applied directly on the work itself in the place where the loose piece is to be fastened, the work in this case being so large that it supports the jig, instead of the jig supporting the work.

At D in the same illustration is shown a jig for locating work by means of a tongue E. This tongue fits into a corresponding slot in the work. This means for locating the work was referred to more completely in connection with locating devices. Finally, at F, is shown a jig where the work is located by a slot G in the jig body, into which a corresponding tongue in the work fits.

CHAPTER III

DESIGN OF CLOSED OR BOX JIGS

In the preceding chapter, the subject of the design of open drill jigs has been dealt with. In the present chapter it is proposed to outline the development of the design of closed or box jigs.

Assume that the holes in a piece of work, as shown in Fig. 1, are to be drilled. Holes A are drilled straight through the work, while holes B and C are so-called "blind holes," drilled into the work from the opposite sides. As these holes must not be drilled through, it is evident that the work must be drilled from two sides, and the guiding bushings for the two blind holes must be put in opposite sides of the jig. The simplest form of jig for this work is shown in Fig. 2. The piece of work D is located between the two plates E, which form the jig, and which, if the jig is small, are made of machine steel and casehardened. If the jig is large these plates are made of cast iron. The work D is simply located by the outlines of the plates, which are made to the same dimensions, as regards width, as the work itself. The plates are held in position in relation to each other by the guiding dowel pins F. These pins are driven into the lower plate and have a sliding fit in the upper one. In some cases, blocks or lugs on one plate would be used to fit into a slot in the other plate instead of pins. These minor changes, of course, depend upon the nature of the work, the principle involved being that some means must be provided to prevent the two plates from shifting in relation to each other while drilling. The whole device is finally held together by clamps of suitable form. The holes A may be drilled from either side of the jig, as they pass clear through the work, and the guides for the drills for these holes may, therefore, be placed in either plate. Opposite the bushings in either plate a hole is drilled in the other plate for clearance for the drill when passing through, and for the escape of the chips.

The two plates should be marked with necessary general information regarding the tools to be used, the position of the plates, etc., to prevent mistakes by the operator. It is also an advantage, not to say a necessity, to use some kind of connection between the plates in order to avoid such mistakes as, for instance, the placing of the upper plate in a reversed position, the wrong pins entering into the dowel pin holes. This, of course, would locate the holes in a faulty position. Besides, if the upper plate be entirely loose from the lower, it is likely to drop off when the jig is stored, and get lost. Some means of holding the two parts

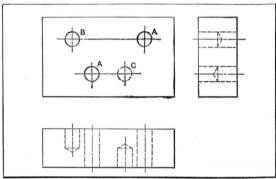

Fig. 1.   Work to be Drilled

together, even when not in use, or when not clamped down on the work, should therefore be provided. Such a means is employed in Fig. 2, where the screw *G* enters into the guiding dowel pin at the left and holds the upper plate in place. A pin *H*, fitting into an elongated slot in the dowel pin, as shown at the left, could also be used instead of the screw. The design shown presents the very simplest form of box jig, consisting, as it does, of only two plates for holding the necessary guiding arrangements, and two pins or other means for locating the plates in relation to each other.

In manufacturing, where a great number of duplicate parts would be encountered, a jig designed in the simple manner shown in Fig. 2 would, however, be wholly inadequate. The simplest form of a jig that would be used in such a case would be one in which some kind of locating means is employed, as indicated in Fig. 3, where three pins are provided, two along the side of the work and one for the end of the work, against which the work

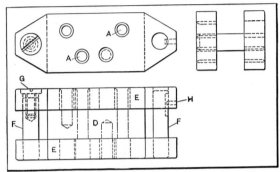

Fig. 2. Simple Form of Closed Jig for Drilling Work
shown in Fig. 1

may be pushed prior to the clamping together of the two jig-plates. In this illustration, the jig bushings are not shown in the elevation and end view, in order to avoid confusion of lines. The next improvement to which this jig would be subjected would

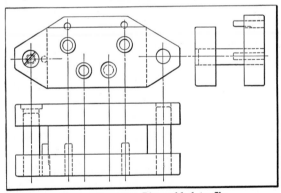

Fig. 3. Locating Pins added to Jig

be the adding of walls at the end of the jig and the screwing together of the upper and lower plate, the result being a jig as shown in Fig. 4. This design presents a more advanced style of closed jig — a type which could be recommended for manufacturing purposes. While the same fundamental principles are still in evidence, this jig embodies most of the requirements necessary for rapid work. This design provides for integral clamping means within the jig itself, provided, in this case, by the screws J. The upper plate K is fastened to the walls of the lower plate L by four or more screws M and two dowel pins N. The cover K could also be put on, as shown in Fig. 5, by making the two parts a good fit at O, one piece being tongued into the other. This gives greater rigidity to the jig. In this jig, also, solid locating lugs F are used instead of pins.

Referring again to Fig. 4, by providing a swinging arm P with a set-screw Q, the work can be taken out and can be inserted

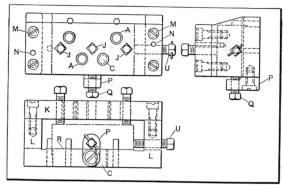

Fig. 4.   Jig Suitable for Manufacturing Purposes

from the side of the jig, which will save making any provisions for taking off or putting on the top cover for every piece being drilled. If there is enough clearance between the top cover and the piece being drilled, the screw Q could, of course, be mounted in a solid lug, but it would not be advantageous to have so large a space between the top plate and the work, as the drill would have to extend unguided for some distance before it would reach the work. The set-screws Q and U hold the work against the locating points, and the set-screws J on the top of the jig, previously referred to, hold the work down on the finished pad R on the bottom plate. These screws also take the thrust when the hole C is drilled from the bottom side. It is immaterial on which side the bushings for guiding the drills for the two holes A are placed, but by placing them in the cover rather than in the bottom plate, three out of the four bushings will be located in the top part, and when using a multiple-spindle drill, the face R will take the greater thrust, which is better than to place the thrust on the binding screws J. In the designs in Figs. 4 and 5 the whole top and bottom face of the jig must be finished, or a strip marked f in Fig. 6, at both ends of the top and bottom surfaces, must be provided, so that it can be finished, and the jig placed on parallels D as illustrated.

While the jig itself, developed so far, possesses most of the necessary points for rapid production and accurate work, the

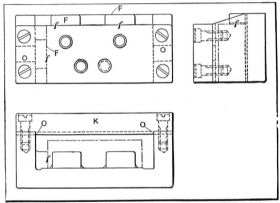

Fig. 5. Alternative Design of Jig shown in Fig. 4

use of parallels, as indicated in Fig. 6, for supporting the jig when turned over so that the screw-heads of the clamping screws point downward, is unsatisfactory. Therefore, by adding feet to the jig, as shown in Fig. 7, the handling of the jig will be a great deal more convenient. The adding of the protruding handle S will still further increase the convenience of using the jig. The design in Fig. 7 also presents an improvement over that in Fig. 4, in that, besides the adding of feet and handle, the leaf or strap E is used for holding screw Q instead of the arm P. This latter is more apt to bend if not very heavy, and would then bring the set-screw in an angle upwards, which would have a tendency to tilt the work. The strap can be more safely relied upon to clamp the work squarely. Two set-screws J are shown for holding the work in place. The number of these set-screws, of course, depends entirely upon the size of the work and the size of the holes to be drilled. Sometimes one set-screw is quite sufficient, which, in this case, would be placed in the center, as indicated by the dotted lines in Fig. 4.

The type of jig shown in Fig. 7 now possesses all the features

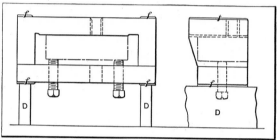

Fig. 6. Jig in Fig. 4 used in Combination with Two Parallels

generally required for a good jig, and presents a type which is largely used in manufacturing plants, particularly for medium and heavy work. The jig shown in Fig. 8, however, represents another type, somewhat different from the jig in Fig. 7. The

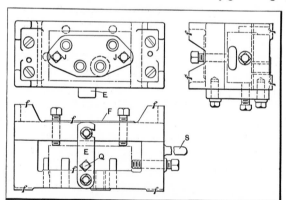

Fig. 7. Jig improved by Adding Feet opposite Faces
containing Drill Bushings

jig in Fig. 7 is composed of two large separate pieces, which, for large jigs, means two separate castings, involving some extra expense in the pattern-shop and foundry. The reason for making the jig in two parts, instead of casting it in one, is because it makes it more convenient when machining the jig. The locat-

ing points, however, are somewhat hidden from view when the
piece is inserted. The jig shown in Fig. 8 consists of only one
casting L, provided with feet, and resembles an open drill jig.
The work is located in a manner similar to that already described,
and the leaf D, wide enough to take in all the bushings except
the one for the hole that must be drilled from the opposite side,
is fitted across the jig and given a good bearing between the
lugs in the jig wall. It swings around the pin E and is held down
by the eye-bolt F with a nut and washer. Sometimes a wing-
nut is handier than a hexagon nut. Care should be taken that

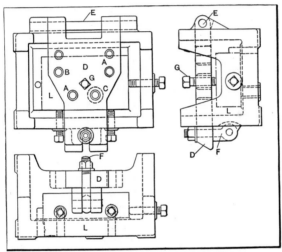

Fig. 8. Alternative Design of Jig in Fig. 7

the feet reach below the top of the nut and screw. The set-
screw G holds the work down, and takes the thrust when the
hole from the bottom side is drilled. The three holes A, A and
B are drilled from the top so that the thrust of the drilling of
these three holes will be taken by the bottom of the jig body L.
If one set-screw G is not sufficient for holding the work in place,
the leaf may be made wider so as to accommodate more binding
screws.

It is, however, an objectionable feature to place the clamping
screws in the bushing plate. If the leaf has not a perfect fit in
its seats and on the swiveling pin, the screws will tilt the leaf

one way or another, and thus cause the bushings to stand at an
angle with the work, producing faulty results.   In order to avoid
this objectionable feature, a further improvement on the jig,
indicated in Fig. 9, is proposed.   In the jig body, the locating
points and the set-screws which hold the work against the locating pins are placed so that they will not interfere with two straps
G, which are provided with elongated slots, and hold the work
securely in place, also sustaining the thrust from the cutting
tools.   These straps should be heavily designed, in order to be
able to take the thrust of the multiple-spindle drill, because in
this case all the bushings, except the one for hole B, are placed

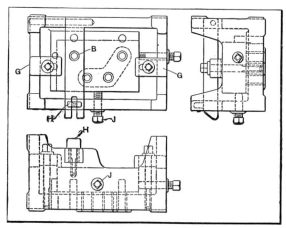

**Fig. 9.   Jig in which Thrust of Drilling Operations
is taken by Clamps**

in the bottom of the jig body.   The leaf is made narrower and
is not as heavy as the one shown in Fig. 8, because it does not,
in this case, take any thrust when drilling, and simply serves the
purpose of holding the bushing for hole B.   The leaves and loose
bushing plates for jigs of this kind are generally made of machine
steel, but for larger sized jigs they may be made of cast iron.
The leaf in Fig. 9 is simply held down by the thumb-screw H.

If the hole B comes near to one wall of the jig, it may not
be necessary to have a leaf, but the jig casting may be made with
a projecting lug D, as shown in Fig. 10, the jig otherwise being
of the same type as the one illustrated in Fig. 9.   The projecting

part *D*, Fig. 10, is strengthened, when necessary, by a rib *E*, as indicated. Care must be taken that there is sufficient clearance for the piece to be inserted and removed. Once in a while it happens, even with fairly good jig designers, that an otherwise well-designed jig with good locating, clamping, and guiding arrangements, is rendered useless, for the simple reason that there is not enough clearance to allow the insertion of the work.

Fig. 11 shows the same jig as before, but with the additional feature of permitting a hole in the work to be drilled from the end and side as indicated, the bushings *E* and *F* being added

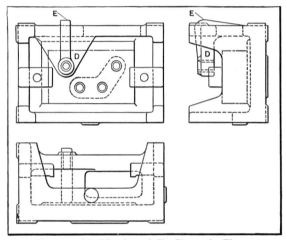

Fig. 10.   Modification of Jig Shown in Fig. 9

for this purpose. The bushings, in this case, extend through the jig wall for some distance, in order to guide the drill closely to the work. Bosses may also be cast on the jig body, as indicated by the dotted lines, to give a longer bearing for the bushings.

Feet or lugs are cast and finished on the sides of the jig opposite the bushings, so that the jig can be placed conveniently on the drill-press table for drilling in any direction. When drilling the holes from the bushings *E* and *F*, the thrust is taken by the stationary locating pins. It is objectionable to use set-screws to take the thrust, although in some cases it is necessary to do so. When designing a jig of this type, care must be taken that strapping arrangements and locating points are placed so that they, in no way, will interfere with the cutting tools or guiding means. In this case the strap H is moved over to one side in order to give room for the bushings F and the set-screw K. Strap G should then be moved also, because moving the two straps in opposite directions still gives them a balanced clamping action on the work. If the strap G had been left in place, with the strap H moved sideways, there would have been some tendency to tilt the work.

Sometimes one hole in the work comes at an angle with the faces of the work. In such a case the jig must be made along

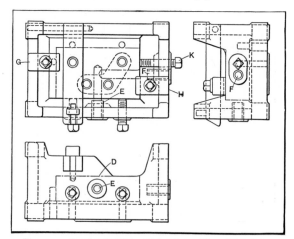

Fig. 11.   Jig for Drilling Holes from Two Directions

the lines indicated in Fig. 12, the feet on the sides opposite to where the drill bushings are placed being planed so that their faces will be perpendicular to the axis through the hole A. This will, in no way, interfere with the drilling of holes which are perpendicular to the faces of the work, as these can be drilled from the opposite side of the work, the jig then resting on the feet B. Should it, however, be necessary to drill one hole at an angle and other holes perpendicular to the face of the work from the same side, an arrangement as shown in Fig. 13 would be used. The jig here is made in the same manner as the jig shown in Fig. 11, with the difference that a bushing A is placed at the required angle. It will be seen, however, that as the

other holes drilled from the same side must be drilled perpendicu-
larly to the faces of the work, it would not be of advantage to
plane the feet so that the hole A could be drilled in the manner
previously shown in Fig. 12. Therefore the feet are left to suit
the perpendicular holes, and the separate base bracket B, Fig.
13, is used to hold the jig in the desired inclined position when
the hole A is drilled.

Stand B in Fig. 13 is very suitable for this special work. It
is made up as light as possible, being cored at the center, so as
to remove superfluous metal. These stands are sometimes pro-

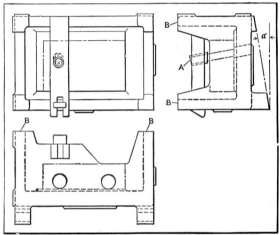

Fig. 12. Jig for Drilling Holes at an Angle

vided with a clamping device for holding the jig to the stand.
Special stands are not only used for drilling holes at angles with
the remaining holes to be drilled, but sometimes such stands
are made to suit the jig in cases where it would be inconvenient
to provide the jig with feet, finished bosses, or lugs, for resting
directly on the drill-press table.

When a jig of large dimensions is to be turned over, either for
the insertion or removal of the work, or for drilling holes from
opposite sides, it is, in cases where the use of a crane or hoist
can be obtained, very satisfactory to have a special device attached to the jig for turning it over. Fig. 14 shows such an
arrangement. In this illustration, A represents the jig which is

4J

to be turned over. The two studs B are driven into the jig in convenient places, as nearly as possible in line with a gravity axis. These studs then rest in the yoke C, which is lifted by the crane hook placed at D. The jig, when lifted off the table, can then easily be swung around. The yoke is made simply of round machine steel.

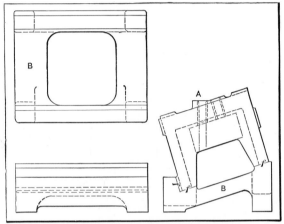

Fig. 13.   Jig and Stand for Drilling Holes at an Angle

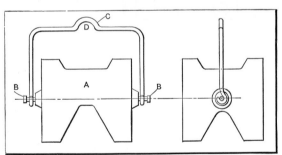

**Fig. 14.   Device for Turning over and Handling
Heavy Jigs**

Examples of Closed or Box Jigs. — The development of a closed or box jig has now been treated. In the following pages a number of examples of closed jig designs will be shown and described. There is, however, no distinct division line between open and closed drill jigs, so that in many cases it is rather inconsistent to attempt to make any such distinction.

In Fig. 15, for instance, is shown a box jig which looks like a typical open jig. The jig body *A* is made in one solid piece, cored out as shown, in order to make it lighter. The piece to be drilled *B*, shown inserted in the jig, has all its holes drilled in this jig, the holes being the screw holes *C*, the dowel pin holes *D*, and the large bearing hole *E*. The bosses of the three screw holes *C* are also faced on the top, and the bearing is faced on both sides while the work is held in the jig. The work is located against two dowel pins driven into the holes *F*, and against two lugs at *G*, not visible in the illustration, located on either side of the

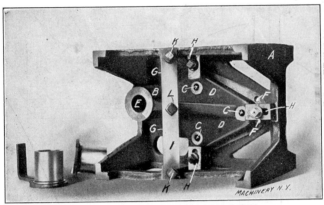

Fig. 15. Box Jig which Resembles the Open Type

work. In these lugs are placed set-screws or adjustable sliding points. It may seem incorrect not to locate the bracket in regard to the hole *E* for the bearing, so as to be sure to bring the hole concentric with the outside of the boss. This ordinarily is a good rule to follow, but in this particular case it is essential that the screw holes be placed in a certain relation to the outline of the bracket in order to permit this to match up with the pad on the machine on which the bracket is used. Brackets of this shape may be cast very uniformly, so that locating them in the manner described will not seriously interfere with drilling the hole *E* approximately in the center of its boss. The work is firmly held in the jig by the three straps *H*, care being taken in designing the jig that these straps are placed so they will not interfere with the facing tools.

The swinging strap *I*, which really is the only thing that makes this jig a closed jig, serves the sole purpose of taking the thrust of the heavy cutting tools when drilling the hole *E* and of steadying the work when facing off the two ends of the hub. The two collar-head screws *K* hold the strap to the jig body and the set-

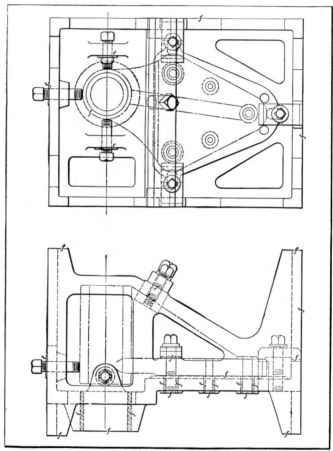

Fig. 16. Plan and Elevation of Jig Shown in Fig. 15

screw *L* bears against the work. This strap is easily swung out of the way by loosening one of the collar-head screws, a slot being milled at one end of the strap to permit this. Stationary bushings are used for the screw hole and dowel holes, but for the bearing hole *E* three loose bushings and a lining bushing are employed.

The hole E is first opened up by a small twist drill, which makes the work considerably easier for the so-called rose-bit drill. The latter drill leaves $\frac{1}{16}$ inch of stock for the rose reamer to remove, which produces a very smooth, straight, and concentric hole. The last operation is the facing of the holes. The holes just drilled are now used to guide the pilots of the facing tools, and, as the operation is performed while the work is held in the jig, it is important that the locating or strapping arrangements should not be in the way.

In connection with the opening up of a hole with a smaller drill, it may be mentioned that it is not only for large holes that this method of procedure will save time, but the method is often a time-saving one also for smaller holes, down to $\frac{1}{4}$ inch in diameter, when drilled in steel.

The use of lubrication in jigs is a very important item, the most common lubricant being oil or vaseline, but soap solution is also used. The objection to the latter is that unless the machine and tools are carefully cleaned it is likely to cause rusting. Using a lubricant freely will save the guiding arrangements, such as the drill bushings, the pilots on counterbores, etc., to a great extent.

The jig in Fig. 15 is shown in Fig. 16 and a clear idea of the design of the jig will be had by studying this line engraving. The bracket B, in Fig. 15, could have been drilled in a different way than described, which would sometimes be advantageous. It could be held in a chuck, and the hole E reamed and faced in a lathe, which would insure that the hole would be perfectly central with the outside of the boss. Then a jig could be designed, locating the work by a stud entering in hole E, as indicated in Fig. 17, additional dowel pins and set-screws being used for locating the piece sidewise. The whole arrangement could be held down to the table by a strap and bolt, a jack-screw supporting it at the overhanging end.

Fig. 18 shows another jig of the closed type, with the work inserted. The piece A is a casing, and the holes to be drilled vary greatly in size. The casing rests on the flat, finished bottom surface of the jig and is brought up squarely against a finished pad at B. It further locates against the finished lug C, in order to insure getting the proper amount of metal around the hole D. At the bottom it is located against the sliding point E, the latter being adjustable, because the location of the work is determined by the other locating points and surfaces. The work is held against the locating points by the long set-screw shown to the left. This clamping arrangement, however, is not to be recommended, because this screw must be screwed back a considerable distance in order to permit insertion and removal of the work.

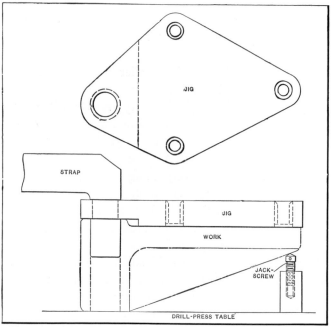

Fig. 17.   Simple Plate Jig for Drilling Bracket shown in Fig. 15, after Hole E has been Bored in the Lathe

An eye-bolt used in the manner described in a preceding chapter would have given better service. The three straps G hold the work against the bottom surface, and the two straps H hold it against the finished surface at B. There is not a long finished hole through the casting, as would be assumed from its appearance, but simply a short bearing at each end, the remaining part of the hole being cored out. For this reason, the hole is drilled and reamed instead of being bored out, as the latter operation would be a slower one. Although the two short bearings are somewhat far apart, the guiding bushings come so close to these bearings that the alignment can be made very good. The screw holes and dowel pin holes at the bottom of the casing are not shown in the illustration, as the inserted casing is not yet drilled. The hole drilled from bushing I is a rather important hole, and the bushing requires a long bearing in order to guide the drills straight when drilling. When this jig was made, the projecting lug which was provided solid with the jig body, to give a bearing

Fig. 18. Box Jig for Casing drilled from Five Directions

to the jig bushing, came so much out of the way in the rough casting for the jig that half of the lining bushing would have been exposed. It was therefore planed off and a bushing of the type shown in Fig. 5, in the chapter on "Jig Bushings," inserted instead, in order to provide for a long bearing.

Leaf K, which carries the bushings for drilling the hole D, fits into a slot planed out in the jig body and is held down by the eye-bolt L. Two lugs M are provided on the main casting for holding the pin on which the leaf swivels. Around the hole

D there are three small tap holes *O* which are drilled by the
guiding afforded by the bushing *P*, which is made of cast iron
and provided with small steel bushings placed inside as illustrated
in Fig. 14, in the chapter on "Jig Bushings." In the bushing *P*
is another hole *Q* which fits over a pin located in the top of the
leaf and which insures that the three screw holes will come in
the right position. It should be noted that large portions of the

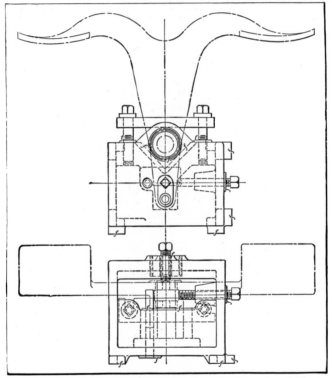

Fig. 19. Box Jig for Drilling Work shown by Dash-dotted Lines

jig body are cored out at top and bottom in order to make it
light and easy to handle. Of course some metal is also saved
by the construction of jigs in this manner, but comparing the
price of cast iron with the total price of a finished jig of this type,
the saving in this respect is so insignificant that it is not worth
while mentioning. The leaf *K* is also made of cast iron, being of

particularly large size, and it is planed at the places where it has
a bearing on the jig body.

Fig. 20 shows a closed jig about which there can be no doubt
but that it should be classified as a box jig. The piece of work
drilled, the foot trip A, has two holes B and C which are drilled
in this jig. The cylindrical hub of the work is located against
V-blocks and held in place by a swinging strap D. The work is
further located against a stop-pin placed opposite the set-screw
E. The trip is located sidewise by being brought against another

Fig. 20. Jig shown in Detail in Fig. 19

stop by the set-screw F. One-quarter of a turn of the collar-head
screw on the top of the jig releases the swinging strap which is
then turned out of the way; this permits the trip to be removed
and another to be inserted. Half a turn or less of the set-screws
is enough to release and clamp the work against the stops mentioned. A line engraving of this jig is shown in Fig. 19 which
gives a better idea of some of the details of the construction.

In Figs. 21 and 22 are shown two views of another type of
closed drill jig. The work A, to be drilled, is shown at the left

in both illustrations, and consists of a special lathe apron with large bearing holes, screw holes, and dowel pin holes to be drilled. The apron is located in the jig body in the same manner as it is located on the lathe carriage, in this case by a tongue which may be seen at B in Fig. 22. This tongue fits into the slot C in the jig,

Fig. 21.   Jig of Typical Design, and Work for which it is Used

Fig. 22.   Another View of the Jig in Fig. 21

care being taken in the construction of the jig that the slot is made deep enough to prevent the tongue from bearing in the bottom of the slot. A good solid bearing should be provided, however, for the finished surface on both sides of the tongue. The surface D should also have a solid bearing on the surface E in the jig the difference in height between the two bearing surfaces in the jig being exactly the same as between the two bearing surfaces on the lathe carriage where the lathe apron is to be fitted. The work is brought up against, and further located by, a dowel **pin** at the further end of the slot, by the set-screw in the block F, Fig. 21. As it is rather difficult to get the tongues on all the pieces exactly the correct width for a good fit in the slot, the latter is sometimes planed a little wider and the tongue is brought up against one side of the slot by set-screws. In the case in hand, a few thousandths inch clearance is provided in the slot, and the set-screw G in Fig. 22 is used for bringing the work against the further edge, which stands in correct relation to the holes to be drilled. The apron is held down against the bottom surface of the jig by four heavy set-screws H.

It will be noticed that the jig is open right through the sides in order to facilitate the finishing of the pads at the ends of the

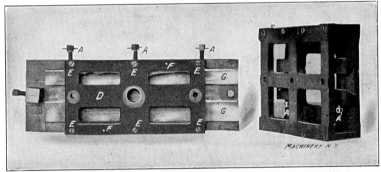

Fig. 23. Jigs in which the Work is Located by Means of Beveled Surfaces

work, and a swinging leaf, like the one previously described, reaches across one side for holding the lining and loose bushings for the hole K which is drilled and rose-reamed in the usual way. The large hole V, Fig. 21, is bored out with a special boring tool M, as there are no standard drills obtainable for this large size of hole. This special boring tool is guided by a cast-iron bushing which fits into the lining bushing; it is provided with two cutters, one for roughing and one for finishing. The small screw holes O around the large hole V are drilled from the bushing P. For drilling the rest of the holes, except the hole Q, stationary bushings are used. The screw holes ought to be drilled simultaneously in a multiple-spindle drill. The jig is provided with feet and cored out in convenient places in order to make it as light as possible to handle. Lugs project wherever necessary to give ample bearings to the lining bushings and, in turn, to the loose guiding bushings.

Fig. 23 shows two closed jigs made up of two main parts which are planed and assembled by screws and dowels as indicated, the reason for making the jigs in this way being the ease of planing the bottom section. The work drilled in these jigs, some special slides, is located by the dovetail and held up against one dovetail side by set-screws A, as shown in the illustration. In the jig

Fig. 24.   Jig for Drilling Holes at other than 90-degree Angles

to the left, the work is located endwise against a dowel pin and is held up against this stop by a set-screw through the block shown to the left. This block must be taken out when the slide is inserted, this being the reason why a lug cast directly in place, through which the set-screw could pass, is not used. The top plate D is held down on the main body by six fillister-head screws E, and two dowel pins F prevent it from shifting. No clamping arrangements, except the set-screws A, are necessary. The holes being drilled from the top, the main body of the jig takes the thrust. These jigs are also used in multiple-spindle drills.

One objectionable feature of the jig to the right in Fig. 23 is that set-screws A are difficult of access. There are, therefore, holes piercing the heads of the set-screws in two directions in order to allow a pin to be used when tightening the screws. A better idea, however, is to have the screw-heads extend out through the wall and, if this is solid, to have cored or drilled holes through which the heads of the screws may pass.

In Fig. 24 is another closed drill jig in which the work is located against the finished seats and held down by the set-screws *A* in the straps *B*. All the holes, except those marked *C*, are drilled

Fig. 25. Jig in Fig. 24 in Position for Drilling Holes at an Oblique Angle with Jig Base

in the usual manner, the jig standing on its own feet, but when drilling the holes *C*, which come on an angle, the special stand *D* is employed, which brings the holes in the right position for drilling, as illustrated in Fig. 25. If only the holes *C* were to be drilled, the feet on the side opposite the guiding bushings for these holes could have been planed off, so that they would have been in a plane perpendicular to the axis of the holes. This last jig has a peculiar appearance, on account of the end walls coming up square, as shown in the illustrations, but this design was adopted only to simplify matters for the patternmaker, it being easier to make the pattern this way.

CHAPTER IV

JIG BUSHINGS

The drills, counterbores, reamers, etc., used in connection with drill jigs are guided by steel bushings, which are hardened and ground, and placed in the jig body in their proper location. These bushings may be of two kinds: stationary and removable, the latter usually being known as "loose" bushings. The most common and the preferable form for the stationary bushing is shown in Fig. 1. This bushing is straight both on the inside and on the outside, except that the upper corners A on the inside are given a liberal radius, so as to allow the drill to enter the hole easily, while the corners B at the lower end of the outside are slightly rounded for the purpose of making it easier to drive the bushing into the hole, when making the jig, and also to prevent the sharp corner on the bushing from cutting the metal in the hole into which the bushing is driven.

Removable Bushings. — When removable bushings are used, they should never be placed directly in the jig body, except if the jig be used only a few times, but the hole should always be provided with a lining bushing. This lining bushing is always made of the form shown in Fig. 1. If the hole bored in the jig body receives the loose or removable bushing directly, the inserting and removing of the bushing, if the jig is frequently used, would soon wear the walls of the hole in the jig body, and after a while the jig would have to be replaced, or at least the hole would have to be bored out, and a new removable bushing made to fit the larger-sized hole. In order to overcome this, the hole in the jig body is bored out large enough to receive the lining bushing referred to, which is driven in place. This lining bushing then, in turn, receives the loose bushing, the outside diameter of which closely fits the inside diameter of the lining bushing, as shown in Fig. 2, in which A is the jig body, B the

lining bushing, and *C* the loose bushing. Both of these bushings are hardened and ground so that they will stand constant
use and wear for some length of time. When no removable
bushings are required, the lining bushing itself becomes the
drill bushing or reamer bushing, and the inside diameter of the
lining bushing will then fit the cutting tool used. The bushing
shown in Fig. 1 is cheaper to make, and will work fully as well,
when driven in place in the hole receiving it, as do bushings
having a shoulder at the upper end, such as the loose bushing
shown in Fig. 2. It was the practice some years ago to make
all bushings with a shoulder, but this is unnecessary, and simply
increases the cost of making the bushing.

Material for Jig Bushings. — Bushings are generally made of
a good grade of tool steel to insure hardening at a fairly low
temperature and to lessen the danger of fire cracking. They

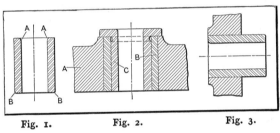

Fig. 1.   Fig. 2.   Fig. 3.

can also be made from machine steel, which will answer all
practical purposes, provided the bushings are properly casehardened to a depth of about $\frac{1}{16}$ inch. Sometimes bushings for
guiding tools may be made of cast iron, but only when the cutting tool is of such a design that no cutting edges come within
the bushing itself. For example, bushings used simply to support the smooth surface of a boring-bar or the shank of a reamer
might, in some instances, be made of cast iron, but hardened
steel bushings should always be used for guiding drills, reamers,
taps, etc., when the cutting edges come in direct contact with
the guiding surfaces. If the outside diameter of the bushing is
very large, as compared with the diameter of the cutting tool,
the cost of the bushing can sometimes be reduced by using an
outer cast-iron body and inserting a hardened tool steel bush-

ing. Occasionally a bushing having a large outside diameter is required as, for example, when a large counterbore must be used in a small hole, which makes it necessary to have a large opening in the jig body. If the jig wall is thin, the bushing may project out as shown in Fig. 3, so as to give the cutting tool the proper guiding and support as close to the work as possible.

American Standard Jig Bushings. — Dimensions of the American Standard jig bushings are given in Tables 1, 2, and 3. This standard was approved by the American Standards Association in 1935 and revised in 1941. It was formulated by the Sectional Committee on the Standardization of Small Tools and Machine Tool Elements, under the procedure of the American Standards Association and sponsored by the National Machine Tool Builders Association, the Society of Automotive Engineers, and The American Society of Mechanical Engineers.

Renewable Bushings. — Renewable wearing bushings to guide the tool are for use in liners which in turn are installed in the jig. (Table 1.) They are used where the bushing will wear out or become obsolete before the jig or where several bushings are to be interchangeable in one hole. Renewable wearing bushings are divided into two classes, "Fixed" and "Slip."

Fixed renewable bushings are installed in the liner with the intention of leaving them in place until worn out. Slip renewable bushings are interchangeable in a given size of liner and, to facilitate removal, they are usually made with a knurled head. They are most frequently used where two or more operations requiring different inside diameters are performed in a single jig, such as where drilling is followed by reaming, tapping, spot facing, counterboring, or some other secondary operation.

Press Fit Bushings. — Press fit wearing bushings to guide the tool are for installation directly in the jig without the use of a liner and are employed principally where the bushings are used for short production runs and will not require replacement. (See Table 2.) They are intended also for use where the closeness of the center distance of holes will not permit the installation of liners and renewable bushings. Press fit bushings are made in two types, with heads and without.

Liner Bushings. — Liner bushings are provided with and without heads and are permanently installed in a jig to receive the renewable wearing bushings. They are sometimes called "master bushings." (Table 3.)

Bushing Specifications. — The dimensions and tolerances of jig bushings shall conform to the specifications given in

Table 1. American Standard Renewable Wearing Bushings — Slip and Fixed Types

Hole Size A		Body Diameter B			Head Diameter F
From	To and Incl.	Nominal	Max.	Min.	
0.0000	0.1562	5⁄16	0.3125	0.3123	5⁄8
0.1610	0.3125	1⁄2	0.5000	0.4998	15⁄16
0.3160	0.5000	3⁄4	0.7500	0.7498	1 1⁄4
0.5156	0.7500	1	1.0000	0.9998	1 5⁄8
0.7656	1.0000	1 3⁄8	1.3750	1.3747	2
1.0156	1.3750	1 3⁄4	1.7500	1.7497	2 1⁄2
1.3906	1.7500	2 1⁄4	2.2500	2.2496	3

Hole Size A		Width D of Chamfer	Max. and Min. Hole, Size A		
From	To and Incl.		Nominal Size A	Max. = Size A Plus	Min. = Size A Plus
0.0000	0.1562	1⁄32	0 to 1⁄4 incl.	0.0004	0.0001
0.1610	0.3125	5⁄64	1⁄4 to 3⁄4 incl.	0.0005	0.0001
0.3160	0.5000	7⁄64	3⁄4 to 1 1⁄2 incl.	0.0006	0.0002
0.5156	0.7500	7⁄64	1 1⁄2 up	0.0007	0.0003
0.7656	1.0000	9⁄64	....	....	....
1.0156	1.3750	9⁄64	....	....	....
1.3906	1.7500	7⁄32	....	....	....

All dimensions given in inches. Tolerance on fractional dimensions where not otherwise specified shall be ±0.010 inch. The head design shall be in accordance with the manufacturer's practice. The angle of chamfer, E, shall be 59 deg ± 1 deg and a slight radius shall be provided at the intersection of this chamfer with the hole, A. Head of slip type is usually knurled. When renewable wearing bushings are to be used with liner bushings of the head type, the length under head, C, should be increased over the jig plate thickness by the thickness of the liner bushing head. Hole sizes conform to the American Standard for Twist Drills.

the tables and notes. The standard lengths of the press-fit portion of these jig bushings are based on standardized or uniform jig plate thicknesses of 5/16, 1/2, 3/4, 1, 1 3/8, and 1 3/4 inches.

Table 2. American Standard Press Fit Wearing Bushings — Headless and Head Types

Hole Diam. A*		Diam. B, Unfinished			Diam. B, Finished		Width Chamfer D
From	To Incl.	Nom.	Max.	Min.	Max.	Min.	D
0.0156	0.0625	5/32	0.166	0.161	0.1578	0.1575	1/32
0.0630	0.0995	13/64	0.213	0.208	0.2046	0.2043	1/32
0.1024	0.1378	1/4	0.260	0.255	0.2516	0.2513	1/32
0.1406	0.1875	5/16	0.327	0.322	0.3141	0.3138	1/32
0.1910	0.2500	13/32	0.421	0.416	0.4078	0.4075	1/16
0.2520	0.3125	1/2	0.520	0.515	0.5017	0.5014	5/64
0.3160	0.4219	5/8	0.645	0.640	0.6267	0.6264	3/32
0.4375	0.5000	3/4	0.770	0.765	0.7518	0.7515	7/64
0.5156	0.6250	7/8	0.895	0.890	0.8768	0.8765	7/64
0.6406	0.7500	1	1.020	1.015	1.0018	1.0015	7/64
0.7656	1.0000	1 3/8	1.395	1.390	1.3772	1.3768	9/64
1.0156	1.3750	1 3/4	1.770	1.765	1.7523	1.7519	9/64
1.3906	1.7500	2 1/4	2.270	2.265	2.2525	2.2521	7/32

Hole A From	To and Incl.	C Short	C Med.	C Long	Diam. F	Height G	Hole Size A above Nominal
0.0156	0.0625	5/16	....	1/2	1/4	3/32	+.0001 to +.0004
0.0630	0.0995	5/16	....	1/2	5/16	3/32	+.0001 to +.0004
0.1024	0.1378	5/16	....	1/2	3/8	3/32	+.0001 to +.0004
0.1406	0.1875	5/16	1/2	3/4	7/16	1/8	+.0001 to +.0004
0.1910	0.2500	5/16	1/2	3/4	17/32	5/32	+.0001 to +.0004
0.2520	0.3125	5/16	1/2	3/4	5/8	7/32	+.0001 to +.0005
0.3160	0.4219	1/2	3/4	1	13/16	7/32	+.0001 to +.0005
0.4375	0.5000	1/2	3/4	1	15/16	7/32	+.0001 to +.0005
0.5156	0.6250	3/4	1	1 3/8	1 1/8	1/4	+.0001 to +.0005
0.6406	0.7500	3/4	1	1 3/8	1 1/4	5/16	+.0001 to +.0005
0.7656	1.0000	3/4	1	1 3/8	1 5/8	3/8	+.0002 to +.0006
1.0156	1.3750	1	1 3/8	1 3/4	2	3/8	+.0002 to +.0006
1.3906	1.7500	1	1 3/8	1 3/4	2 1/2	3/8	+.0003 to +.0007

* Hole sizes A conform to the American Standard for twist drill sizes. The body diameter, B, for unfinished bushings is larger than the nominal diameter in order to provide grinding stock for fitting to jig plate holes. Tolerance on fractional dimensions where not otherwise specified shall be ±0.010 inch. The length, C, is the overall length for the headless type and the length underhead for the head type. The head design shall be in accordance with the manufacturer's practice. The angle of chamfer, E, shall be 59 deg ± 1 deg and a slight radius shall be provided at the intersection of this chamfer with the hole, A.

Miscellaneous Types of Drill Bushings. — As mentioned, it was general practice formerly to provide even stationary bushings with a shoulder or head, as shown in bushing C, Fig. 2. This will prevent the bushing from being pushed through the jig by the cutting tool, but this seldom happens if the bushings are made to fit the tool correctly. Sometimes the shoulder is used to take the thrust of a stop-collar, which is clamped on the drill, to allow it to go down to a certain depth, as shown in Fig. 4, in which C is the stop-collar, D the wall of the jig, and E the stationary bushing; F is the work.

Table 3. American Standard Liner Bushings — Headless and Head Types

Range of Hole Size in Renewable Wearing Bushings*		Inside Diameter A of Liner Bushing			Body Diameter B Unfinished		
From	To and Incl.	Nom.	Max.	Min.	Nom.	Max.	Min.
0.0000	0.1562	5⁄16	0.3129	0.3126	1⁄2	0.520	0.515
0.1610	0.3125	1⁄2	0.5005	0.5002	3⁄4	0.770	0.765
0.3160	0.5000	3⁄4	0.7506	0.7503	1	1.020	1.015
0.5156	0.7500	1	1.0007	1.0004	1 3⁄8	1.395	1.390
0.7656	1.0000	1 3⁄8	1.3760	1.3756	1 3⁄4	1.770	1.765
1.0156	1.3750	1 3⁄4	1.7512	1.7508	2 1⁄4	2.270	2.265
1.3906	1.7500	2 1⁄4	2.2515	2.2510	2 3⁄4	2.770	2.765

Range of Hole Size in Renewable Wearing Bushings*		Body Diameter B Finished		Jig Plate Thickness C			Head Diam. F
From	To and Incl.	Max.	Min.	Short	Medium	Long	Max.
0.0000	0.1562	0.5017	0.5014	5⁄16	1⁄2	3⁄4	5⁄8
0.1610	0.3125	0.7518	0.7515	5⁄16	1⁄2	3⁄4	15⁄16
0.3160	0.5000	1.0018	1.0015	1⁄2	3⁄4	1	1 1⁄4
0.5156	0.7500	1.3772	1.3768	3⁄4	1	1 3⁄8	1 5⁄8
0.7656	1.0000	1.7523	1.7519	3⁄4	1	1 3⁄8	2
1.0156	1.3750	2.2525	2.2521	1	1 3⁄8	1 3⁄4	2 1⁄2
1.3906	1.7500	2.7526	2.7522	1	1 3⁄8	1 3⁄4	3

* For detail dimensions of renewable wearing bushings see Table 1. Hole sizes A conform to the American Standard for Twist Drills.

Minimum body diameter, B for unfinished bushings, is 0.015 to 0.020 inch larger than nominal diameter to provide grinding stock for fitting to jig plate holes. Tolerance on fractional dimensions where not otherwise specified shall be ±0.010 inch. The head design shall be in accordance with the manufacturer's practice. The length, C, is the overall length for the headless type and the length under head for the head type.

If the work to be drilled is located against a finished seat or boss on the wall of the jig, and the wall is not thick enough to take a bushing of standard length, then it is common practice to make a bushing having a long head, as shown in Fig. 5. The length A of the head can be extended as far as necessary to get the proper bearing. As the bushing is driven in place and the shoulder of the head bears against the finished surface of a boss on the jig, it will give the cutting tool almost as rigid a bearing as if the jig metal surrounded the bushing all the way up.

Removable bushings (Fig. 6) are frequently used for work which must be drilled, reamed, and tapped, there then

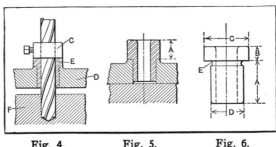

Fig. 4.   Fig. 5.   Fig. 6.

being one bushing for each of the cutting tools. They are also used when different parts of the same hole are to be drilled out to different diameters, or when the upper portion of the hole is counterbored, or when a lug has to be faced off. In this case, each tool, of course, has its own guide bushing. The outside is made to fit the inside of the lining bushing with a nice sliding fit, so that it can be gently pressed into the lining bushing by the hand. The distance A under the head of the bushing, and the diameter C for different bushing diameters D, are given in Table 1, although the letters differ from those shown in Fig. 6. A groove E is cut immediately under the head, so that the grinding wheel can pass clear over the part being ground.

Means for Preventing Loose Bushings from Turning. — In order to prevent the bushings from turning, in some shops a collar, with a projecting tail, as shown in Fig. 7, is forced

turning and from rising out of the hole. At the same time
it can easily be removed when required, and there is no
projection on the jig of any kind that can be broken off
while handling. It is not always necessary to tap a hole
for the pin in the jig bushing. A plain drilled hole is sufficient when the bushing is at least 3/8 inch thick. If the
wall of the bushing is thinner than this, the pin cannot be
driven in tightly enough to stay in place securely.

Screw Bushings. — Sometimes removable bushings are
threaded on the outside and made to fit a tapped hole in the
jig, as shown in Fig. 10. The lower part of the bushing is

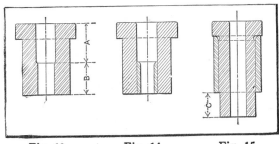

Fig. 13.   Fig. 14.   Fig. 15.

usually turned straight, and ground, in order to center the
bushing perfectly in the hole in the jig. The head of the
bushing is either knurled or milled hexagon for a wrench.
When these bushings are used, they are, as a rule, not used
for the single purpose of guiding the cutting tool, but they
combine with this the purposes of locating and clamping
the work. For such purposes they are quite frequently
used. These bushings are not commonly used as removable
bushings, as it would take considerable time to unscrew,
and to again insert, a bushing of this type into the jig body.

Special Designs of Guide Bushings. — When the guide bushings are very long, and consequently would cause unnecessary friction in their contact with the cutting tools, they
may be recessed, as shown in Fig. 13. The distance A of
the hole in the bushing is recessed enough wider than the
diameter of the tool so as not to bear on it. The length B,
being about twice the diameter of the hole, gives sufficiently

long guiding surfaces for the cutting tool, to prevent its running out. If the outside diameter of the bushing is very large compared with the diameter of the cutting tool, as indicated in Fig. 14, the expense of making the bushings may be reduced by making the outside bushing of cast iron, inserting into this a hardened tool-steel bushing, driven in place. The steel bushing is then given dimensions according to Table 3 for stationary bushings. The reason why there may be a necessity of a bushing having so large an outside diameter and so small a hole may be that the bushing is required to be removed for counterboring part of the small hole being drilled by a counterbore of large diameter, in which case the hole in the jig body has to be large enough to accommodate the large counterbore.

If a loose or removable bushing is longer than the lining bushing, as illustrated in Fig. 15, it will prove advantageous to make the size of the projecting portion of the bushing about 1/32 inch smaller in diameter than the part of the loose bushing which fits the lining bushing. This lessens the amount of surface which has to be ground, and, at the same time, makes it easier to insert the bushing, giving it, so to say, a point, which will first enter the lining bushing, and it interferes in no way with the proper qualities of the bushing as a guide for the cutting tool. In some cases, the holes in the piece to be drilled are so close to one another that it is impossible to find space for lining bushings in the jig. If this happens, it is necessary to make a leaf, or a loose wall, or the whole jig, of machine steel or tool steel, hardening a portion or the whole jig thus made.

Locating and Machining Holes for Jig Bushings. — The method of locating and machining holes in jig plates depends upon the equipment at hand. Machines designed expressly for jig boring or similar work are very efficient and accurate. These machines are so arranged that the part to be bored and the boring spindle or spindles can be adjusted to accurately locate the holes at given center-to-center distances without preliminary measurements or laying out. One design of jig-boring machine has a single spindle adjustable on a cross-rail located above a horizontal work-table, which may be adjusted along its bed in a direction at right angles to the cross-rail. Another larger and more elaborate design has three spindles—one vertical and two horizontal—for boring the top of the jig and opposite sides. The vertical spindle may be adjusted along a cross-rail which, in turn, may be raised or lowered to suit the work. The horizontal spindles are carried by slides adjustable vertically along the cross-rail uprights. These lateral and vertical adjustments of the three spindles, in conjunction with the longitudinal movement of the work-table, make it possible to bore holes in any position within the limits of spindle and table travel. Measurements may be made with great accuracy by the means provided and there is an automatic compensating device to eliminate small residual errors in the screws for moving the table and spindles.

Among the different methods employed for accurately locating jigs, etc., especially on the faceplate of a lathe, one of the most commonly used is known as the "button method." This method is so named because cylindrical bushings or buttons are attached to the work in positions corresponding to the holes to be bored, after which they are used in locating the work.

Methods of Making Jig Bushings.—There are several methods followed in turning jig bushings. Some toolmakers prefer to "chuck out" the hole to the desired size and then finish the outside of the bushing by placing it on an arbor; others prefer to turn up the bushings two at a time, end to end, cut them apart, and then bore as the final operation. This is an excellent method to follow when making large bushings. The most rapid method, however, is to chuck out the hole and finish the outside at one setting, using bar stock held in the chuck of a rigid engine lathe. This method is not always practicable on large bushings.

In making allowances for grinding and lapping, many toolmakers use too small limits, which is the cause of many bushings having to be made over again on account of not

Table 4. Allowances for Grinding and Lapping Bushings

Operation	Diameter of Bushings in Inches					
	½	1	1½	2	2½	3
A	0.008	0.010	0.013	0.016	0.020	0.025
B	0.0005	0.0005	0.0007	0.0008	0.0009	0.001
C	0.008	0.010	0.013	0.016	0.020	0.025
D	0.0003	0.0005	0.0007	0.0008	0.0009	0.001

A—Grind outside; B—Lap outside after grinding; C—Grind inside; D—Lap inside after grinding.

"finishing out." On the other hand, many toolmakers leave too liberal an allowance for finishing, thereby causing unnecessary trouble and labor. The allowances given in Table 4 can be safely used when the bushings are made somewhere near the standard proportions but for extra long bushings more liberal allowances should be made.

Hardening Jig Bushings. — When hardening bushings made of tool steel they should be brought to an even red heat in a clean fire; the heating should never be hurried. When bushings are heated quickly, they are apt to heat unevenly, which results in warping or distortion that makes it impossible to finish them to the required size. Gas furnaces are excellent for heating, but a clean charcoal fire will answer the purpose. As soon as the bushing has been brought to an even red heat, it should be dipped in water just warm enough to take off the chill. The bushing should then be heated to a "sizzling" heat, after which it is left in the air to cool. Some toolmakers draw bushings to a medium straw color. This is a mistake as it only tends to shorten their life.

Grinding and Lapping. — There are four methods in common use for finishing holes in jig bushings: 1. Lapping with a lead lap. 2. Lapping with a lead lap followed by a cast-iron or copper lap. 3. Internal grinding. 4. Internal grinding followed by a cast-iron or copper lap for removing the last 0.0005 inch. The first method is erroneous, as it invariably results in bell-mouthed holes, especially when the toolmaker charges the lap while in use, which is an unsatisfactory but very common method. The second method is correct for holes too small to be ground conveniently. The third method is inadvisable, as the grinding wheel, no matter how fine, leaves innumerable very fine scores and high spots. These high spots soon wear away leaving the hole oversize. The last method is correct and should be used whenever possible.

In Fig. 16 is shown a lead lap with a steel tapered spindle, and a convenient mold for casting the laps. This mold is pro-

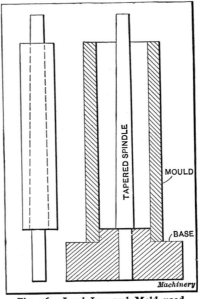

vided with a base having a hole to receive the spindle that the lap is cast on. A number of laps can be cast in this mold at one heating of the metal, and the laps are afterwards turned to the size required. Fig. 17 represents a familiar form of cast-iron lap. This lap is split in three places and provided with a taper-end screw for expanding it to compensate for wear.

Laps should be charged before using — not while they are in use. A good way to charge a lap is to lay it on a cast-iron plate on which some of the abrasive mate-

Fig. 16. Lead Lap and Mold used for Casting it

rial has been sprinkled. A cast-iron plate small enough to be conveniently handled is then held on the lap and moved back and forth with a regular motion. The lap being rolled between the two surfaces picks up a certain amount of the abrasive material. A lead lap can be charged in this manner very rapidly, as the grains of abrasive material readily imbed themselves in the soft metal. A cast-iron lap, being of a harder material, requires more time to properly charge.

Until the last few years emery was the abrasive generally used for lapping. At the present time, however, artificial abra-

sives, products of the electric furnace, are displacing emery, as
they cut faster, producing excellent results in a comparatively
short time as compared to emery. Nos. 90 to 150 are used in
connection with lead laps for roughing operations. For the
final finishing with cast-iron laps, flour abrasive is used. When
not in use, any abrasive used for lapping should be kept in a
covered box to protect it from dirt and other foreign substances.
A small chip or piece of grit will often cut a deep score in a piece
of work.

Laps should always be run at a fairly low speed. Fifteen to
twenty feet surface speed for a lead lap used for roughing and

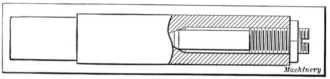

Fig. 17.   Usual Form of Cast-iron Lap

twenty to twenty-five feet surface speed for a cast-iron lap used
for finishing are about right. A high surface speed causes the
lap to wear out without cutting as rapidly as it should. Many
toolmakers make the mistake of running laps too fast, often
causing unsatisfactory work. For light lapping, the work can
be held by hand, but for a heavy roughing cut it is best to hold
the work with an ordinary lathe dog, care being taken to see
that the dog is not clamped so tightly as to spring the work
out of shape. Lead laps should be split to compensate for wear,
and the spindles should have a groove cut along their entire
length to prevent the lap from turning.

Before testing with a size plug, the work should be washed
with benzine or gasoline to remove all traces of the abrasive
material, a few grains of which will wear the size plug below
standard size in a surprisingly short time.

Many toolmakers look on the finishing of jig bushings by
internal grinding as a rather uncertain method, whereas it is a
comparatively simple process when the following important
factors are carefully considered. First, proper selection of grinding wheels; second, correct wheel speeds or at least as nearly

correct as the design of the machine will permit; third, correct alignment of the headstock in regard to the travel of the platen; and fourth, proper truing of wheels.

Wheels for internal grinding should be of a medium grit, soft grade and open bond. As a rule the grit should never be finer than 60 grit; in fact, a coarser grit can often be used to advantage. Wheels with fine grit cut slowly, and fill up readily, glazing and invariably heating the work, and causing chattering and other troubles. In fact, the only argument in favor of a fine grit wheel is that it leaves a smooth surface. However, no matter how smooth the surface appears, even under a powerful glass, it must be lapped to remove the wheel marks.

For the internal grinding of jig bushings, aloxite wheels, $1\frac{1}{2}$ inch in diameter, $\frac{3}{8}$-inch face, 60 grit, P grade, D-495 bond, may be used with good results, the wheel speed being 12,000 R.P.M. For bushings averaging $2\frac{1}{2}$ inches long, $1\frac{3}{4}$-inch hole, the holes rough-bored, 0.015 inch being left for grinding, the grinding time per bushing, including chucking and truing up, would be about twelve minutes each, and the finish left good, 0.0005 inch being sufficient to lap out the wheel marks. Reference is made to the holes being rough-bored; this is good practice, as the rather rough surface tends to wear the wheel just a little while removing the fire scale, thus preventing the wheel from glazing. Once the scale is removed from the hole, the wheel should not glaze readily, provided it is of the proper grit and grade.

Wheels for internal grinding should be run at a surface speed of 5000 feet per minute. This, however, is a general rule open to exceptions. A safe practical rule to follow is to speed up the wheel if it wears away too readily, and to reduce the speed where the wheel shows a tendency to glaze. Attention to this rule will often save much trouble. The toolmaker should bear in mind the fact that it is easier to adjust the speed to suit the wheel than it is to try to keep on hand a large variety of wheels to suit all speed conditions.

Assuming that the work in question is to be done on an ordinary universal grinder, the headstock must be set parallel with the travel of the platen to produce straight holes. A practical way to determine parallelism is to clamp a piece of round stock in the headstock chuck, letting it project from the jaws a little farther than the length of the holes to be ground. This piece should have a groove turned in it for the wheel to dwell in during reversal. This test piece is then ground in the regular way with the wheel used for cylindrical work, the headstock being adjusted by means of its swivel base until the test piece is ground parallel. Before calipering, the wheel should be allowed to grind until very few sparks are visible. When once this test piece has been ground straight the setting can be depended upon to produce straight holes, provided, of course, that the swivel adjustment of the headstock and the angular adjustment of the platen are not disturbed. To try to align the headstock by calipering the work while the internal grinding is in process is, at best, difficult, and the operator is never sure of accurate results.

It is common practice to true wheels for internal grinding with a diamond fed by hand, using the eye as a guide. This is poor practice, as the wheel is seldom turned parallel, one edge being left to do all the cutting, which glazes it readily. A more practical way to true these comparatively soft wheels is to feed them past the end of a carborundum rub, in 20 grit, H grade. The rub can be held in a suitable holder strapped to the platen of the grinder or held firmly by hand against the end of the work. A carborundum rub shows high efficiency when used for this purpose.

In holding work in the chuck for internal grinding, it is well to exercise due care to see that the work is not clamped hard enough to spring it out of shape. As a rule it does not require much pressure to hold work of this nature, as the grinding cut is comparatively light. As it is general practice to grind internal work dry, a certain amount of expansion from frictional heat is always present. For this reason considerable care has to be used in calipering the work with the sizing plug. As the plug is many degrees cooler than the work, it is liable, on being inserted, to contract the bushing suddenly, causing bushing and plug to "freeze" together firmly. This can be avoided by cooling the work with a plug that is known to be undersize before calipering with a plug of the desired size.

When a wheel of 60 grit is used, a hole one inch or under in diameter should be left approximately 0.0005 inch undersize. This amount is sufficient to lap out the wheel marks and leave a "dead smooth" mirror finish to the hole. This is a general rule based on the fact that a certain amount (in this case 0.00025 inch) is enough allowance to lap out the marks left on a surface by a grinding wheel, and that should suffice for all holes regardless of size. With comparatively large holes, one and one-half inch diameter or over, it is better, however, to make allowance for finishing, owing to the fact that the area of contact of wheel

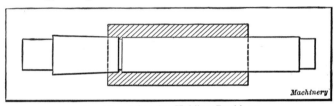

Fig. 18.   Arbor for Holding Bushings

and work is generally not so great and the ground surface is not quite so smooth.

In regard to the external grinding of bushings, there are two important points that should be given consideration: the selection of wheels and the method of holding the work. The wheel should be fast cutting and at the same time it should hold its shape and leave a good finish. For this work good results may be obtained with an aloxite wheel of 12 inches diameter, $\frac{1}{2}$-inch face, 5-inch hole, 405 grit, N grade, D-497 bond, the wheel being run at a speed of 1800 R.P.M.

When a number of bushings are to be ground one after another it is best to mount them on arbors of the same length, when practicable to do so, thus saving considerable time generally spent in re-setting the platen, which has to be done whenever the tailstock is moved to accommodate arbors of different lengths. An arbor for holding bushings should be made as shown in Fig. 18. The straight part should be a good fit in the bushing, a slight taper on the remainder of the arbor being sufficient to prevent the bushing from turning on the arbor. When bushings are held on an ordinary arbor or mandrel the operator is never quite sure that the hole and the outside of the bushing are concentric, as one end of the arbor, owing to its taper, does not quite fill the hole. This is illustrated in Fig. 19. Both Figs. 18 and 19 are somewhat exaggerated to illustrate the principle.

In grinding lining and solid bushings, due allowance must be made for a driving fit in the body of the jig. There are three methods in common use for making driving fits on this class of work: First, grinding the bushing until the lower end just enters the hole, the bushing being slightly tapered to bring it to a snug fit when pressed into place; second, grinding the

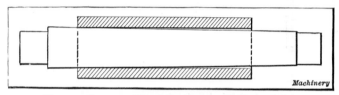

Fig. 19. Improper Fit of Bushing on Ordinary Arbor

bushing straight for its entire length, leaving it just enough oversize to make a good driving fit; and third, grinding the bushing for nearly its entire length just enough oversize to make a good driving fit, and grinding about one-eighth its length just enough undersize to enter the hole.

The first method is not considered very good practice, as the bushing contracts more at the top than elsewhere, owing to the taper, which leaves the hole in the bushing tapered. The second method is very poor practice, as the bushing is liable to cramp while being forced in place, which results in an unsatisfactory job, as the hole in the jig is generally sheared by the sharp end of the bushing. The third method is correct, as the part that is ground to fit the hole acts as a pilot, thus insuring the proper starting of the bushing, and the body, being straight, insures even contraction.

In making allowances for driving fits, 0.001 inch for each

inch diameter of the bushing is considered practical where the holes are one inch or over, and where the holes in the jig are bored smooth. If the holes are rough-bored, a more liberal allowance is required. After the lining bushings are driven in place, they require re-lapping, as they always contract a little.

The outside of the removable bushings should be finished by lapping to a "dead smooth" finish, as otherwise they will soon wear loose. This should never, under any circumstances, be done with emery cloth, but with a cast-iron lap as illustrated in Fig. 20. The abrasive used in this case should be of flour grit with lard oil as a lubricant, the abrasive and oil being applied through a hole in the top of the lap. The work should be lapped with a regular even motion to insure its being

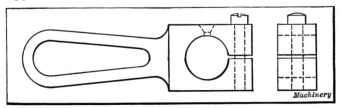

Fig. 20. Lap for Finishing Outside of Slip Bushings

straight, and should be brought to the temperature of the room by being cooled in benzine or gasoline before testing for a fit. The lapping should be carried to a point where the bushing is a wringing fit in its liner, but not tight enough to stick when left for a moment.

After the grinding and lapping of the removable bushings, their tops can be finished by lapping on a carborundum stone, in medium grit, wet with gasoline. A regular motion should be used across the face of the stone without turning or altering the relative position of the bushing. This lapping gives the bushings a good appearance, and, as the dimensions stamped are left black from the action of the fire in hardening, they can be read at a glance.

Driving Fit Allowances for Jig Bushings. — Standard dimensions for driving fit allowances for jig bushings, arranged according to the outside diameter of the bushing, are given in

Table V   Oftentimes difficulty is experienced in assembling the bushings on account of not having allowed the proper amount of stock for fitting.

Plate Bushing Holders for Multiple Drilling. — When a number of holes are to be drilled and reamed on a multiple-spindle machine, the most simple method is to place the piece in a suitable jig and use individual slip bushings, so that after the holes are drilled the bushings can be replaced with reamer-

Table V   Allowances for Driving Fit for Drill Bushings

Outside Diameter, Inches	Allowance for Drive Fit, Inch	Outside Diameter, Inches	Allowance for Drive Fit, Inch	Outside Diameter, Inches	Allowance for Drive Fit, Inch
3/16	0.001	7/8	0.0015	1 5/8	0.0025
5/16	0.001	1	0.0015	1 3/4	0.0025
7/16	0.001	1 1/16	0.002	1 15/16	0.0025
1/2	0.001	1 1/8	0.002	2 1/8	0.003
9/16	0.0015	1 3/16	0.002	2 1/4	0.003
11/16	0.0015	1 5/16	0.002	2 7/16	0.003
3/4	0.0015	1 3/8	0.002	2 5/8	0.0035
13/16	0.0015	1 7/16	0.002	2 3/4	0.0035

size bushings, the jig moved under the reamers, and the holes machined. The loss of time in handling these slip bushings is so great that the production costs increase very rapidly, especially when the operator has to stop to pry up bushings with a screwdriver or some other tool, as is often the case. This style of bushing will frequently catch the drilling or reaming tool and turn with it, thus wearing the bushing plate. To prevent its turning, the groove-cut bushing is sometimes used. This consists of an ordinary slip bushing in which a slot is cut spirally around one-quarter of the outer periphery. This slot engages a pin in the bushing plate, so that, when the bushing starts to slip, the pin prevents its making a full turn. A modification of this method was described in connection with Fig. 12.

One source of trouble from individual slip bushings is the accumulation of chips, which must be carefully removed before the bushings are changed; another is the possibility of interchanging the drilling and the reaming bushings (even though they are carefully marked) and thus spoiling the tools or the work. An improvement over the individual slip bushings is

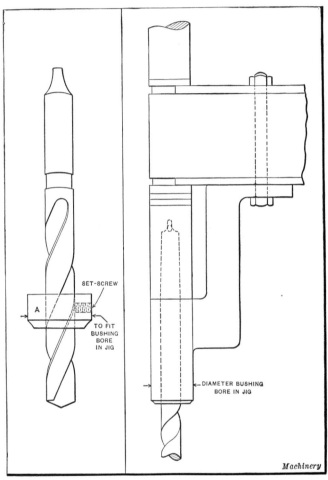

Fig. 21. Drill with Guide Bushing attached **Fig. 22. Stationary Guide for Multiple Drilling and Reaming Tools**

the plate bushing holder, which is especially useful on such work as crankcases, cylinders, etc., and in practically all work where six or more holes are to be drilled. The work is placed in a box jig or frame in which there are either two dowel-pins or two slots. The removable bushing plates used with this frame have holes or hinged binders to correspond with these pins or slots and so are correctly located.

Guide Bushings attached to Drills. — When several small holes necessitating two or more operations are to be machined, the following plan works well from a production standpoint. Guide bushings of the same diameter are fastened to the drills, reamers and other tools to locate them in the bushings in the plate, which are uniform in diameter. Thus, when drilling or reaming, the tools will be guided from the bushing A, Fig. 21. This method is not recommended for holes over one inch deep, as there is a tendency for the drills to spring out of alignment, especially if the drilling is done against a rough surface, since the end of the drilling tool will be some distance from the auxiliary bushing guiding it. This arrangement is effective for drilling steel, as the space between the jig plate and the work allows room for the curled chips. The diameter of the guide bushing, however, must be kept as small as possible, since this piece has a tendency to heat and stick owing to the peripheral speed. This sticking and the wear on the bushing plate may be avoided by using a stationary pilot similar to that shown in Fig. 22. A Z-shaped casting with a bore equal to the tool size and a nose equal to the jig bushing diameter is secured to the arm of the multiple-spindle drilling machine by a bolt that extends through the slot in the arm, as shown in the illustration.

General Notes on Bushings. — When accurate work is necessary, the bushings should support the cutting tool to within one diameter of the tool from the work. If a $\frac{5}{16}$-inch drill is used, the end of the bushing should not be more than $\frac{5}{16}$ inch from the work, and it may be carried to within $\frac{1}{8}$ inch of the work. Bushings should not be located close to the work with the object of carrying the chips up through the bushing. It is much better to provide other means in the jig for the removal of the chips.

The shape of the work frequently requires bushings of considerable length in order to carry the cutting tool close to the work. When the length exceeds four diameters of the tool to be guided, the bushing presents considerable friction surface.

A length equal to two diameters of the cutting tool is usually sufficient for a bearing surface in the bushing. The remainder of the length of the hole in the bushing may be counterbored or relieved. The end that should be relieved is, of course, that which is farthest from the work into which the tool is to be guided.

Screw bushings are generally avoided when accurate work is required. There must be a certain amount of clearance in the ordinary tapped hole, and a threaded bushing is likely to be out of true on that account. Sometimes, however, it happens that no other type of bushing can be used for the work in hand.

The headed or flanged bushing is preferred by many tool designers as a lining bushing, whenever it is possible to utilize it. If it is desired to have the head of the bushing flush with the surface of the jig, the jig is counterbored to receive the head.

As previously mentioned, slip bushings are employed when several operations are to be performed through the same lining bushing. For example, when it is desired to drill and ream a hole to finish a boss or spot around the hole while the work is still in the jig, a lining bushing is selected that will guide a counterbore $\frac{1}{16}$ inch larger than the boss to be finished. A slip bushing is then made to guide the drill, the body of which is a sliding fit in the lining bushing. Another slip bushing is made for the reamer which is also a sliding fit in the lining bushing. The slip bushing walls may have any thickness, providing they are not too thin. Should the conditions require bushings with too thin walls, the counterboring operation in the jig must be abandoned and some different method of procedure adopted.

CHAPTER V

LOCATING POINTS AND ADJUSTABLE STOPS

The locating points in a jig usually consist of finished pads, bosses, seats, or lugs, cast solid with the jig, as illustrated in Fig. 1. In this engraving the surfaces marked f are the locating points, which bring the piece to be machined in correct relation to the bushings guiding the drills, or to the gages to which other cutting tools may be set. This method of locating the work is satisfactory when the work done is finished in a uniform way and where there is very little variation in the parts inserted in the jig.

Pins and Studs used as Locating Means. — Another commonly used method for locating the work in jigs is by means of dowel pins, as shown at A and B in Fig. 2. The sides of the dowel pins which rest against the work are usually flattened, as indicated, so as to give more bearing than a mere line contact with the pins could give, and, at the same time, prevent too rapid wear on the locating pins, as would be the case if the work bear against the pins along a line only.

Sometimes pins or studs are inserted in jigs to act as locating points, instead of having lugs cast directly on the jig as shown in Fig. 1. A case where a pin is used for this purpose is shown in Fig. 3, where B is the body of the jig, A the pin inserted to act as a locating and resting point, and C the work located against this point. Locating pins of this character should always be provided with a shoulder or collar, so that they will firmly resist the pressure of the work they support, without possibility of moving in the hole in which they are inserted.

Locating by Means of V-blocks. — A common method of locating cylindrical pieces or surfaces is that of placing the cylindrical surface in a V-block, as shown in Fig. 4. This V-block, as a rule, is stationary, and is held in place by screws and dowel pins, as indicated in the engraving, but sometimes this V-block may also be made adjustable, in order to take up the variations of the pieces placed in it, and also in order to act as a clamp. A V-block of this character is shown in Fig. 5. In this, *A* is the adjustable V-block, having an oblong

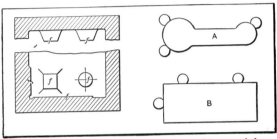

Fig. 1. Locating Pads in Jigs   Fig. 2. Pins used for Locating Work

hole *B* to allow for the adjustment. The block is held down in place by a collar-head screw *C*, which passes through the elongated hole. The under side of the block is provided with a tongue *D*, which enters into a slot in the jig body itself, the V-block being thereby prevented from turning sideways. The

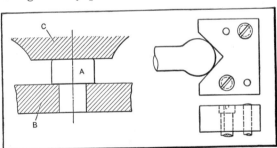

Fig. 3. Inserted Pin used for Locating and Support- ing Work   Fig. 4. V-block for Locating Round Work or Cylindrical Surfaces

screw *E* passes through the wall of the jig, or through some lug, and prevents the V-block from sliding back when the work is inserted into the jig. It is also used for adjusting the V-block and, in some cases, for clamping the work. The V-blocks are usually made of machine steel, but when larger sizes are needed they may be made of cast iron. Little is gained, however, in making these blocks of cast iron, as most of the surfaces have to be machined, and the difference in the cost of material on such a comparatively small piece is very slight.

Cup and Cone Locating Points. — When it is essential that a cylindrical part of the work be located centrally either with the outside of a cylindrical surface or with the center of a hole

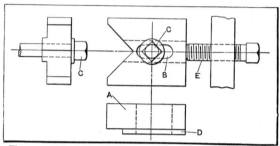

Fig. 5.   Adjustable V-block used for Locating Purposes

passing through the work, good locating means are provided by the designs shown in Figs. 6 and 7.   In Fig. 6, the stud A is countersunk conically to receive the work.   The stud A is made of machine or tool steel, and may, in many cases, serve as a bushing for guiding the tool.   In Fig. 7, the stud is turned conically in order to enter into a hole in the work.   These two

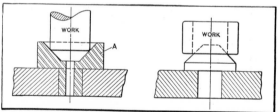

Fig. 6.   Recessed Stud used   Fig. 7.   Conical Stud used
for Locating Round Work   for Locating Work in Re-
in a Jig with Relation to   lation to the Center of
the Center   a Hole

locating appliances are always made stationary, and are only used for locating the work, never for binding or clamping.

Screw Bushings and Sliding Bushings used as Locating Means. — Screw bushings may be used for locating and clamping purposes by making them long enough to project through the walls of the jig and by turning a conical point on them, as shown in Fig. 8, or by countersinking them, as shown in Fig. 9. In all cases where long guide bushings are used, the hole in the bushing ought to be counterbored or recessed for a certain distance of its length.

Another type of bushing which serves the same purpose as a screw bushing is illustrated in Fig. 10. This bushing, together with the forked lever D and clamping bolt and wing-nut shown, will serve not only to locate but also to clamp the work in place. This sliding bushing gives very good results and is preferable to the screw bushing in cases where accurate work is required; but, as a rule, where extreme accuracy would be required, this kind of locating means is not used.

In Fig. 10 the sliding bushing A has a close sliding fit in the lining bushing B. In the head of the bushing A there are two

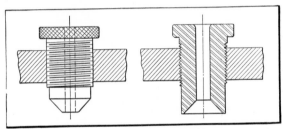

Figs. 8 and 9. Screw Bushings

screws with hardened heads, which fit into elongated slots in the forked lever or yoke D, which, in turn, swivels around pin E. The eye-bolt F fits into a slot G in the yoke, and the wing-nut tightens down the bushing against the work as clearly indicated in the engraving. A comparatively long bearing for the bushing is required in order to produce good results. On work that varies considerably in size, this arrangement works somewhat quicker than does a screw bushing, but it is clearly evident that it is a rather expensive appliance and that the construction of the jig does not always permit of its application.

In some instances it is necessary to have the screw bushing movable sideways, for instance, when the piece of work to be made is located by some finished surfaces, and a cylindrical part is to be provided with a hole drilled exactly in the center

of a lug or projection, the relation of this hole to the finished
surfaces used for locating being immaterial.   The piece of work,
being a casting, would naturally be liable to variations between
the finished surfaces and the center of the lug, particularly if
there are other surfaces and lugs to which the already finished
surfaces must correspond, and in such a case, the fixed bushing
for drilling a hole that ought to come in the center of the lug,
might not always suit the casting.   In such a case, so-called
"floating" bushings, as shown in Fig. 11, are used.   The screw

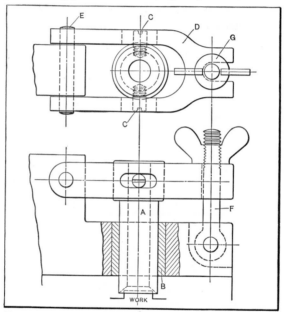

Fig. 10.   Sliding Bushing for Locating and Clamping Work

bushing A is conically recessed and locates from the projection
on the casting.   It is fitted into another cylindrical piece B,
provided with a flange on one side.   The piece B, again, sets
into the hole C in the jig body D, this hole being large enough
to permit the necessary adjustment of the jig bushing.

When the bushing has been located concentric with the lug
E on the work, the nut F, having a washer G under it, is tightened.
The flange on piece B and the washer G must be large enough
to cover the hole C even if B is brought over against the side

of the hole. It is not often necessary, however, to use this floating bushing, because it is seldom that a drilled hole in a piece of work can be put in without having any direct relation to other holes or surfaces.

Adjustable Locating Points. — The most common form of adjustable locating points is the set-screw provided with a check-

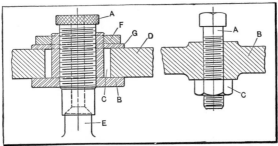

Fig. 11. Floating Drill Bushing   Fig. 12. Adjustable Locating Point

nut, as shown in Fig. 12. The screw *A* is a standard square-head set-screw, or, in some cases, a headless screw — with a slot for a screw driver; this screw passes through a lug on the jig, or the jig wall itself, and is held stationary by a check-nut *C*

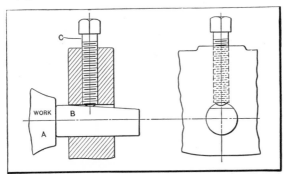

Fig. 13. Adjustable Locating Point consisting of a Flatted Stud held in Place by a Set-screw

tightened up against the wall of the jig. Either end of this screw may be used as a locating point, and the check-nut may be placed on either side. By using a square-head screw, adjustment is very easily accomplished, but unless the operator is familiar with the intentions of the designer of the jig, locating

points of this kind are often mistaken for binding or clamping
devices, and the set-screws are tightened up and loosened to
hold and release the work, when the intention is that these
screws should be fixed when once adjusted. It is not even
possible to depend upon the check-nut stopping the operator
from using the screw as a binding screw. A headless screw,
therefore, is preferable, as it is less apt to be tampered with.

The sliding point, as illustrated in Figs. 13 and 14, is another
adjustable locating point which is used to a great extent in jig
work. A flat piece of work or a plate which is not perfectly
level will always rock if put down on four stationary locating

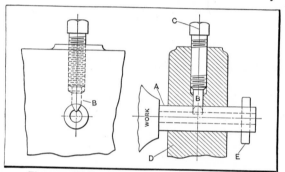

Fig. 14. Sliding Point used for Locating Work

points, but the difficulty thus encountered is very easily overcome by making one of the locating points adjustable, and, as a
rule, the sliding point is used for this purpose.

One design is shown in Fig. 13, where A represents the work
to be located, B the sliding point itself, and C the set-screw,
binding it in place when adjusted. The sliding point B fits a
hole in the jig wall and is provided with a milled flat slightly
tapered, as shown, to prevent its sliding back under the pressure
of the work or the tool operating upon the work. This design
of sliding point is frequently used, but it is not as efficient as
the one illustrated in Fig. 14. In this design the sliding point
A consists of a split cylindrical piece, with a hole drilled through
it, as illustrated in the engraving, and a wedge or shoe B tapered
on the end to fit the sides of the groove or split in the sliding
point itself. This wedge B is forced in by a set-screw C, for the

purpose of binding the sliding point in place. Evidently, when the screw and wedge are forced in, the sliding point is expanded, and the friction against the jig wall *D* is so great that it can withstand a very heavy pressure without moving. Pin *E* prevents the sliding point from slipping through the hole and into the jig, when loosened, and also makes it more convenient to get hold of. In the accompanying table are given the dimensions most commonly used for sliding points and binding shoes and wedges.

Special Types of Adjustable Stops. — Adjustable stops are used to a greater extent in milling fixtures than in drill jigs, but

Dimensions of Sliding Points and Shoes or Binders

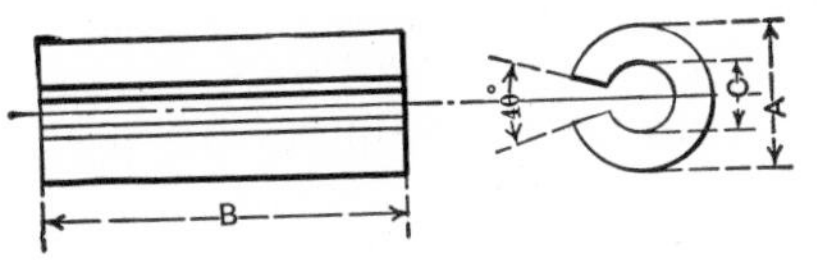

A	3/8	1/2	5/8	3/4
B	2¼ to 3	2¼ to 3	2¼ to 3	2¼ to 3
C	3/16	1/4	5/16	3/8

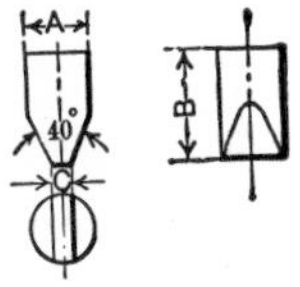

Screws	5/16	3/8
A	1/4	9/32
B	1/2	5/8
C	1/16	3/32

the principles employed are the same. The examples shown in connection with the following description of adjustable stops have been applied to milling fixtures, and, in some cases, to drill jigs. In Fig. 15 is shown the simplest type of adjustable stop, provided with a helical spring beneath the plunger, to press it against the work. The objection to this type of stop is that the plunger *A* will slip back under the pressure of the clamps or cutting tools upon the work. There is also danger of the milled flat on the plunger clogging with dirt, so that the stop will not work properly. Considerable time is, therefore, lost in using jigs or fixtures with this type of stop. The method of clamping the plunger is also slow, as it is necessary to use a wrench in tightening or loosening the set-screw *B*. In Fig. 16 is shown an adjustable stop which is an improvement over that shown in Fig. 15. The flat on the side of plunger *A* is milled at a slight

[redacted]

angle instead of parallel with the center-line, as in Fig. 15. This prevents the plunger from slipping after being clamped. A piece of hardened drill rod B, which is kept from turning by a small pin C, engaging a flat milled in piece B, is used between the plunger A and the clamp. A wing-nut D is fastened to the

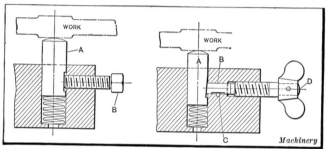

Fig. 15.   Simple Type of   Fig. 16.   Improvement on Stop
   Adjustable Stop   shown in Fig. 15

end of the screw as shown, in order to eliminate the use of a wrench.

In Fig. 17 is shown another adjustable stop which presents a further improvement over that shown in Fig. 16. A bronze bushing B is driven into the base of the jig and allowed to pro-

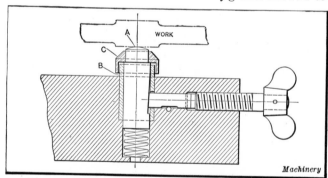

Fig. 17.   A Further Improvement upon the Adjustable Stops
                shown in Figs. 15 and 16

ject above the base, as indicated. Plunger A is a sliding fit in the bushing. A cap C is driven onto the end of the plunger and extends down over the outside of the bushing, as indicated, making the stop dirt-proof. This stop, however, as well as that shown in Fig. 16, is not entirely satisfactory, because it will shift at the time it is tightened, although when once tightened it will remain in position.

In Fig. 18 a different arrangement is shown. Here the thumb-screw and spring plunger used in the preceding device is abandoned, and the sliding wedge A is used to obtain the pressure upon plunger C. The wedge is provided with a handle B attached so that it can easily be operated, and is held in place by two shoulder screws that are inserted through two elongated slots milled in the wedge. These screws are tightened after the stop has been brought up to position. The difficulty met with in using this stop is that the wedge is liable to slip back, owing to

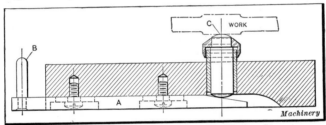

Fig. 18. **Simple Form of Adjustable Wedge Stop**

the vibration of the machine while in operation, so that plunger C drops down.

In Fig. 19 is shown a further development of the method indicated in Fig. 18. In this case, means are provided for preventing wedge A from slipping back. A stud is riveted into the wedge A, this stud extending up through an elongated slot cut in the base of the fixture. The end of the stud is threaded for the knurled nut B, which also acts as a handle for shifting the wedge. When this nut is tightened, it clamps the wedge A and the shoe C against the base. The friction between shoe C and the base prevents the slipping of wedge A. Shoe C also acts as a covering for the slot cut in the base, and thus acts as a dirt and chip shield. It is prevented from turning, when the nut B is tightened or loosened, by a stud D, driven into it and sliding in a slot cut in the base. The difficulty with this design is that wedge A rests upon the table of the machine, and, if there is slight unevenness in the table, the plunger is liable to spring down slightly under the pressure of the cut.

In order to overcome this difficulty, an adjustable stop, as shown in Fig. 20, has been designed. The flat style of wedge is abandoned, and the wedge A is made of drill rod and slides in a hole drilled in the base of the fixture. The stud at the back end of the wedge is screwed into it instead of being riveted, as in the previous example. Bushing C is provided with a shoulder and a headless set-screw D is added to prevent plunger E from dropping out when the fixture is not in use. The wedge A is subjected to considerable friction and the fixture is, therefore, not so sensitive to the touch of the operator as would be desir-

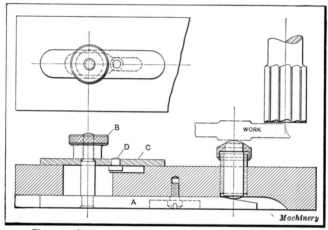

Fig. 19.   Improvement upon the Adjustable Wedge Stop
shown in Fig. 18

able. It is difficult for the operator to feel when the stop is against the work, when tightening the wedge in position.

Fig. 21 shows a modification of the design shown in Fig. 20, the only change made being in bushing A, which has been lengthened so that it will act as a support for the end of wedge B. The bushing is made of cold-rolled steel and casehardened. The bottom part of the base is cut away in order to reduce the friction between the base and the wedge. This design is better than that shown in Fig. 20.

In Fig. 22 is shown a somewhat complicated and expensive adjustable stop which, however, has the advantages of almost perfect operating conditions. Bushing A is lengthened and has a much larger shoulder in order to take the thrust to which it will be subjected when the device is operated. A small pin B replaces the headless set-screw used in the designs in Figs. 20 and 21. The arrangements for clamping the wedge have been considerably changed, and bronze casting C is added. A hole is cut in the base into which the casting is inserted, clearance

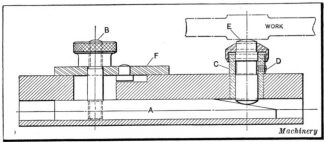

Fig. 20. A Further Improvement upon the Adjustable Wedge
Stops shown in Figs. 18 and 19

being permitted all around so that the casting can be aligned easily with the wedge. The casting is held in place by two fillister-head screws and two dowels; a hole is drilled through the lower part of it which acts as a support for the back end of the wedge, as indicated. The front end is supported in the bushing A in such a manner that the friction is reduced to a

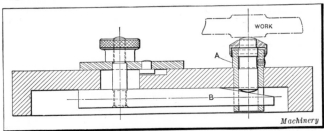

Fig. 21. A more Satisfactory Form of Adjustable Wedge Stop
than that shown in Fig. 20

minimum. Casting C also supports the shoe D and raises it from the base of the fixture. A tongue is cut on the lower side of shoe D which fits into a groove in casting C, thereby preventing the shoe from turning when the nut is tightened or loosened. Stud E is screwed into the side of the knurled nut and a small pin F is driven into the shoe. This pin acts as a stop for the stud, preventing the operator from turning the nut more than is necessary in tightening or loosening.

The adjustable stop shown in Fig. 22 meets practically all requirements placed on an adjustable stop. It will not slip back under the pressure of the stop; it will not slip in tightening; it is dirt-proof; all the parts form integral parts of the jig; and it will not become loose, due to vibration of the machine, or spring down under the pressure of the cut, due to unevenness of the tables of the machines on which the fixture is used. It can be rapidly operated and is so sensitive that the operator feels instantly when plunger *G* is in contact with the work.

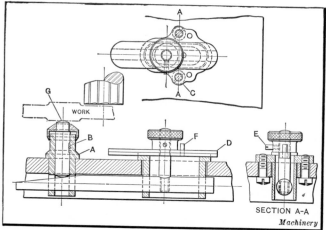

Fig. 22.   Principle of the Final Improvement in the Adjustable
Wedge Stop

The only objection to this design is that so much of the metal of the base has been cut away that it is seriously weakened, and the design shown in Fig. 23 is superior in this respect. In the making of the fixture, difficulties were also encountered in aligning the holes in bushing *A* with the holes in casting *C*, Fig. 22. This was remedied by making the bushing an easy fit and adding a small pin *D* and the round-head screw *C*, Fig. 23, to keep the bushing from turning or working loose. The wedge was also jointed and made in two parts, as indicated, in order to take care of the variations that might occur in drilling the holes in the bushing A and casting C, Fig. 22, in which the wedge slides. This practically makes the wedge self-aligning.

Locating from Finished Holes. — If the work to be finished in the jig has some holes already finished, it is sometimes most satisfactory to locate the work by these holes, which may be done by means of studs or plugs similar to the one shown in Fig. 3, which then enter the holes; preferably, these studs should be ground and hardened to the standard size of the hole. If the finished hole should be of a character that varies somewhat in size, expansion studs with bushings may be used. These studs

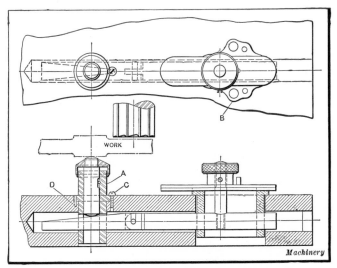

Fig. 23. The Adopted Form of Adjustable Wedge Stop

may be of a great many different designs and styles, but, as a rule, they always work on the same principle as the one shown in Fig. 24. In this, A is the bushing, fitting the finished hole in the work. This bushing is split in several different ways, either by having one slot cut entirely through it, and two more slots cut to within a short distance of the outside periphery, or by having several slots cut from the top and from the bottom, alternating, but not cut entirely through the full length of the bushing. The method of splitting, however, in every case, accomplishes the same object, that of making the bushing capable of expansion, so that when the stud *B*, which is turned to fit the tapered hole in the bushing, is screwed down, the bushing is expanded.

Locating by Keyways in the Work. — Sometimes the work to be finished in the jig is provided with a keyway or a slot, or with some other kind of a seat, by means of which it is located on its component part on the machine for which it is ultimately in-

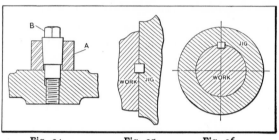

Fig. 24.   Fig. 25.   Fig. 26.

tended, and it is always essential that the work be located in the same way in the jig as it is to be located on the machine on which it is to go; thus, if the work has a keyway suitable for locating, a corresponding keyway ought to be put into the jig, and the work located by means of a key, as shown in Figs.

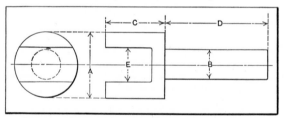

Fig. 27.   Work which is Milled as Indicated at E

25 and 26. Instead of a loose key, a tongue may be planed or milled solid with the jig, but, as a rule, it is more satisfactory to have the loose key, as, if it should happen to wear, it is possible to replace it; and if the width of the keyway should vary in different lots of the parts made, it is possible, with little expense, to make a new key to fit the variation, whereas if the key is made solid with the jig, and found to be either too large or too small, the trouble of fixing this would be considerably greater.

Common Defects in Jig Design. — The first consideration of the jig designer should be to determine what degree of accuracy is essential in the part that is to be produced, and also whether absolute interchangeability is necessary. This information will be a guide for the economical production of the jig. The designer must also consider any operations which are to be performed on the work prior to the one for which the jig under consideration is intended; for while this preliminary machining may not need to be accurately done, inaccuracy or uniformity may result in improperly locating the work in the next jig,

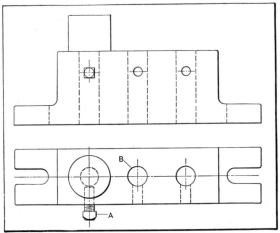

Fig. 28. Defective Design of Fixture for Holding Piece
shown in Fig. 27

which should be so designed as to locate the part with the required accuracy.

The locating points of any jig should be such as to allow as wide a range of inaccuracy on any preceding operation as is compatible in the part. For example, if the part has to be turned to, say, a limit of 0.001 inch, it will require more skill and time than if a limit of 0.005 inch is allowable. Again, as far as practicable, the portion of the work that requires to be the most accurate should be used in locating it in the jig for the succeeding operation. Often a surface is selected to locate from, which, in consequence, must be machined to an accurate limit, when accuracy otherwise would be unnecessary. This, of

course, only adds to the cost of production. After considering
the points mentioned, the best method of arranging the details
of the jig, so that it has as few dimensions as possible requiring
absolute accuracy, should also receive attention; that is, the
jig should be as simple as possible, and still be so designed as
to accurately locate the parts to be machined.

In Figs. 28 and 29 are shown two jig designs which will serve
to illustrate these points. The part for which a jig is required
is shown in Fig. 27. In the preliminary machining operation
the work is turned to diameters A and B and to lengths C and
D. The limit of accuracy required on end A is $-\frac{1}{64}$, or any
diameter from $1\frac{39}{64}$ inch as a minimum to $1\frac{5}{8}$ inch. For end B a

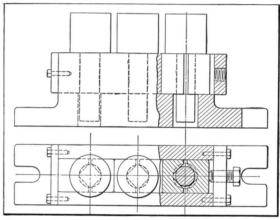

Fig. 29. Fixture which will hold a Number of Pieces, Fig. 27,
properly, even when Diameters of Locating Parts vary

finer limit of -0.002 is necessary, so that this end should be used
as the locating part for the next operation; *viz.*, the milling out
of the slot E which must be central with the part B. A design
such as shown in Fig. 28 is not uncommon for this operation,
and with it fairly accurate results will be secured; but if the
locating diameter on the work is slightly small, say 0.002 inch,
then the forcing of the piece over to one side by the locking
screw A will result in an inaccuracy in the milling operation.
The locating holes B must be the exact size of the locating part
of the work, and unless every piece is a push fit (which is un-

necessary accuracy in the part) the location is not accurate, as
the work is clamped against a small area on one side of the hole
and the point of the set-screw on the other. This can be avoided
by locating the part against V-blocks, as shown in Fig. 29,
which locate each shank central, irrespective of the variations
in their diameters. The construction of this jig illustrates the
points which have been referred to. The V-blocks provide
four lines of contact, and the part is secured very rigidly in a
central position irrespective of the variations in the diameter of
the locating part. This jig, though more expensive than the
one shown in Fig. 28, is quite simple in its construction. A
central slot is machined to a width which need not be to any
particular dimension as the steel V-blocks will be accurately
fitted to this slot. Steel plates are secured to the ends of the

Fig. 30. The Way the V-blocks for the Jig, Fig. 29, are planed

jig after machining the slot as shown. By closing these ends
after the slot is machined, the tool has a clear passage through,
which, of course, would be impossible were the ends cast on.
The V-blocks are planed in one piece, as shown in Fig. 30.
The only important dimension is the width of the block. The
exact position of the V in relation to the sides is immaterial
provided that after the blocks have been sawed off they are
inserted in the slot in the jig with the long or short sides together. To avoid trouble from this source, one side of the slot
and a corresponding side on the blocks should be marked to
insure the correct insertion of the latter. In the event of a
design requiring the V's to be strictly central with the sides,
the cost would, of course, be increased, as much more care
would be required in machining. The jig shown in Fig. 29 is
for holding three of the pieces shown in Fig. 27 at one time;
this number could be increased as desired.

CHAPTER VI

JIG CLAMPING DEVICES

The clamping devices used in connection with jigs and fixtures may either clamp the work to the jig or the jig to the work, but very frequently the clamps simply hold in place a loose or movable part in the jig, which can be swung out of the way to facilitate removing the work from, and inserting it in. the jig. The work itself is in turn clamped by a set-screw or other means passing through the loose part, commonly called the leaf.

Types of Clamps. — The simplest form of clamping device is the so-called clamp, of which a number of different forms are commonly used. Perhaps the most common of all clamps is the one shown in Fig. 1. This kind of clamp is also commonly termed a strap. It is simple, cheap to make, and, for most purposes, it gives satisfactory service. The clamp shown in Fig. 2 is made on practically the same principle as the one shown in Fig. 1, but several improvements have been introduced. The clamp is recessed at the bottom for a distance b, to a depth equal to a, so as to give a bearing only on the two extreme ends of the clamp. Even if the strap should bend somewhat, on account of the pressure of the screw, it would be certain to bear at the ends and exert the required pressure on the object being clamped. This strap is also provided with a ridge at D, located centrally with the hole for the screw. This insures an even bearing of the screw-head on the clamp, even if the two bearing points at each end of the clamp should vary in height, as illustrated in Fig. 3. The clamp in Fig. 1 would not bind very securely, under such circumstances, and the collar of the screw would be liable to break off, as the whole strain, when tightening the screw, would be put on one side.

A further improvement in the construction of this clamp may be had by rounding the under side of the clamping points

A, as shown in Fig. 4. When a clamp with such rounded clamp-ing points is placed in a position like that indicated in Fig. 3, it will bind the object to be held fully as firmly as if the two clamping surfaces were in the same plane.

The hole in these straps is very often elongated, as indicated by the dotted lines in Figs. 1 and 2. This allows the strap to

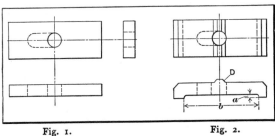

Fig. 1.   Fig. 2.

be pulled back far enough so as to clear the work, making it easier to insert and remove the piece to be held in the jig. In some cases, it is necessary to extend the elongated hole, as shown in Fig. 5, so that it becomes a slot, going clear through to the end of the clamp, instead of being simply an oblong hole. Aside from this difference, the clamp in Fig. 5 works on exactly the same principle as the clamps previously shown.

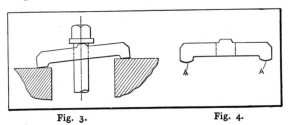

Fig. 3.   Fig. 4.

The clamps described may be given a number of different shapes to suit different conditions. Instead of having the strap or clamp bear on only two points, it is sometimes necessary to have it bear on three points, in which case it may be designed similar to the strap shown in Fig. 6. In order to get an equal pressure on all the three points, a special screw, with a half-spherical head like the one shown, may be used to advantage. The half-spherical head of this screw fits into a concave recess of the same shape in the strap. When the bearing for the screw-head is made in this manner, the hole through the clamp must have plenty of clearance for the body part of the bolt.

When designing clamps or straps of the types shown, one of the most important considerations is to provide enough metal around the holes, so that the strap will stand the pressure of the screw without breaking at the weakest place, which naturally is in a line through the center of the hole. As a rule, these straps are made of machine steel, although large clamps may sometimes be made from cast iron.

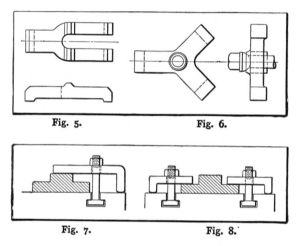

Fig. 5.   Fig. 6.

Fig. 7.   Fig. 8.

Figs. 7 and 8 show clamps bent to meet the requirements, and also indicate the application of this type of clamp, the part shown in cross-section being the work. These clamps are commonly used for clamping work in the planer and milling machine, but are also frequently used in jig and fixture design.

The screws used for clamping these straps are either standard hexagonal screws or standard collar-head screws. When it is not necessary to tighten the screws very firmly, thumb-screws are frequently used, especially on small jigs.

Sometimes the strap or clamp is arranged as shown in Fig. 9, the screw passing through it at the center and bearing upon the work, either directly, as indicated, or through the medium of a collar fitted to the end of the clamping screw, as shown in

Fig. 10. This type of clamping arrangement is commonly used for holding work in a drill jig when one screw is sufficient. The strap used in this type of arrangement can be improved upon by making it in one of the forms shown in Fig. 11. Here the ends

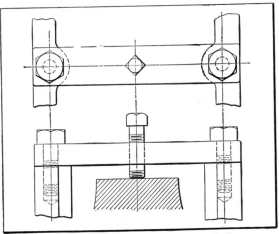

Fig. 9. Clamping Strap for Open-end Jigs

of the straps are slotted in various ways, so as to make it easy to rapidly remove the strap when the work is to be taken out of the jig. Fig. 12 illustrates a method which is not often found in use. This type of clamp is adapted to box jigs; it has the

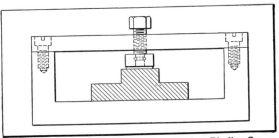

Fig. 10. Common Form of Clamps with One Binding Screw

advantage of being easily removed, which is accomplished by sliding it longitudinally. By glancing at the detailed view to the right, which shows the end of the clamping bar and its retaining grooves, the way in which it is held in place and removed will be clearly understood. Figs. 13 and 14 show clamps which are very much alike, but that of Fig. 14 is simpler and more rapidly operated when the work is to be removed. When the clamp is slotted as shown in the plan view of Fig. 14, fixed studs may be used instead of the swinging bolts.

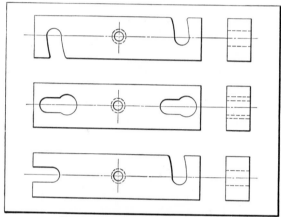

Fig. 11. Types of Clamping Straps

The type shown in Fig. 15 is often found in machine shops, on milling fixtures, drill jigs, lathe fixtures, etc. The clamp and bolts can be removed by loosening the nuts and pulling out the slip washers which allow the nuts to pass through the large

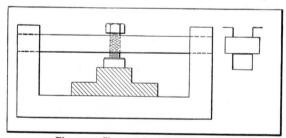

Fig. 12. Clamp Adapted to Box Jigs

holes. Fig. 16 illustrates a method which is commonly used on milling fixtures when light milling is to be done. The design of clamp shown in Fig. 17 is not frequently seen in use, as it is a method which a mechanic will not use if he can see another way out of it; but at times it is found almost impossible to use a clamp of a different type.

A style of clamp that is somewhat similar to the one illustrated in Fig. 12 is shown in Fig. 18. In this case, however, two clamping bolts are used and the clamp is removed from the end of the jig. This is a good as well as a quick method of clamping work in open-end drill jigs. Fig. 19 illustrates the use of bolts only, for holding down work. The illustration is self-

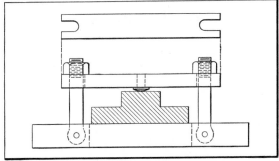

Fig. 13.   Clamp with Swinging Bolts

explanatory. Fig. 20 shows a good design of clamp for holding work in a milling fixture. It binds the work both horizontally and vertically and is the very best type for its purpose when it can be used.

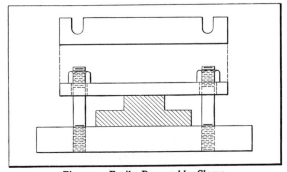

Fig. 14.   Easily Removable Clamp

Hook-bolts. — The hook-bolt shown in Fig. 21 is better adapted for some classes of work than any other clamping device. At the same time, it is very cheap to make and easily applied. The bolt A passes through a hole in the jig, having a good sliding fit in this hole, and is pushed up until the hook or

Dimensions of Collar-head Screws used on Jigs

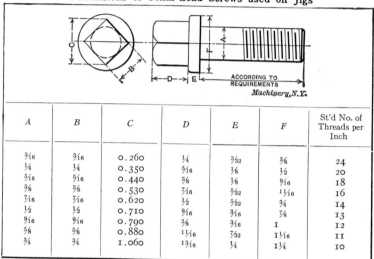

A	B	C	D	E	F	St'd No. of Threads per Inch
3/16	3/16	0.260	1/4	3/32	3/8	24
1/4	1/4	0.350	5/16	1/8	1/2	20
5/16	5/16	0.440	3/8	1/8	9/16	18
3/8	3/8	0.530	7/16	5/32	11/16	16
7/16	7/16	0.620	1/2	5/32	3/4	14
1/2	1/2	0.710	9/16	3/16	7/8	13
9/16	9/16	0.790	5/8	3/16	1	12
5/8	5/8	0.880	11/16	7/32	1 1/16	11
3/4	3/4	1.060	13/16	1/4	1 1/4	10

Dimensions of Shoulder Thumb-screws used on Jigs

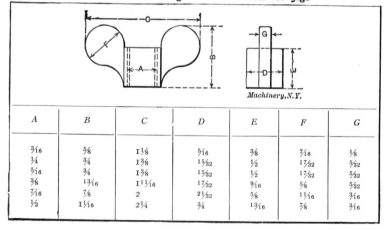

A	B	C	D
3/16	9/16	1/2	3/32
1/4	1	11/16	1/8
5/16	1 1/8	3/4	5/32
3/8	1 1/4	13/16	5/32
7/16	1 1/2	15/16	3/16
1/2	1 5/8	1 1/8	3/16

Dimensions of Wing- or Thumb-nuts for Jigs

A	B	C	D	E	F	G
3/16	5/8	1 1/8	5/16	3/8	7/16	1/8
1/4	3/4	1 3/8	15/32	1/2	17/32	5/32
5/16	3/4	1 3/8	15/32	1/2	17/32	5/32
3/8	13/16	1 11/16	17/32	9/16	5/8	5/32
7/16	7/8	2	21/32	5/8	11/16	3/16
1/2	1 1/16	2 1/4	3/4	13/16	7/8	3/16

head *B* bears against the work, after which the nut is tightened. When great pressure is not required, the thumb- or wing-nut provides a satisfactory means for tightening down upon the work, and permits the hook-bolt to be applied more readily. The thumb- or wing-nut is preferable to the knurled nut, shown in Fig. 24, which sometimes is used. It is possible to get a better

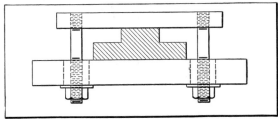

Fig. 15. Clamp with Slip Washers beneath Nuts

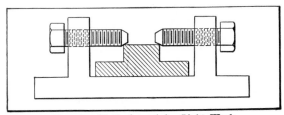

Fig. 16. Method used for Light Work

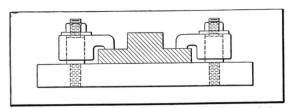

Fig. 17. Clamping Method not to be Recommended

grip and to tighten the bolt more firmly with a wing-nut than with a knurled nut. When the work is removed from the jig, using the hook-bolt clamping device, the nut is loosened and the head or hook of the bolt is turned away from the work, thus allowing it to be taken out and another piece of work to be placed in position. The hook-bolts are invariably made of machine steel. Fig. 25 shows an application of a bent hook-bolt. Generally speaking, the type shown in Fig. 21 is better suited to its purpose, because the bearing point on the work is closer to the bolt body.

Screw Tightening Devices. — In a box jig, or a jig where the work is entirely, or almost entirely, surrounded by the jig, the work is easily held in place by set-screws which are used when-

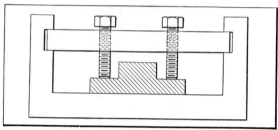

Fig. 18.   Simple Clamping Method

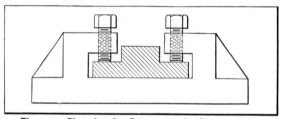

Fig. 19.   Clamping by Set-screws in Open-end Jig

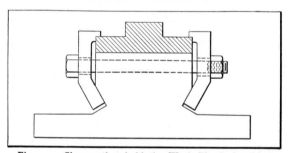

Fig. 20.   Clamps that hold the Work Firmly in place

ever great clamping pressure is required, the square head allowing the use of the wrench.   Sometimes screws of this kind may be tightened enough for the purpose by hand if a pin is put through the head of the screw, as shown in Figs. 22 and 23. This means is used not only when great pressure is not necessary, but also when the work is liable to spring if the screws are tightened too hard. In such a case, if a pin is inserted, it is obvious that the screw-head is not intended for a wrench, but that the pin is intended for getting a good grip by the hand for tightening the screw, without resorting to any additional means. Usually it is not possible to use an ordinary machine wrench on such a screw. Wing-nuts are generally most satisfactory for jigs where only a light binding pressure is required.

Wing-nuts are used on hook-bolts or swiveling eye-bolts, when a comparatively light pressure is required. The thumb-

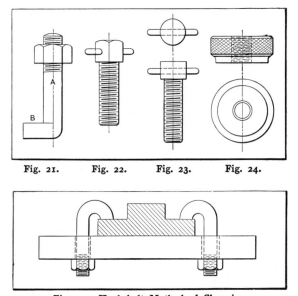

Fig. 21.   Fig. 22.   Fig. 23.   Fig. 24.

Fig. 25.   Hook-bolt Method of Clamping

or wing-nut is preferable to a knurled nut, as it gives a better grip and makes it possible to tighten the bolt more firmly. The dimensions of an excellent design of handwheel for use on jigs, etc., are given in an accompanying table. These wheels have a rather long stem or hub which provides a good length of thread and brings the grip or handle far enough from the jig body to prevent the fingers or knuckles from striking it. The "star" design of handle also permits a good grip. By having the casting solid, these handwheels can be tapped out for any size thread, or a plain hole can be drilled when it is desired to attach the handles to round stock.

If screws are to be firmly tightened without the use of a wrench, the method of using a pin through the screw-head should be used only on large fixtures, where the pin is $\frac{1}{2}$ inch

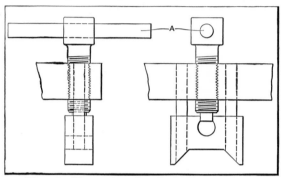

Fig. 26. Pin used as Handle for Binding Screw

in diameter and requires the use of both hands, an application of which is shown in Fig. 26. On smaller sizes of fixtures where the pin is about $\frac{1}{4}$ inch in diameter by 4 inches long, and must be used with one hand, the pressure is concentrated across the

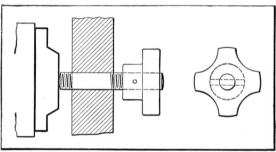

Fig. 27. Hand Knob for Binding Screw

palm of the hand, and if the fixture is used frequently it is likely to develop a sore spot.

In the case of the hand knob shown in Fig. 27, however, it is evident that the pressure is distributed over the palm of the hand, and therefore the likelihood of producing a sore is much less. Tables of sizes of two different types of knobs for different classes of fixtures are given herewith.

Dimensions of Latch Nuts

	A	B	C	D
	5/8	7/16	5/16	5/32
	3/4	1/2	3/8	5/32
	7/8	9/16	7/16	3/16
	1	5/8	1/2	3/16
	1 1/8	3/4	5/8	1/4
	1 1/4	7/8	3/4	5/16

Star Handwheels for Jigs

	A	B	C	D	E	F	G	H	I
	3/4	1 3/4	1	1	3/8	3/16	5/16	1/8	1/8
	1	1 7/8	1 1/4	1 1/8	7/16	5/16	7/16	1/8	1/8
	1 1/8	2	1 1/2	1 3/8	1/2	3/8	9/16	3/16	3/16
	1 1/2	2 1/8	2	1 5/8	9/16	1/2	11/16	3/16	3/16
	1 5/8	2 1/4	2 1/2	1 3/4	5/8	7/8	7/8	3/16	1/4

Dimensions for Cast-iron Knobs

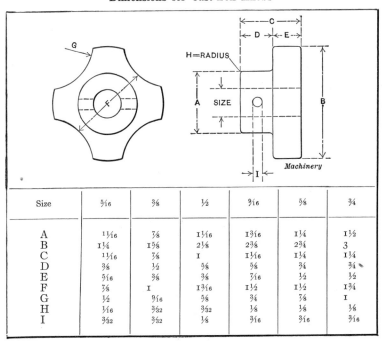

Machinery

Size	5/16	3/8	1/2	9/16	5/8	3/4
A	1 1/16	7/8	1 1/16	1 3/16	1 1/4	1 1/2
B	1 1/4	1 5/8	2 1/8	2 3/8	2 3/4	3
C	1 1/16	7/8	1	1 1/16	1 1/4	1 1/4
D	3/8	1/2	5/8	5/8	3/4	3/4
E	5/16	3/8	3/8	7/16	1/2	1/2
F	7/8	1	1 3/16	1 1/2	1 1/2	1 3/4
G	1/2	9/16	5/8	3/4	7/8	1
H	1/16	3/32	3/32	1/8	1/8	1/8
I	3/32	3/32	1/8	3/16	3/16	3/16

Dimensions of Jig-screw Latches

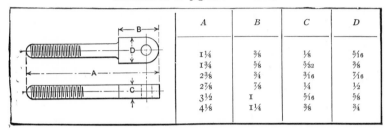

	A	B	C	D
	1¼	⅜	⅛	5/16
	1¾	⅝	5/32	⅜
	2⅜	¾	3/16	7/16
	2⅞	⅞	¼	½
	3½	1	5/16	⅝
	4⅛	1¼	⅜	¾

Dimensions of Regular Thumb-screws

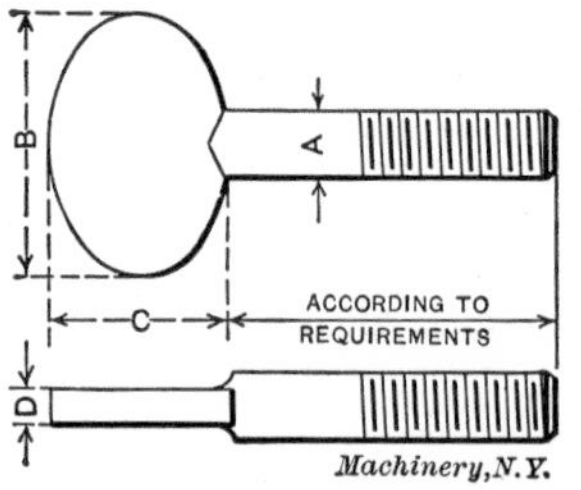

A	B	C	D
3/16	¾	⅝	3/32
¼	15/16	¾	⅛
5/16	1⅛	⅞	5/32
⅜	1¼	15/16	5/32
7/16	1½	1 1/16	3/16
½	1⅝	1 3/16	3/16

Machinery, N.Y.

Dimensions of Thumb-screws with Wide Grip

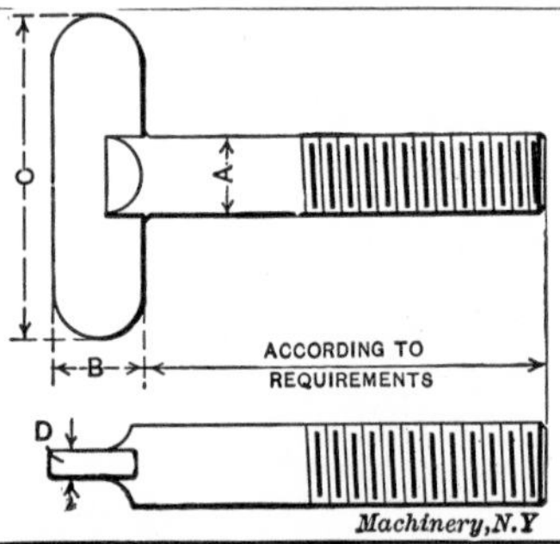

A	B	C	D
3/16	¼	⅞	3/32
¼	5/16	1	⅛
5/16	⅜	1¼	5/32
⅜	7/16	1½	5/32
7/16	½	1¾	3/16
½	9/16	2	3/16
9/16	⅝	2¼	3/16
⅝	11/16	2½	7/32

Machinery, N.Y.

The questions naturally arise, how much pressure can a man exert with his fingers in operating a knurled-head screw, how much pressure can he develop with a screw and hand knob, and how much pressure can he exert in operating a screw with a pin through it? It is quite safe to say that for continuous operation on jigs or fixtures all that can be depended upon with a knurled-head screw is to bring the screw up to steady the work, but, with a screw and pin through it, it is not uncommon to bend the pin. With a hand knob the amount of pressure is doubtful and depends largely upon the position of the screw, which governs the grip obtainable on the knob.

Swinging Leaves. — The elementary principles involved in the swinging-leaf clamping construction are shown in their simplest form in Fig. 28. Loose leaves which swing out, in order

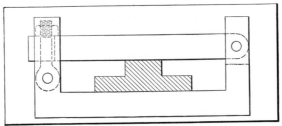

Fig. 28.   Principle of Commonly used Clamping Method

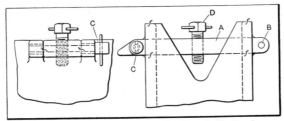

Fig. 29.   Another Common Design of Jig Leaf

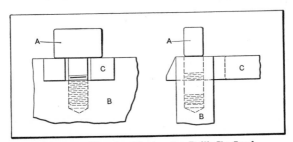

Fig. 30.   Clamping Device for Drill Jig Leaf

to permit the work to be inserted and removed, are usually constructed in some manner similar to that shown in Fig. 29, in which *A* represents the leaf, being pivoted at *B* and held by a pin at *C*, which goes through the two lugs on the jig wall and passes through the leaf, thus binding the leaf and allowing the tightening of the set-screw D, which bears against the work. The holes in the lugs of the castings are lined with steel bushings in order to prevent the cast-iron holes from being worn out too soon by the constant pulling out and putting in of the pin.   This kind of leaf, when fitted in nicely, is rather expensive, but is used not only for binding purposes, but also for guiding purposes, making a convenient seat for the bushings.   If leaves are fitted well in place, the bushings in the leaves will guide the cutting tools in a satisfactory manner.

Another method of clamping down the leaf is shown in Fig. 30, in which A is a thumb-screw, screwed directly into the wall B of the jig, and holding the leaf C down, as indicated.   To swing the

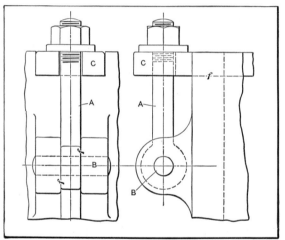

Fig. 31.   Eye-bolt used for Clamping Drill Jig Leaf

leaf out, the thumb-screw is turned back about a quarter of the turn, so that the head of the thumb-screw stands in line with the slot in the leaf, this slot being made wide and long enough to permit the leaf to clear the head of the thumb-screw.   This is a very rapid way of clamping, and is frequently used.   The lower side of the head of the screw will wear a long time before the head finally comes in line with the slot when binding.   It can then easily be fixed for binding the leaf again when standing in a position where the head of the thumb-screw is at right angles to the slot, by turning off a portion of the head on the under side

The size of these thumb-screws is made according to the strain on the leaf and the size and design of the jig. No standard dimensions could be given for this kind of screw.

The hinged bolt or latch bolt, shown in Fig. 31, is also commonly used. Here *A* represents an eye-bolt, which is connected with the jig body by the pin *B*. The leaf or movable part *C* of the jig is provided with a slot in the end for the eye-bolt, this slot being a trifle wider than the diameter of the bolt. The threaded end of the eye-bolt is provided with a standard hexagon nut, a knurled-head nut or a wing-nut, according to how firmly it is necessary that the nut be tightened.

When the leaf is to be disengaged, the nut is loosened up

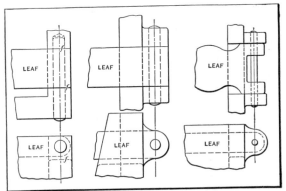

Fig. 32. Detail Designs of Hinged Leaves

enough to clear the point at the end of the leaf, and the bolt is swung out around the pin *B*, which is driven directly into lugs projecting out from the jig wall, a slot being provided between the two lugs, as shown, so that the eye-bolt can swing out with perfect freedom. At the opposite end, the leaves or loose parts of the jig swing around a pin the same as in Fig. 29, the detailed construction of this end being, most commonly, one of the three types shown in Fig. 32. It must be understood that to provide jigs with leaves of this character involves a great deal of work and expense, and they are used almost exclusively when one or more guide bushings can be held in the leaf.

Quite often drill jigs have a bushing plate in the form of a leaf which swings on a hinge out of the way so that the piece

to be drilled can be put in place in the jig. This requires a
locking device which can be depended upon to hold the bushing
plate exactly in place while drilling. The locking device shown
in Fig. 33, and also shown applied to a jig in Fig. 34, answers
this purpose admirably. To open the jig so as to put in the
piece to be drilled, all that is necessary to do is to push the

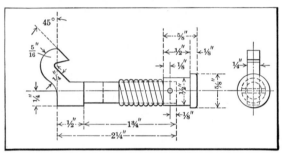

Fig. 33. A Jig Locking Trigger

button on the end of the lock trigger and lift the leaf up. When
the piece is in place in the jig, the leaf is again pressed down
into place. The pressure springs the locking device, and the
trigger grips the pin shown. The part of the trigger which

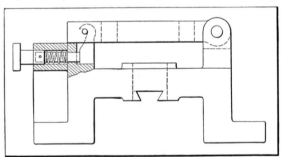

Fig. 34. Locking Device in Fig. 33 applied to Jig

fits against the pin should taper slightly. This makes it hold
much more tightly, and also takes up what little wear there
may be on it. The device can be fitted to a great variety of
jigs and fixtures. It is very simple and inexpensive to make,
is quick and simple to operate, and is positive in its action.

A hinged jig cover may also be conveniently held in place by
means of a spring latch of the form shown in Fig. 35, which is

semi-automatic in its action. In this illustration, the body of
the jig is shown at A and the hinged cover at B. This cover
swings on the pivot C and drops onto the latch D which takes
the place of the locking screw arrangement shown in Fig. 36,
and which shows an application of the principle illustrated in
Fig. 30. In cases where the cover is merely used to carry bushings, a latch of this kind is entirely satisfactory, although it
is not recommended for use on jigs where screws for holding
down the work are carried by the cover. The method of using
is evident from the illustration. To swing the cover clear of

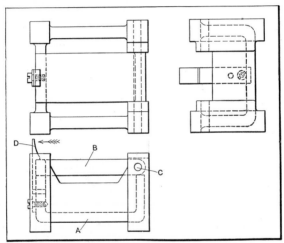

Fig. 35. Jig with Cover held by Spring Latch

the work in the jig, the latch D is pushed back in the direction
of the arrow. After the cover has been raised, the latch springs
back into place ready to catch over the top of the cover, when
it is dropped back onto the jig. When the cover is dropped,
the latch catches it automatically, requiring no attention from
the operator.

A number of applications that vary in details only are shown
in Figs. 37 to 40. Fig. 37 shows the style of clamp that is used in
connection with box drill jigs when it is desired to support a part
to be drilled on two points. As will be seen, these two bearing
points are self-adjusting. The design of Fig. 38 is generally
used when it is desired to support the work in two places in

an open-end drill jig. Figs. 39 and 40 show types which are quite similar, but there are many cases where one type can be used to advantage and not the other. For instance, the clamp, Fig. 39, is intended for box jigs, but the type shown in Fig. 40 could not be used for such a jig, because the latter is altogether too slow. However, its advantages over Fig. 39, in case

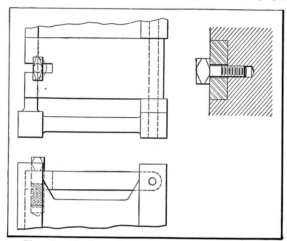

Fig. 36. Jig Cover Locked by Quarter-turn Screw

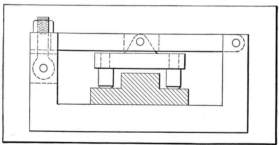

Fig. 37. Jig Cover with Two-point Self-adjusting Clamp

it is desired to have an open-end jig, are apparent. The relation of the first cost of a jig to the quantity of work to be done is a factor which sometimes makes a jig which is not perfect, from a purely mechanical standpoint, more desirable than one which represents better design, but greatly increased cost.

The ordinary jack-screw is employed quite commonly as a clamping device in drill jigs, but the objection to its use is that, not being an integral part of the jig, it is very apt to get lost. In Fig. 41 are shown two simple devices working on the same principle as the jack-screw, but having the advantage of being connected to the jig by the pin shown at *B*. At *A*, a set-screw screws directly into the end of the eye-bolt, and at *C* a long

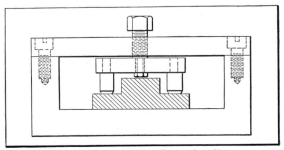

Fig. 38. Compensating Two-point Clamp

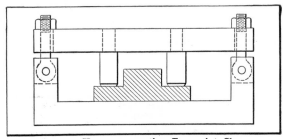

Fig. 39. Non-compensating Two-point Clamp

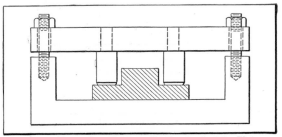

Fig. 40. Alternative Design, Similar to that in Fig. 39

square nut is threaded on the eye-bolt. These nuts must be made of special length, and be made up especially for this purpose. The eye-bolts are fastened, as shown, directly to the wall of the jig, and the set-screw or nut is tightened against the work. The eye-bolt can be set at different angles to suit the work, thereby providing a clamping device which may be said to possess double adjustment. This device makes a very convenient clamping arrangement. It works satisfactorily and has the advantage of being easily swung out of the way.

Wedge or Taper Gib. — The principle of clamping work in the jig by means of a wedge or taper gib is shown in Fig. 42 and two applications are illustrated in Figs. 43 and 44. In Fig. 43,

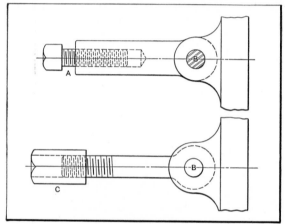

Fig. 41. Clamping Devices Working on the Jack-screw
Principle

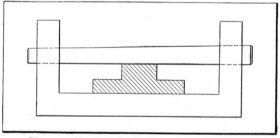

Fig. 42. Simplest Application of Wedge Clamp

the work is located between the wedge *A* and the wall *B* of the jig and pressed against the wall by the wedge, which can be driven in by a hammer, or screwed in place when the jig is constructed as shown. It is preferable to have the wedge screwed in place, as it is then less likely to loosen by the constant vibrations to which it is subjected, and at the same time the wedge

is less likely to get lost, being an integral part of the jig. The
ear for the screw may be placed in any direction in regard to
the gib, as indicated by the dotted lines in the end view of
Fig. 43. This tightening device is, in particular, adapted to
work of dovetail shape, as shown in Fig. 44. In this case the
wedge is made similar to the common taper gib used for taking
up the wear in dovetail slides. It is sometimes of advantage
to relieve the bearing surface opposite the wedge, as shown in

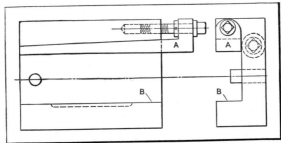

Fig. 43. **Wedge or Taper Gib used for Clamping**

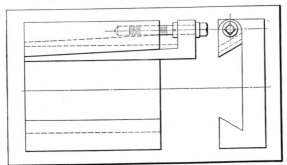

Fig. 44. **Wedge for Clamping Dovetailed Work**

dotted lines in Fig. 43, in order to provide two distinct bearing
points, which prevent the work from rocking. The hole in the
ear of the gib, through which the screw passes, must be oblong,
so that when the screw is adjusted, and the gib moved in or
out, there is ample allowance for the sidewise movement of the
ear, due to the taper of the gib.

If it is required to get a bearing on two points of a surface
that is likely to vary in its dimensions, a yoke can be used,
designed on the principle of that shown in Fig. 45. In the

engraving, *A* is the work to be clamped, and *B* is the yoke which fits into a slot in the center of the strap or clamp *C*. The yoke is held by a pin *D*, around which it can swivel to adjust itself to the work. It is evident that the amount of pressure at the two points *E* and *F* will be equal, or at least near enough so for all practical purposes, even though the screws at the ends of the strap may not be equally tightened. In this device the

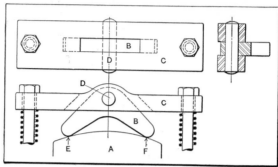

Fig. 45. Equalizing Clamp

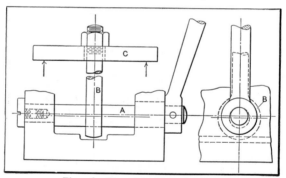

Fig. 46. Eccentric Clamping Bolt

pin *D* takes the full clamping strain, and should therefore be designed strong enough, and the strap, which is weakened by the slot and the hole in the center, should be reinforced, as indicated, at this place. It is preferable to have spiral springs at each end of the strap to prevent the strap from slipping down when the work is taken out. The strap may be made either of cast iron or machine steel, the yoke being made of machine steel.

Eccentric Clamping Arrangements. — Eccentric clamps and shafts for binding purposes are often used. In Figs. 46 and 47 are shown two applications of the principle of the eccentric shaft. In Fig. 46 the eccentric shaft A has a bearing at both ends, and the eye-bolt B is connected to it at the center and is forced down when the eccentric shaft is turned. This causes the two end points of the clamp C to bear on the work. This clamping arrangement has a very rapid action and gives good satisfaction. The throw of the eccentric shaft may vary from $\frac{1}{16}$ inch to about $\frac{1}{4}$ inch, depending upon the diameter of the shaft and the accuracy of the work. In cases where it is re-

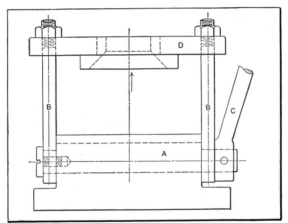

Fig. 47. **Another Example of Eccentric Clamping Bolt**

quired that the clamp should bear in the center, an arrangement like the one shown in Fig. 47 may be used. Here the eccentric shaft A has a bearing in the center and eye-bolts B are connected to it at the ends. As the eccentricity is the same at both ends, the eye-bolts or connecting-rods will be pulled down evenly when the lever C is turned, and the strap D will get an even bearing on the work in the center. If the force of the clamping stress is required to be distributed equally at different points on the work, a yoke like that shown in Fig. 45 may be used in combination with the eccentric clamping device shown in Fig. 47.

When it is essential that strap D should also be used for locating purposes, necessary guides must be provided for the strap, so as to hold it in the required position.   These guiding arrangements may consist of rigid rods, ground and fitted into drilled and reamed holes in the strap, or square bars held firmly in the jig, and fitted into square slots at the ends of the strap.   The bars may also be round, and the slots at the ends of the strap half round, the principle in all cases remaining the same; but the more rigid the guiding arrangement is, the more may the accuracy of the locating be depended upon.

The ordinary eccentric lever works on the same principle as the eccentric rods just described.   There are a great variety of eccentric clamping devices, but they are not as commonly used

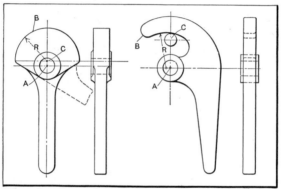

Figs. 48 and 49.   Cams or Eccentrics used for Clamping

in present-day jig design as they were a few years ago.   The eccentric clamping levers, however, provide good and rapid clamping action.   In Fig. 48 is shown one especially intended for clamping finished work.   It is not advisable to use this kind of lever on rough castings, for the reason that the latter may vary so much that the cam or eccentric would require too great a throw for rigid clamping to suit the rough castings.   The extreme throw of the eccentric lever should, in general, not exceed one-sixth of the length of the radius of the eccentric arc, if the rise takes place during one-quarter of a complete turn of the lever.   This would give an extreme throw of, say, $\frac{1}{4}$ inch for a lever having $1\frac{1}{2}$ inch radius of the cam or eccentric. It is plain that as the eccentric cam swivels about the center A,

the lever being connected to the jig with a stud or pin, the face
B of the cam, which is struck with the radius R from the center
C, recedes or approaches the side of the work, thereby releasing
it from, or clamping it against, the bottom or wall of the jig.
The lever for the eccentric may be placed in any direction, as

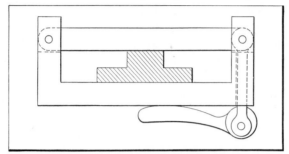

Fig. 50. Application of Clamping Cam

indicated by the full and dotted lines in Fig. 48. In Fig. 49 is
shown another eccentric lever, which is used frequently on small
work for holding down straps or leaves, or for pulling together
two sliding pieces, or one sliding and one stationary part, which
in their turn hold the work. These sliding pieces may be

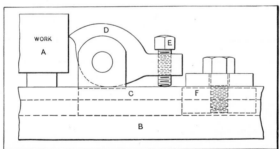

Fig. 51. The " Gripping Dog " Method of Clamping

V-blocks or some kind of jaws. The cam lever is attached to
the jig body, the leaf, or the jaw, by a pin through hole A.
The hook B engages the stud or pin C which is fastened in the
opposite jaw or part, which is to be clamped to the part into
which the pin through hole A is fastened. The variety of
design of eccentric cam levers is so great that it is impossible
to show more than the principles, but the examples shown

9 J

embody the underlying action of all the different designs.   An
elementary application is shown in Fig. 50.

Irregular shaped castings which must be machined often
present no apparently good means of holding by ordinary gripping appliances for drilling, shaping, or milling.   In such cases
a gripping dog, as illustrated in detail in Fig. 51, may be used.
The base block C of the dog is slotted to receive jaw D, which
is fulcrumed on a cross-pin.   In the tail of the dog is threaded
a set-screw E, and by turning in this set-screw the jaw is caused
to "bite" inward and downward at the same time, firmly grip-

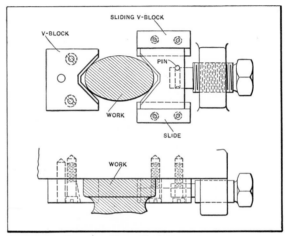

Fig. 52.   Work Held by V-clamps

ping the casting and forcing it down on the table.   A backstop
F is bolted behind each dog, so that there is no chance for slipping away from the work.

Applications to Jig Design. — The preceding description and
illustrations indicate the principles embodied in jig clamping
devices.   The following typical illustrations show a number of
applications that are merely modifications of the various methods
already reviewed.   Most of the devices described may be
quickly operated, the purpose being to show a collection of
efficient designs that will hold the work securely.   They possess
the further advantage of being relatively simple, so that the
jigs can be made at a moderate cost in all cases where there are

a sufficient number of pieces to be machined to warrant making a good tool.

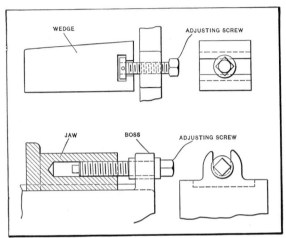

Fig. 53. Sliding Clamps

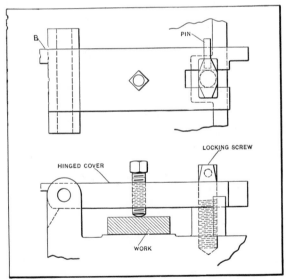

Fig. 54. Hinged Cover with Locking and Clamp Screw

A method of holding a piece of work with an oval-shaped flange is shown in Fig. 52. This piece is held between V-blocks, one of which is stationary while the other is moved by a screw.

A pilot on the end of the adjusting screw enters a hole in the V-block, the two members being held together by a pin which fits in a groove in the pilot. The movable V-block is held to the body of the jig by two steel straps. Fig. 53 illustrates, in the upper view, another method of attaching a screw to a sliding clamp member. In this case, the sliding piece is used for forcing the work down into place. This screw runs in a tapped hole in a stationary part of the fixture, while the collar at the end of the screw fits into the movable wedge to push it forward or draw it back. The lower view shows a movable clamp

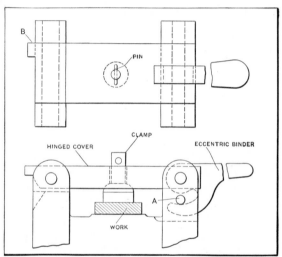

Fig. 55. Hinged Cover with Floating Stud

member that has a tapped hole to receive the adjusting screw. Here two collars on the screw are located at each side of a boss on the fixture and the adjustment is obtained by the screw turning in the tapped hole.

Two examples of hinged covers are shown in Figs. 54 and 55. The cover shown in Fig. 54 (same principle as in Figs. 30 and 36) is held in place by a locking screw, while the work is secured by a set-screw carried by the cover. The hinged cover illustrated in Fig. 55 is provided with a floating stud that secures the work, the cover which carries the stud being held in place by an eccentric binder with a hook which slides under the pin *A*.

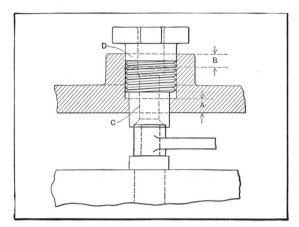

Fig. 56. Bell-mouthed Screw Bushing.

This provides a very quick-acting jig. The lug *B* at the oppo-site end of the cover prevents it from swinging back too far and breaking the hinge.

Fig. 56 shows the application of a bell-mouthed bushing, which is screwed down onto the hub of a lever, thereby locat-ing the work and at the same time providing a guide for the drill which is to operate upon it. The objection to this type of bushing is that it requires an extra long drill, and if made with two sizes of holes, as shown, particular care will have to be taken in using small drills, to prevent breaking a num-ber of them. Another objectionable feature of this clamp-ing device is that chips work into the threads and prevent turning the bushing easily, which also shortens the life of the thread. This difficulty can be overcome, however, by not tapping the hole all of the way through, as indicated at *A*; by counterboring the hole at the top marked *B*; and then grinding the pilot *C* and shoulder *D* on the bushing to a snug running fit. The bushing is then held true and chips are excluded from the thread. The average tool designer, nevertheless, avoids screw bushings whenever possible, but such bushings are frequently selected after careful con-sideration because of their neat appearance and effective operation.

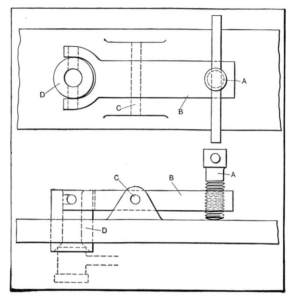

Fig. 57. An Improvement on the Screw Bushing.

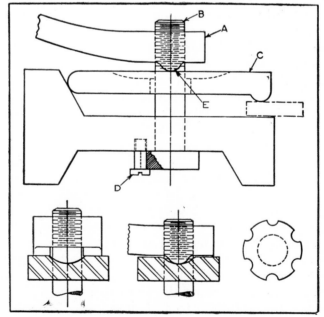

Fig. 58. Clamp with Cam Action for Quick Operation.

Fig. 57 shows a clamping device which, although a little more expensive than a screw bushing, would probably pay for itself in saving the breaking of drills, as the bushing on this jig can be made shorter and with a one-size hole. The screw A swings the lever B about pin C and pushes down the bushing D which is a slip fit in the body of the jig.

The quick-acting jig clamp, Fig. 58, has a handle A threaded to fit screw B, and a cam lobe E which engages strap C. As handle A is turned, cam E applies pressure to strap C. A movement of approximately 90 degrees of handle A produces the clamping action on the work. This allows for a variation in the thickness of the piece to be clamped equivalent to one-fourth the lead of the screw thread advancement. For example, with a 5/8-11 screw, a tolerance of plus or minus 0.011 inch would be allowed in the work. A groove is cut in the upper surface of strap C, and when the strap is loose, the cam rests in this groove. (See sectional view.) About 30 degrees movement of handle A is required to cause cam E to ride on top of the strap, as shown by the sectional view at the left.

The head of screw B has six grooves in it (as shown by the plan view in lower right-hand corner), which are engaged by set-screw D to keep screw B from turning. To adjust the lever or tighten the strap when parts wear, screw B is turned to a new position, and locked in place by set-screw D. Set-screw D also serves to keep screw B from dropping out of the jig. It is advisable to make a positive stop for handle A, so that the cam will not fall into the groove by a 180-degree turn and loosen the strap.

The bayonet-lock type of clamping device, Fig. 59, is fast in operation and positive. The bayonet slot is milled in the ram C, and the point of screw D, which is locked in place by a check-nut, slides in it. In operation, the part is slipped over the stud A with one hand, while with the other hand, the handle E attached to the ram is pushed in and rotated with a single continuous motion. The shoulder stud A extends into the work for about two-thirds of the length of the hole. This insures accurate location of the work and provides ample support against the thrust of the drill. The

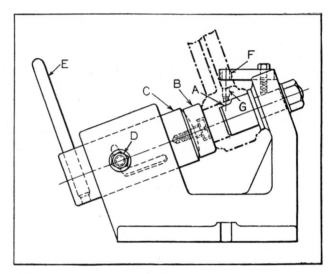

Fig. 59. Jig for Drilling Hole G in Part Shown by Heavy
Dot-and-dash Lines.

stud is flattened, as shown, to give ample drill clearance.
The revolving cap *B* turns on a crown at the end of the
clamping ram *C* and provides for a slight amount of float
to compensate for possible variations in the work. As
clamp *B* remains stationary during the actual turning or
clamping motion of the ram *C*, scoring of the face of the
work is avoided. The drill bushing *F* in the jig illustrated
is permanently fixed to the base.

Fig. 60 shows a special nut for a box wrench, the purpose of which is to permit lifting the wrench off the "hex,"
and moving it back for a new grip. The round part of the
nut serves to keep the wrench in place to be slipped back
onto the hexagon nut, while the pin at the top of the nut
makes the wrench an integral part of the fixture, so that it
cannot get lost.

Two unusual examples of jig and fixture design are illustrated in Figs. 61 and 62. The distance that the clamp had
to be raised in removing the work from between the V's of
these fixtures made it desirable to provide some method of
releasing the clamp more quickly than by turning the screw
back through the necessary distance. The way in which

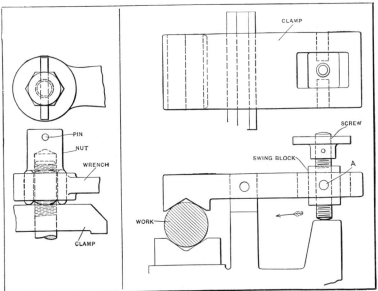

Fig. 60.   Fig. 61. Binding Screw Pivoted in Clamp

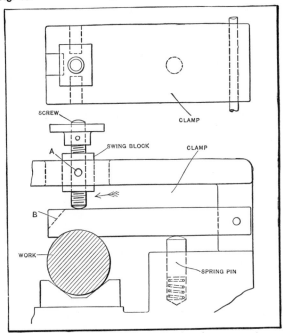

Fig. 62. Quick-releasing Clamping Arrangement

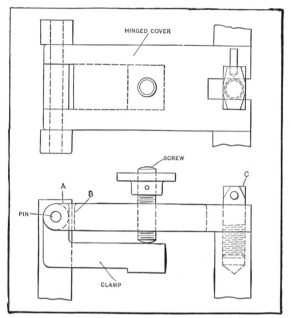

Fig. 63. Hinged Cover with Attached Clamp

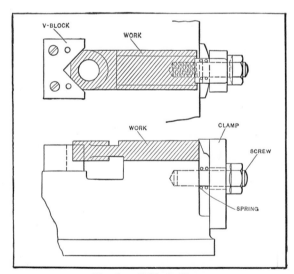

Fig. 64. V-block Clamp

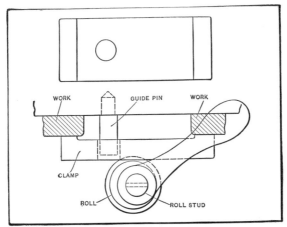

Fig. 65. Cam Clamping Device

this was accomplished is clearly shown in the illustrations, and will be seen to consist of loosening the screw and then swinging the block which carries the screw on the pivot A, the direction being indicated by the arrow. This moves the screw off its bearing on the casting in the case of the jig shown in Fig. 61, while in Fig. 62 the binding screw is removed from the clamp. The clamp shown in Fig. 62 has been cut away at B to permit the point of the screw to clear it; a spring-pin holds the clamp against the screw at all times.

Fig. 63 shows a hinged cover with the clamp attached to it. This is a convenient arrangement to remember when considering the design of jigs and fixtures. The clamp and cover are held by the same pin and both parts are swung out of the way at the same time by means of the corner of the clamp, which catches on the hinged cover at B. The design is such that the fixture has sufficient clamping range when the cover is held in place by the screw C. The clamping is effected by means of the screw in the cover which forces the clamp down on the work. Fig. 64 shows a clamp beveled at the end to pull the work down flush and push it into the V at the same time. The clamp is tightened by a screw and a spring forces it open when the screw is

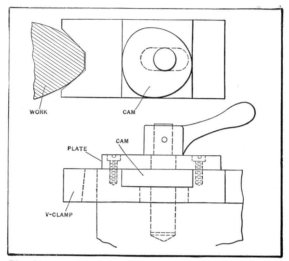

Fig. 66. Another Application of a Cam Clamping Device

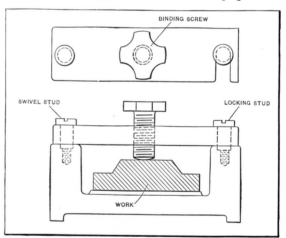

Fig. 67. Quick-acting Clamp of Simple Design

loosened. This type is often used when it is desirable to keep the clamp out of the way of the cutter.

Two examples of the use that can be made of cams are shown in Figs. 65 and 66. The device shown in Fig. 65 is simply an eccentric stud operated by a handle. This device pushes the clamp against the work; a hole is drilled in the

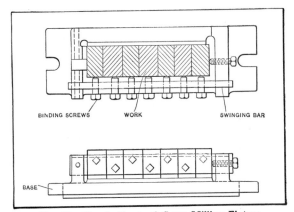

Fig. 68. Simple Form of Gang Milling Fixture

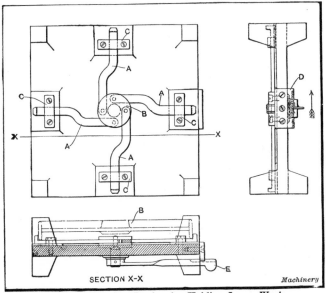

Fig. 69. Clamping Device for Holding Large Work

clamp to slide over the guide pin mounted in the frame of the jig. Fig. 66 shows a cam for operating a sliding V, the method being evident from the illustration. Another form of quick-acting clamp is shown in Fig. 67. This device consists of a bar that is hinged on a stud at one end and has a slot cut in the opposite end to slip under a second stud. The

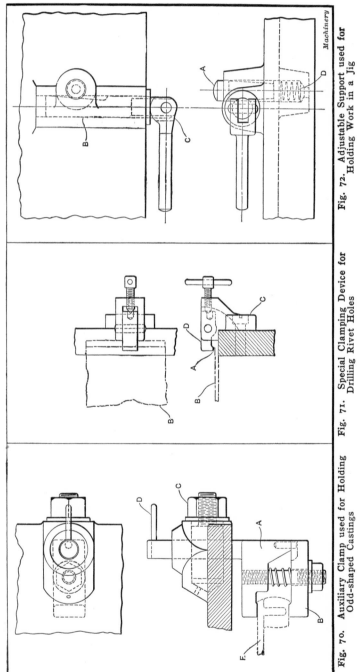

Fig. 72. Adjustable Support used for Holding Work in a Jig

Fig. 71. Special Clamping Device for Drilling Rivet Holes

Fig. 70. Auxiliary Clamp used for Holding Odd-shaped Castings

Machinery

screw that clamps the work also serves to secure the clamp in place.

A simple form of gang milling fixture is shown in Fig. 68, where the different pieces are clamped by separate screws held in a bar that can be swung out of the way to enable the work to be removed from the jig. This also makes it possible to brush the chips out at the side of the jig.

In Fig. 69 is shown a clamping device that has been found useful on large work. It consists of four arms A with the ends bent to a right angle and knurled so as to hold the work firmly in place. These arms are pivoted on the stud B and their action is guided by the blocks C. The spring handle E is pinned to the shank of the stud, and the upper edge of the handle is beveled to fit the rack D, which is fastened to the side of the base. By turning the handle in the direction indicated by the arrow the work is securely clamped and, if necessary, ordinary straps may be added for holding the work.

When making tools for tin castings of odd shapes, it is often desirable to use an adjustable clamping device that can be easily moved out of the way when reloading the fixture. Such a floating clamp is shown in Fig. 70, where the piece of work to be drilled was properly located and clamped, with the exception of one arm E, for which no ordinary clamp could be used. By pushing the support A down against the work and clamping the strap B, the work is held tight without springing it; and by tightening the nut C the clamp is held in place by the bunter and the work is securely supported. When reloading the fixture, the clamp is brought out of the way by means of the handle D.

In Fig. 71 is shown a small clamping device used when drilling the rivet holes through the beading A and the plate B. The steel bracket C is fastened by screws to the side of the fixture. The front face of the clamp bracket is used as a stop for the plate and the beading, and the clamp D with a small hole drilled in one end is fitted loosely in the milled slot in the bracket. The set-screw is located a little higher than the hole in the clamp and by a few turns of the screw the clamp is brought down against the work and forces the beading up against the stop ready to be drilled.

Spring bunters are often used in designing fixtures where adjustable supports are necessary, and the form of bunter shown in Fig. 72 has proved very efficient. The bunter *A* and the binder *B* fit freely in the holes in the casting. The bunter is slightly tapered and a tapered flat is milled on one side of the binder. When the fixture is loaded the spring *D* forces the bunter up against the work, and by means of the cam *C* the binder is pulled outward and holds the bunter firmly in place. The double taper on both bunter and binder makes it impossible to press the bunter downward away from the work.

Conclusion.—When designing clamping devices, as few operating screws or handles should be used as will accomplish the desired result. Making the screw with a double or triple thread is sometimes done to advantage in decreasing the number of turns necessary to release the piece. Jig lids should be hung on taper pins in order that wear in the hinge may be compensated for and the resulting inaccuracy due to the lost motion in the hinge prevented. The included angle of taper on hinge pins should be only one or two degrees. The hinge pin should be a tight fit in the central portion of the hinge, which is usually the jig body, and a bearing fit in the ears of the lid.

All clamping screws and similar parts should be long enough and so located as to be conveniently taken hold of to operate, and of sufficient size to prevent hurting the operator's hands on account of the pressure necessary to manipulate them. The screws should be located so that they will resist the tilting action of the block, and the dowel pins should be fairly close to the screws and of liberal dimensions in order to resist the shearing strains to which they will be subjected. When clamping or locating the work in the jig, it is essential to have the clamping pressure exerted in a direct line against some solid point of support to prevent the tilting tendency, and the thrust should also come on such a point of the work that it will be resisted by solid metal.

CHAPTER VII

EXAMPLES OF DRILL JIG DESIGN

As jigs and fixtures are now used wherever machines and tools are constructed, the number of designs in use is practically endless, although a great many of the simpler jigs are constructed on the same general principle and differ chiefly in regard to form. There are, however, many distinct types which have been developed to handle different classes of work to the best advantage. Since the jig or fixture is designed around the part for which it is intended, the form and size naturally vary accordingly; but aside from such changes, there are many details for insuring accuracy of location and rapidity of clamping or releasing, which give the designer an opportunity for the display of judgment and ingenuity in producing a jig that is effective, and at the same time not unnecessarily complicated and expensive. In order to illustrate the relation between the work to be done and the design of the jig or fixture for that work, this chapter and those which follow will be confined largely to illustrated descriptions of designs taken from practice. In selecting these designs, the object has been to show as many types of jigs and fixtures as possible.

Drill Jig having Automatic Locating Devices. — In Fig. 1 is shown a combination flywheel and driving pinion *A* which is to be drilled and tapped for four hollow-point set-screws as shown. All the surfaces marked with dotted lines, as well as the bore, are finished before the wheel comes to the drilling machine. The problem was to construct a jig by which any unskilled laborer or boy could drill and tap these wheels quickly and correctly without any previous laying out of the holes. The jig had to be constructed so that it would be practically impossible to make any mistake in drilling when the work was properly clamped.

10 J

The jig shown in Fig. 2 fulfills all these conditions and gives very good results. It consists of a cast-iron angle-plate base B, which is fastened upon the drilling machine table. A bracket C is fastened to this base by countersunk fillister-head screws. This bracket, which is of U-shape, is provided with a stud L fitting into the finished bore of wheel A. The two arms of the U-shaped bracket serve as supports for the drill guides M. At one side the pin P passes through bracket C, while the opposite side of C is provided with an indentation to receive the pin N which connects the drill guides M. Pin N is held in

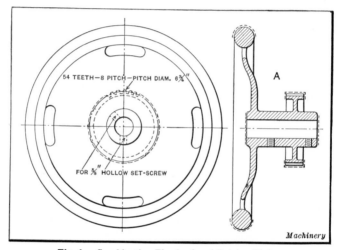

Fig. 1.   Combination Flywheel and Driving Pinion

place by headless set-screws S which also hold the drill guides to pin P as shown. One end of pin N forms a handle by means of which the guides may be conveniently swung out about pin P as a fulcrum. Bracket C fits tightly between drill guides M at both ends, thus holding them firmly in place. A screw O having its center located somewhat above the center of pin N prevents this pin and also the drill guides from coming up with the drill, and breaking the latter. Bracket C is provided with a slot in which slides a rack D, a detail view of which is shown at Y, which is provided with teeth of the same pitch as those in pinion A that are cut before the wheel comes to the drilling machine. The bottom of rack D has a narrow slot V cut in it extending from F to G.

A hardened stop-pin E is driven tightly into base B which protrudes into slot V as shown, thus determining the length of movement of rack D in each direction. A safety latch H is fastened to bracket C, swinging about screw J and resting with its tapered nose upon the taper end T of the low offset

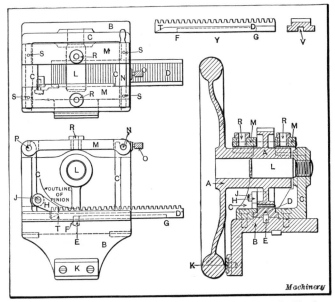

Fig. 2. Jig for Drilling Set-screw Holes in Work shown in Fig. 1

portion of rack D. Latch H is held in constant contact with D by its own weight.

To use the jig drill guides M, bushings R are swung out and the wheel is slipped upon pin L until the finished rim of A comes against the finished steel supporting plate K. If the operator should fail to push the wheel far enough, it will be impossible to close the drill guides M, as the slot between the guides that fits over the pinion will only pass over it when the wheel is in the proper place. Thus the correct location of the holes is assured. The guides are closed and the first two holes drilled and tapped. A quick-acting chuck is used to hold the drill and tap. The wheel is now revolved, causing the rack, the teeth of which mesh with those of the pinion, to move until the stop-pin E terminates its motion at point G. The wheel will then have turned 135 degrees and is ready for the drilling and tapping of the other two holes. After these are finished, the wheel is turned back until stop-pin E comes against point F. The operator cannot take the wheel off nor

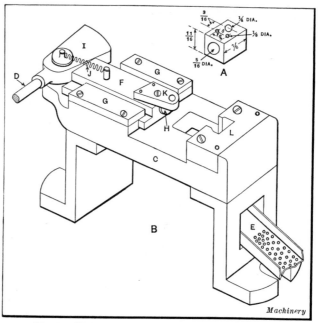

Fig. 3.   Jig for Holding Cast-iron Blocks while drilling

put it on until the rack is in the correct starting position, because safety latch H will be lifted by rack D, thus preventing the pinion which just passes it when in the lowest position from being taken off or put on. The operator must, therefore, start at the proper point for turning the full 135 degrees, and cannot make the mistake of not turning the wheel back far enough to achieve that result.

Cam-operated Clamping Slide on Drill Jig. — Two jigs were required for drilling 50,000 blocks of the size shown at A in Fig. 3. These blocks were of gray iron, and, when received, were machined all over and accurate within ± 0.005 inch. The drilling was performed in two operations; the two $\frac{1}{8}$-inch holes and the $\frac{1}{4}$-inch hole were drilled simultaneously in the first operation, the $\frac{5}{16}$-inch hole being drilled in the second operation. This order of drilling was necessary, as the $\frac{1}{8}$-inch drills would have been deflected by cutting into the larger hole, but the $\frac{5}{16}$-inch drill having a larger diameter was not affected by cutting into the smaller holes.

The first problem was to design jigs for holding the blocks that would require the minimum amount of time in loading and unloading. At B is shown the jig that was used successfully for drilling the $\frac{5}{16}$-inch hole. It is similar in design and operation to the one that was used for drilling the two $\frac{1}{8}$-inch holes and the $\frac{1}{4}$-inch hole. The jig consists of the cast-iron body C, which is set on legs five inches high in order to provide hand room for using the handle D, and also to give a sharper angle to the discharge chute E, and at the same time to provide clearance for the receiving box at the end of the chute.

The slide or movable jaw F is made a close sliding fit in the body C and is held in place by pieces G. Jaw F carries at the forward end the hardened wearing piece H and the templet K for guiding the drill, the templet K being attached to the movable jaw in this case to allow greater freedom in loading. Sliding jaw F is closed upon the work by the movement of the cam I, which is of such shape as to give a powerful grip to the jaws, a wide loading space, and a quick movement. Tension spring J holds the slide back, leaving the jaws always in an open position, except when forced together by means of pressure exerting on the hand-lever D. A carbon steel locating piece L is doweled to the body to receive the blocks; it is accurately lined up with the hole in templet K. The block when in place rests on a half floor extending across and in front of the opening in L. Just in front of this is the large opening into which the blocks fall, and beneath which the chute E is placed. A light spring, not shown, knocks the blocks off into the opening when the slide F is withdrawn, and they slide down the chute into the receiving box. It is only necessary for the operator to place the block in the jig and feed the drill to the work. Brushes are unnecessary, as the chips clear themselves and the blocks are freed from chips as they slide over the perforated section of chute E.

For drilling the three holes in the sides, a multiple drill head is used and the piece is held in a jig which is a duplicate of the one shown, except that the templet which guides the drills is

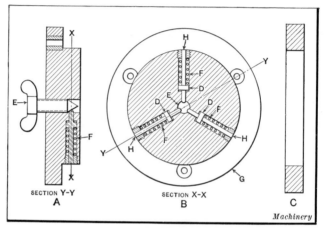

Fig. 4.   Jig for Holding Ring while drilling

attached to the stationary jaw and is provided with three holes for guiding the three drills.

Jig for Drilling Ring. — The jig shown in Fig. 4 at A and B is used for drilling the ring shown at C. Referring to the illustration at B, it will be seen that there are three plungers D held against the conical point of wing-screw E by springs F. In operation, the wing-screw E is turned back until the plungers D are just within the body G at points H. The ring C is then slipped on and the wing-screw turned down until the plungers D are forced out and into contact with the inside surface of the ring. The ring is then drilled on a sensitive drilling machine.

Indexing Jig operated by Hand-lever and Foot-treadle. — The drill jig shown in Fig. 5 was designed for drilling four angular holes in a brass time-fuse cap. (See sectional view of cap at lower part of illustration.) The principle of this jig can

easily be applied to other work. The jig consists of a hardened
steel locating plate A, mounted on a hardened spindle, which
runs in a bushing that is also hardened. A ball bearing B takes
the thrust of the spindle. At the other end of the spindle is an
index plate C, in which are cut four 90-degree notches. Keyed
to the index plate, and also to the spindle, is a ratchet wheel D.

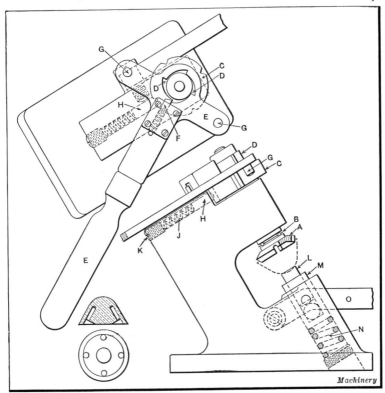

Fig. 5. Indexing Fixture operated by Hand-lever and Foot-treadle

having four teeth. A hand-lever E, which has a bearing and
turns around a hub on the index plate, carries a spring pawl F
that engages with the ratchet wheel D. The lever also carries,
at the outer ends, two pins G that project downward, so that
when it is pushed back and forth the pins strike on the body
of the jig and prevent carrying the index plate beyond the
locking pin H. This locking pin is a hardened steel sliding pin,

one end of which is rounded and engages with the notches in the index plate. Back of the pin and held in place by a headless set-screw K is a coil spring J, which holds the locking pin against the index plate. The tension of this spring is just enough to hold the work from turning while being drilled, but not enough to prevent its being readily indexed by a quick pull on the indexing lever.

The work is held in position against the locating plate A by the plunger L, which rests on a single $\frac{1}{2}$-inch hardened steel

Fig. 6. Jig having Lever- and Spring-operated Clamping Members

ball that acts as a bearing while the work is being indexed. Plunger L is carried in a second plunger M, which is held up by a powerful coil spring N. This spring should be longer and stiffer than the one shown, as an enormous pressure can be obtained with drills as small as the No. 30 used with this work. The outer plunger M is operated by a foot-treadle connected to the lever O. In operation, the foot-treadle is depressed and a piece of work is placed between the plunger L and the locating plate A. When the treadle is released, the work is held by the tension of the spring N while the indexing is done by the lever E. The locating plate A has slots milled in it with a radius cutter of the same radius as the drill to be used. This feature, in connection with the lip on the work, answers the same purpose as a drill bushing, no other means of guiding the drill being necessary. The production of this jig was about 4000 caps per day.

Jig having Lever- and Spring-operated Clamping Members. — The jig shown in Fig. 6 is used for drilling 1.250-inch holes in the motor truck steering arms, shown in Fig. 7. Owing to the means provided for securing work in this jig ready to be

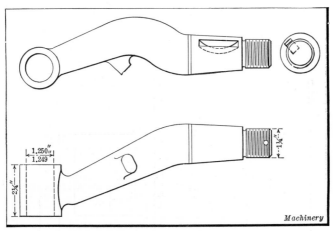

Fig. 7. Type of Steering Arm drilled in Jig shown in Fig. 6

drilled, and for releasing the finished part after the operation has been performed, this is known as a "pump" jig. Bushing A is bell-mouthed on the lower side, and drops down over the top of the boss at the end of the steering arm. The threaded end of the work is supported by means of a slotted block B carried at the end of bracket C.

When it is desired to set up a piece of work in the jig, "pump" handle D is pushed down; this handle swings on pivots E, with the result that rods F raise jig bushing A against the pressure applied by coil springs G. The piece of work is then slipped into place and handle D is released so that springs G apply sufficient pressure to enable bushing A to hold the work in the desired position to be drilled. This arrangement will be

readily understood by comparing the jig with the work. After
the drilling operation has been completed, it is a simple matter
to release the work from the jig by pushing down the handle D
and withdrawing the piece from under the bell-mouthed bushing.

Drill Jig for Fork Links. — The drill jig shown in Fig. 8 was
designed for drilling fork links. The form of these links is
indicated by dot-and-dash lines in both views. The link has a
round boss at one end and rounded forks at the other end. It

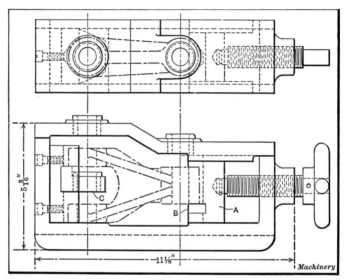

Fig. 8. Drill Jig for Fork Links

is accurately held between two V-blocks, one being adjustable
and the other stationary. The adjustable V-block A is clamped
against the work by the star-wheel and screw shown, and it
travels between finished ways, thus providing an accurate as well
as rapid method of clamping. These V-blocks have inserted
steel plates B and C. The latter, which is in the stationary
V-block, carries a drill bushing for drilling the lower fork, and
an upper shoulder on this plate provides a support for the
upper fork; thus there are two bushings in alignment for drilling the two ends. The inserted plate B in the adjustable block
supports the opposite end of the fork link. With this arrange-

ment, a two V-clamping jig is obtained having a three-point support. This drill jig was accurate, rapid and easily operated.

Drill Jig for Machining Half Holes. — A rather unusual form of jig for drilling a half hole in the work to match a similar half hole in another piece is shown in Fig. 9. Holes are often drilled in such locations when it is desired to assemble two pieces and drive a pin into the hole to act as a driver. To drill such a half hole, it is usually necessary to plug up the hole in the work in some way which will back up the side of the drill that is not cutting. This is accomplished in the present instance

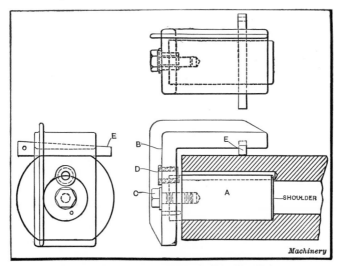

Fig. 9. Useful Form of Jig for Drilling Half Holes

by having a stud *A*, which is a push fit in the work, back up the drill. An angle-iron or plate *B* is attached to the stud *A* and held in position by a bolt *C*, the plate *B* being also doweled in place. A hole is drilled in this angle-iron to receive the bushing *D* which guides the drill in the usual manner. The remainder of the jig consists of the key *E* which locks the jig in place on the work.

In using this tool, the key *E* is pulled back clear of the work and the stud *A* which carries the angle-iron is pushed into the hole until the stud brings up against the shoulder of the work. By pushing the tapered key *E* up until it binds on the flat of the work, and then tapping it lightly, the jig is held securely in place. When drilling one of these half holes it is found that if an ordinary twist drill is used there is a tendency for it to "hog in," which is likely to result in breaking the tool. For this reason, it is desirable to use a straight-fluted or farmer's drill, although good results may also be obtained by grinding a twist drill in such a way that it has no rake or hook resulting from the spiral form of the flutes. A drill which is ground in this way presents a square or slightly obtuse cutting edge to the work, thus doing away with the trouble experienced from drills breaking when ground in the usual way.

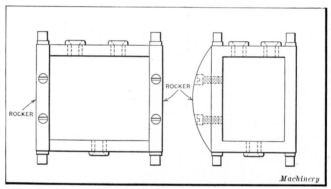

**Fig. 10.   Drill Jig provided with Rockers to Facilitate
Reversing its Position**

When drilling the hole, the work is set up on end on the drill press table and the drill is fed through the bushing in the usual way, the bushing holding the drill in position until it starts to cut. As the drill is fed down, there is a tendency to force it away from the work, but this tendency is resisted by the hardened stud *A* so that the half hole is drilled parallel with the axis of the work. This jig affords a convenient means of quickly accomplishing this work and having the two half holes match up accurately, so that no difficulty is experienced in assembling the work.

Jig having Rockers upon which it is turned over. — The box drill jig shown in Fig. 10 was used for drilling three holes in a certain piece that was to be produced in quantity. The jig is made from a forging, two stationary bushings being inserted in the top and one in the bottom. As the jig and work weighed about twelve pounds, it was hard for the workmen to be constantly lifting the jig and turning it over for the operation on the other side; therefore, two pieces of steel were machined to a radius and attached to the jig between the four feet on the side opposite the leaf. With the aid of these rockers, the jig is easily turned over from one side to the other. They do not interfere in any way with the working parts, and when changing

Fig. 11. Drill Jig designed for Rapid Indexing

work, the jig is supported by the rockers. In this way, the jig is always on the drilling table, and there is less likelihood of the operator letting it fall to the ground or throwing it down and snapping the bushing or legs, which are hardened to glass hardness. In addition, the operator does not have to work so hard and the production is considerably increased.

Drill Jig designed for Rapid Indexing. — The necessity for a drill jig of the indexing type was brought about by a certain design of motorcycle drive pulley. This pulley is of the flat-belt, flanged type, having cork inserts over its entire periphery.

To the right in Fig. 11 is shown a completed pulley with the cork inserts in place. Mounted on the drill jig is shown a pulley being drilled. The pulley is $4\frac{1}{2}$ inches in diameter and has 42 holes, $\frac{1}{2}$ inch deep, arranged in three rows of 14 equally spaced around the periphery. The drill jig is built in such a manner that it will take a large variety of sizes of pulleys.

At the left of the jig is shown a large drum which serves as a means of indexing the drill jig readily, and has three annular grooves on its periphery, spaced the same distance apart longitudinally as it is desired to have the holes drilled on the pulleys. Directly in the center of these grooves and spaced equidistantly around the periphery are 14 tapered index pin holes. At the base of the drill jig is an index pin (not shown), which is tapered on the end to fit the tapered index hole. At the back of this index pin is a light spring which holds it constantly in contact with the index drum.

In operation, the first row of holes is drilled. When enough pressure is applied to the drum to rotate it, the index pin, being correctly tapered, will jump out and allow the drum to revolve to the next index hole. After the first row of holes has been drilled in this manner, the second row is placed in line with the revolving drill by forcibly sliding the index drum and its shaft longitudinally until the index pin jumps into the middle groove. In this position the 14 central holes are drilled as before. To drill the last row of holes it is only necessary to move the index drum over as in the second case.

Where it is essential to drill holes accurately spaced around the periphery, this form of index drum and pin might not be accurate enough. However, in this case and in many other cases it is sufficiently accurate. It has the advantage of being quickly indexed, which is not always true of the ordinary index pin that has to be grasped by one hand while the other hand is employed in rotating the fixture. In this case, the right hand is never moved from the drill spindle lever.

Indexing Jig provided with Work-locating Device. — The jig shown in Fig. 12 is for drilling differential spider arms. Before the drilling operation the forging is chucked and rough-turned, including the arms, and then without centering the ends of the arms the piece is casehardened. A row of hardened spiders is then strung on an arbor and sufficient metal is ground from the ends of the arms to remove the hardened case. This leaves the soft cores exposed for center drilling. By drilling

Fig. 12. Indexing Jig provided with Special Work-locating Device

after hardening, a better working center is obtained, and one that is not full of scale; moreover the centers are not influenced by any distortion that might occur in hardening.

The jig upon which the center drilling is done consists of the angle-iron base A, upon which is swiveled the jig section B. The spider, which is indicated at C, is slipped over the swiveling stud *D*. In order to locate the spider centrally in the jig, that is, so that the arms will come in average alignment with the four bushings, the centering device *E* is employed. By means of a spring *F*, the end of which is attached to the bent end of the part *E*, the two aligning fingers are brought to bear simul-

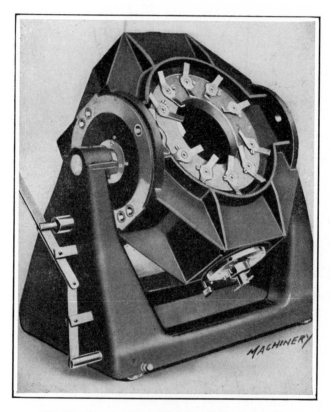

Fig. 13. Trunnion Type of Indexing Jig for Automobile
Rear-axle Housings

taneously against opposite arms of the spider, thus locating the spider in a central position in the jig. After this it is a simple matter to drill and countersink the spider arms one after another, indexing the jig by hand for each arm.

An idea of the facility with which this jig is operated can be gathered from the fact that 500 of these spiders are drilled and countersunk in a day of nine hours, making a total of 2000 holes per day. The most important part, however, is the fact that the method insures that the centering is done with reference to the *hardened* spider arms, thus insuring that the amount of metal removed in grinding will be practically equal at all points.

Indexing Jigs mounted on Trunnions. — A box drill jig for use in drilling, reaming, tapping, chamfering, and spot-facing holes in automobile rear-axle housings is illustrated in Fig. 13.

Fig. 14.   Another Indexing Drill Jig of the Trunnion Type

It will be seen from the illustration that the jig swings on trunnions fitted in the cradle or base, and that the base is equipped with index-pins for locating the jig in any of five positions. There is an index-pin at each side of the base and these pins are operated simultaneously by a single hand-lever.

The rear-axle housing is put in the jig through an opening covered by a hinged and latched lid; and the work is held in place by means of hardened steel plugs which insure positive location. All parts of the jig which are subject to wear are hardened and ground to size, thus greatly reducing the possibility of inaccuracy of the work as a result of wear. The weight of the jig is 1100 pounds and it is equipped with rollers carried

11 J

by hardened and ground steel pins. These rollers run on tracks which carry the jig under the machine and also enable it to be easily run back to remove the work.

It is necessary to drill quite a number of holes in the casting shown in place in the jig illustrated in Fig. 14, and these holes

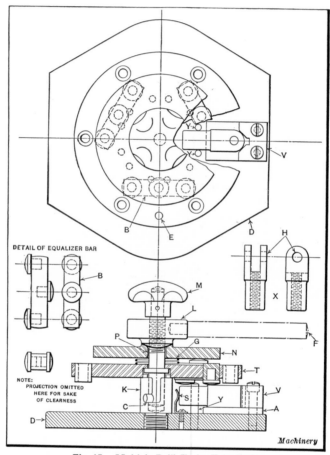

Fig. 15.   Multiple Drill Jig for Yoke Ends

are located on different sides and at various angles to one another. For this reason, an indexing jig is employed. This particular illustration shows the cover *A* of the jig removed in order to illustrate more clearly the position of the casting, which is located in the jig by its trunnions. The main body of the jig is also supported by heavy trunnions at each end, and the large disks B and C enable it to be held in different positions. These disks contain holes which are engaged by suitable indexing plungers D at each end of the fixture.

Multiple Drill Jig for Yoke Ends. — In automobile shops, the part shown at X in Fig. 15 is known as an adjustable yoke end. Even the simplest motor car employs many such parts, and it will therefore be understood that jigs for drilling these yoke ends must be designed with a view to high production. The jig used for drilling the hole H in six yoke ends at the same time by means of a multiple-spindle drill head is rather complicated in detail, but may be operated very rapidly.

It is required that the hole H be practically concentric with the round end, so that the piece is located in a V-block, between the two pins Y, shown in the upper view where the plate is broken away. The locating is accomplished by pushing the yoke end between the V-blocks V and the flat steel springs S. The bushing plate T and the entire clamping assembly is removed at this time to make the jig accessible. After the parts have been placed in position in the jig, the bushing plate and assembly are put back in place, and as the pin C enters the slot, it is pushed down to the bottom of the socket K and locked by turning the knob M clockwise. The bushing plate is brought to the right position by registering with the pin E, which location also brings the lower buttons of the equalizer bars B directly over the yoke ends. Turning the nut L clockwise by means of the removable handle F brings it against the spherical seat of the clamp plate N which, in turn, compresses the helical spring G and brings the equalizer bars against the work. The handle F is then removed and the work drilled. Reversing the process and rapping the baseplate D against the drill table releases the work. The function of the helical spring G is to keep the plate N against the nut L so that a small movement of the handle F will permit of unclamping the plate. A hardened steel plate A is provided for a seat on which the work rests. It should be noted that the slot in the yoke end is milled out in an operation following the drilling.

A Vise Drilling Jig. — Fig. 16 shows a jig for drilling and milling an elongated hole in a piece of work where the limit of accuracy required is not less than ± 0.003 inch. A flanged milling machine vise was fitted with a special jaw having a V-groove cut lengthwise, as shown at *B*. Pin *C* was put into

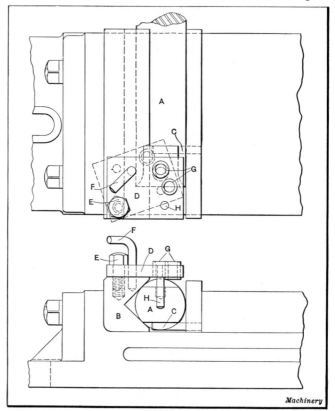

Fig. 16.   Vise Drill Jig with Swiveling Leaf for Forming an Oblong Hole

a soft jaw on the movable slide of the vise and located so that the milled surface of shaft *A* would rest on the upper surface of the pin and hold the shaft level for drilling. Bushing plate *D* was next put on and held in place by a cap-screw *E*. Bushing plate *D* was then laid out and drilled and reamed in position for the locating pin *F* and the drill and counterbore bushings *G*. The stop-pin *H* was located in the bushing plate *D* to insure obtaining the right location of the drilled hole from the end of the shaft A.

After the hole was drilled, the locating pin F was pulled out and the plate D swung around from the first position, as shown by the dotted lines, to the second position, and pin F was inserted in another hole. Each hole for pin F was located so as to bring the bushing plate D into the proper positions for drilling and counterboring. A special counterbore or mill was then used through the bushing G to elongate the hole to the proper size and depth. This counterbore was made from drill rod of the same diameter as the width of the elongated slot in the shaft. Four teeth were cut in the end and it was then hardened and tempered.

After the shaft A was properly drilled and counterbored, it was removed from the vise, and the bushing plate D swung back into the drilling position; this also brings the stop-pin H into position for locating the next shaft. Another shaft is now put into the vise against the stop-pin and the previous operations are repeated.

This device has been used with new bushing plates to suit many different kinds of work. For drilling and tapping, when using a reversible tapping chuck or a drill press that has a reversible spindle, it will be found to be a very handy tool. After the tap hole is drilled in the work, pin F is pulled out and bushing plate D can be swung out of the way.

Jig for Drilling Deep Holes in Studs. — The jig to be described was designed for drilling 50,000 brass studs which were turned from a $\frac{3}{8}$-inch square bar, with a short section of the original square bar left at the center of the finished stud. The drilling operation could not be done conveniently on the automatic screw machine, as it was necessary to drill a $\frac{7}{64}$-inch hole to a depth of $2\frac{3}{4}$ inches.

The machine used is a speed lathe which is provided with both wheel and lever feed for the tailstock. For this work, the tailstock spindle was removed and replaced by a special spindle which is shown at A in the cross-sectional view, Fig. 17. In the illustration it will be seen that the spindle is provided with a threaded nose on which the bracket *B* is screwed. The spindle was bored out to such a size that the work-holder *C* is a sliding fit in the spindle, the movement of the work-holder being accomplished by means of the lever *D* which is pivoted to the bracket *B*. The quadrant *E* is provided with teeth for the purpose of locking the lever in the closed position.

One of the studs to be drilled is shown in position at *F* in the work-holder. It is accurately centered between the tapered drill bushing *G* at one end of the work-holder and the tapered end of the rod *H* at the opposite end of the holder. The drill

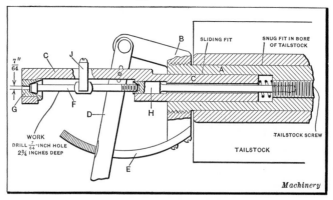

Fig. 17.   Jig for Drilling Deep Holes in Studs

bushing is pressed into the end of the work-holder, and the design of the work-holder and the manner in which the rod *H* is threaded into the tailstock screw are all clearly shown. In setting up a piece of work in the jig, the rod *H* is held stationary by its threaded connection with the tailstock screw, and a movement of the lever *D* releases or re-centers the work by sliding the work-holder *C* in the spindle *A*, the work-holder being prevented from turning by means of a clamp *J* which engages the square which is left at the center of the stud.

The drills used for this operation were of exceptional length and made with an increase in the angle of twist. They were held in the lathe spindle and the work was fed up to the drill by means of the tailstock lever. The use of this lever feed made possible the quick return of the work, which enabled the work to be rapidly backed off. This was an advantage as it was necessary to back off the work several times in drilling each hole in order to clear the chips from the drill to prevent breakage. The average rate of production obtained with this fixture was one piece per minute, the time required for setting the work up in the fixture being not over three seconds.

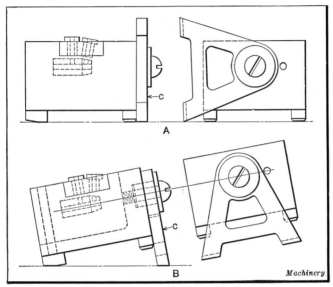

Fig. 18. (*A*) Jig in Position for Drilling Straight Hole. (*B*) Jig in Position for Drilling Angular Hole

Jig for Straight and Angular Drilling. — The jig shown in Fig. 18 was designed for drilling two holes, one of which was on an angle. By the use of this jig, the operator can bring the jig quickly into the correct position for drilling the two holes. When drilling the straight hole, the jig is in the position shown at *A;* when the operator desires to drill the angular hole, he simply lifts the front of the jig, and the swinging leg *C* falls, bringing the jig into the position shown at *B*, and placing the hole to be drilled in a line with the drill. By using this jig, extra parts, such as a cradle or angle-block, are eliminated.

Quick-operating Drill Jig. — The design of quick-operating drill jigs is a difficult matter, particularly when the shape of

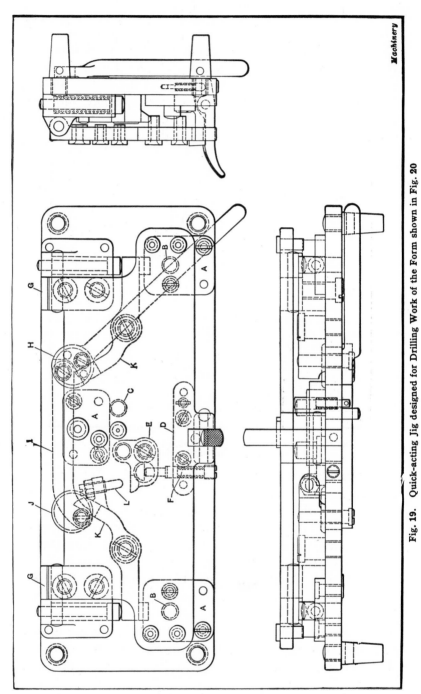

Fig. 19. Quick-acting Jig designed for Drilling Work of the Form shown in Fig. 20

the work is such that it must be located in more than one direction and clamped at several points. If the necessary clamps could be positively operated by a single lever, the greatest possible speed would be obtained, but this ideal condition may not be practicable, owing to the fact that the holding position of each clamp is likely to vary with the size of the work, thus making any combined positive movement of the clamps ineffectual. The clamps may be released by a single lever, but when holding the work their position is fixed by the work itself, and this condition, coupled with variations in the size of the work,

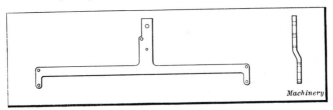

Fig. 20. Work to be drilled in Jig shown in Fig. 19

makes the operation of the clamps by a single lever a difficult matter.

If it were always possible to reverse this condition, making each clamp independent of the others in its closing movement and thus compensating for varying sizes of work, a single lever might be arranged to release all the clamps at once. This desirable result has been accomplished in the jig shown in Fig. 19 by employing spring pressure to close the locating and holding mechanisms. The position of the work is fixed in two directions, and the work is clamped at two points by a single movement of the operating lever to the right, while moving this lever to the left releases the work from the clamping and locating devices. The work (which is shown on a reduced scale in Fig. 20) lies on three hardened steel blocks *A*, and is located behind pins *B* mounted in these blocks and to the left of the pin *C* in the base of the jig.

The block *D* forms a seat for the cover-plate and the latch which holds the cover-plate down is pivoted in this block. The latch is held down by a spring plunger. The bellcrank lever *E*, which carries the fourth locating pin, is pivoted to the base of the fixture and provided with a lug which enters an opening through the base and receives the pressure of the spring plunger F. The brackets G are attached to the base of the fixture and the cover-plate is hinged to these brackets. The brackets are also bored out to receive two spring plungers. The operating lever is fastened to a hub H and a link I is pivoted on this hub, the opposite end of the link being attached to the hub J. The screws which hold the operating lever to the hub H, and the link I to the hub J, are extended to form pins which engage the levers K.

The jig is shown closed with all parts in the positions they would occupy when holding a piece of work. To raise the cover-plate, the latch is pressed back, when the thrust of a spring plunger raises it sufficiently to prevent the latch re-engaging the cover-plate. The cover-plate is raised to the limit of its movement which is a few degrees beyond the perpendicular. The operating lever is then swung to the left until it strikes a limit pin. This movement of the lever turns the hubs H and J, bringing the pins against the tail ends of the levers K and compressing the springs behind the plungers carried in the brackets G. Thus, the ends of the levers K which engage the work are swung back, releasing their grip.

The final movement of the left-hand lever K brings the adjustable stop-screw L carried by this lever against a lug projecting above the lever E, thus compressing the spring F and releasing the work from the pressure of the pin carried by the lever E. The screw L limits the movement of the lever E to the minimum amount necessary to release the work, and the stop-screw may be adjusted to accomplish this after the jig has been locked open. After removing the work from the jig, an undrilled piece is placed in position and the operating lever thrown to the right. This causes the different holding members to go through their sequence of movements in the opposite order to that described for releasing the work from the jig. The result is that the work is clamped in place in a minimum amount of time.

Drill Jig equipped with Milling Attachment. — The drill jig shown in Fig. 21 has mounted upon it a straddle-milling attachment for straddle-milling two bosses and cutting two oil slinger grooves in the lower half of an automobile crankcase. The crankcase is rigidly held in adequate supports in the drill jig, so that the light milling operation can be conveniently performed at the same time. The use of the jig for milling is also desirable, because the bosses must be in an accurate position in relation to the drilled holes.

Fig. 21. Trunnion Type of Drill Jig equipped with Milling Attachment

In Fig. 21 the drill jig is shown in the loading position. The jig templet plate _A_ has to be removed when the crankcase is being loaded on the jig. The crankcase is located by setting the outline to permanently located lines on the face of the jig. When the correct position is obtained, the crankcase is firmly clamped by four straps. After the crankcase is clamped into position, the templet jig _A_ is replaced, being held down by the hand-nut _B_ and located by a keyway in its under surface and a key in the main body of the drill jig. While in the position shown, the holes are drilled and tapped through the templet jig _A_, and this jig is allowed to remain in place, acting as a clamp, while the drilling and milling are being done.

After the completion of the foregoing operation, the drill

jig is indexed to the position shown in Fig. 22. While in this position, 22 holes are drilled in the crankcase, and after these are completed the milling is done. The milling attachment for this drill jig consists of two members D and C. Part C consists of a body member for the milling attachment. In this member are cut vertical ways in which the cutter carrying member D travels up and down. The movable member D carries a horizontal cutter-arbor having a gang of three cutters J and G on each end. In the center of this arbor is a bevel gear which meshes with another bevel gear carried by a vertical

Fig. 22.   Jig in Position for Drilling and Milling Operations

shaft, the upper end of which terminates in a Morse taper shank E. The movable member D is held normally in the upper position by springs.

In operation, the drill spindle is brought down in contact with the taper shank E until it is seated into the taper drill socket. Then the drill spindle is rotated, and the milling arbor, of course, rotates also through the bevel gears. The drill spindle is fed downward the same as for drilling, and in so doing the entire member D is lowered until the right-hand set of cutters G is brought into contact with the boss to be milled at the right-hand side of the crankcase. The cutters continue to be lowered until they come against a previously set stop, in which position the milling of the right-hand boss is completed.

To proceed with the milling of the left-hand boss, it is necessary to loosen the straps that hold the milling fixture in place, grasp the handles H and lift the milling attachment over to the left-hand side of the drill jig, where there are dowel-pins which accurately locate it in its correct relative position. The operation is repeated in the same way as for the right-hand boss, except that cutters J are used instead of cutters G. This milling attachment is never removed from the drill jig, except as explained, for milling the right- and left-hand bosses. The movable member D is moved up out of the way by spring pressure when a new crankcase is being placed in the jig. It would be possible, of course, to equip this drill jig with two milling attachments, one at each end, so that it would not be necessary to move the attachment from one side to the other, but as the changing of the fixture from one side to another was such a simple matter, it was not deemed advisable to go to the extra expense that this would involve.

Jig for Cross-drilling Pistons. — The jig shown in Fig. 23 is used successfully in cross-drilling pistons. The piston is drilled from both sides and not all the way through from one side, which is the common practice, especially when the work is done on some kind of lathe. It is not an easy matter to drill and ream a true hole by starting on one side of the piston, drilling through one boss, and then advancing the tool across the opening between the bosses and expecting the tool to secure a true start in the second boss.

This jig was made in the following manner to insure accuracy. A block of cast iron was milled square and the large hole rough-bored to within $\frac{1}{16}$ inch of size. This block was then milled across one end to receive the stop-bar A. After fitting the stop-bar, it was removed and the seat for the clamp-bar B was bored by using a fly-cutter in the milling machine. This clamp-bar was a piece of two-inch cold-rolled stock, milled flat to form a little more than a half round. During the succeeding boring and grinding operations the clamp-bar was held to its seat by the two screws C which had washers under their heads instead of the springs shown in the illustration. A piece

of 0.005-inch stock was placed between the clamp-bar and
seat while boring and grinding; this shim was taken out later
to allow for a little clearance. After the clamp-bar was fitted
and bored, the holes for the hardened bushings *D* were bored
and the bushings fitted. These bushings were long enough to
reach through the large bore so that they could be ground flush
with the inside of the jig.

The jig was next set up on the table of a Heald cylinder
grinder and the holes in the bushings ground in line and true

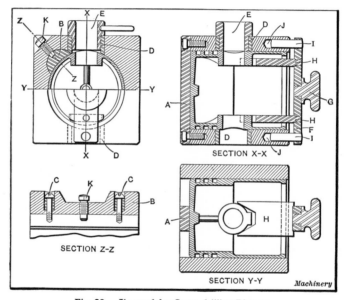

Fig. 23. Jig used for Cross-drilling Pistons

to size. The jig was then placed on one side with the bushings in a horizontal plane and the large hole finished to size
by grinding. To be sure that the holes in the bushings would
be perfectly central with the large bore, an arbor was ground
to a snug fit for the bushings and the large hole was gaged
from it, measuring from the wall of the large hole to the arbor
until both sides were exactly the same. The hole was then
finished 0.003 inch larger than the piston to be worked on.
Two slip bushings *E* were made to fit the bushings in the jig,

one for the three-lipped drill and the other for the reamer. The reamer used was 0.0015 inch under size, so that the holes could be finished with a long hand reamer that reached through both holes of the piston.

To locate the piston in the jig so that the bosses would line up with the holes being drilled, the "locator" shown at the open end of the piston was made and used in the following manner. The locator consists of the cross-bar F, into which are fitted the knob G that is used for a handle, two flat bars H with V-slots in the ends, and the two pilot-pins I. The pilot-pins fit into holes J, bored in the face of the jig in line with the bushings. In using this locator the piston was first put into the jig and then the locator was pushed in until the V-slots came in contact with the bosses. This put the piston in such a position that the bosses were in line with the drill bushings. After locating, the piston was gripped by the clamp-bar by tightening the set-screw K.

In this case the pistons were rough-drilled $\frac{3}{32}$ inch under size before turning, so that in this jig it was only necessary to use one drill and reamer. The drilling operations were as follows: The drill bushing was put in and the drill run through one side. The bushing was then taken out, the jig turned over, and the bushing put in the other side, after which the second boss was drilled. The drill bushing was now replaced by the reamer bushing and the hole reamed; the bushing was then taken out, the jig turned over, the bushing replaced and the second hole reamed. When using this jig two strips were fastened to the drill press table forming a channel in which the jig could slide and which would also hold the jig in line with the machine spindle.

Jig for Facing Bosses in Pistons. — Fig. 24 shows the jig and facing bar used for facing the bosses in the piston after it leaves the cross-drilling jig. It was found advantageous to do this operation in a separate jig because it consisted of top and bottom facing and also because the machine spindle had to be set to a stop. This jig proved to be a very handy and rapid tool. The base and the adjustable top are provided with a pair of jaws bored to the proper size to fit the piston to be worked on. The springs on the upright studs hold up the upper or clamping jaw while the work is being put in or taken out.

In operation, a piston is slipped between the jaws, the facing bar run down through the cross-drilled holes, the cutter fitted into the bar, and the top jaw set by a half turn of the lever-handled nut. A feature of the facing bar is the manner in

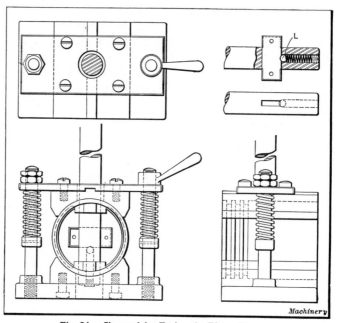

Fig. 24.   Jig used for Facing the Piston Bosses

which the cutter is held. It will be seen that the cutter has a half-round notch in the center of the bottom edge that registers with a steel ball L in the center of the cutter slot. A stiff spring holds the ball to its seat in the bar. The cutter is also provided with two holes near each end that are used for pulling it out of the bar with a stout wire hook. It is double edged, so that both bosses can be faced without reversing it or stopping the machine. This method of holding the cutter would not be desirable in the case of a boring tool, but for a facing tool it serves very well. Of course the cutter must be a nice fit in the bar. When the facing jig is used it can be clamped to the machine table, while the cross-drilling jig is not clamped, because it is necessary to turn it over and over.

Universal Jigs. — While a large percentage of the jigs in common use are designed especially for some part and are used exclusively for that particular part, occasionally jigs are so constructed that they are adjustable and adapted for a variety of work. For this reason they are often called "universal" jigs. Jigs of this type may resemble an ordinary jig somewhat

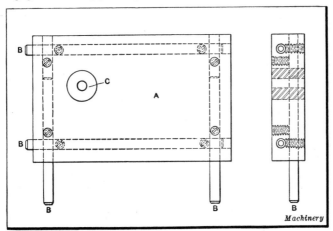

Fig. 25. Toolmakers' Universal Drill Jig

and simply be arranged to locate the guide bushings (in the case of a drill jig) in different positions; or the jig may be in the form of a special attachment for the drilling machine.

An example of universal jig construction is shown in Fig. 25. This is a very simple design and consists of a plate containing one or more drill bushings and adjustable locating rods. It may be used for accurately locating and drilling holes in jigs, dies, and templets. A hardened and ground block *A* is provided with four sliding pins *B*, a set of removable bushings *C*, and eight headless set-screws. Bushings *C* may be made up with various sized holes to provide for guiding different sizes of drills. Small slugs of brass or copper are used between the set-screws and the pins *B* so that adjusting the screws will not tend to change the position of the pins.

To illustrate the use of this jig, suppose that a number of holes must be accurately located, drilled, and reamed in a die-block. After the block has been planed up perfectly square, parallels are clamped to the edges so that they overhang in the manner shown in Fig. 26, allowing the pins B to engage with these parallels when the jig is laid flat against the die-block. The bushing C is located at a known distance from the edges of the jig, and by setting the pins B in the required position by means of a micrometer or micrometer depth gage,

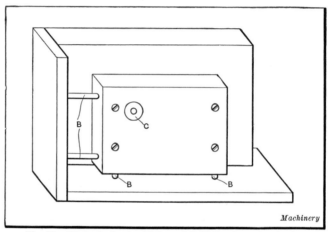

Fig. 26.   Method of using Universal Drill Jig shown in Fig. 25

the bushing is located in position for drilling the hole in the die-block. For this purpose, the jig is clamped to the die-block with a pair of parallel clamps, after which the hole is spotted, drilled and reamed in the usual way. It will, of course, be evident that any number of holes that come within the range of the jig can be located on the die-block in the same way. The usefulness of this tool will be apparent to any toolmaker, and many uses will be found for it that may not be seen at the first glance.

A universal jig which is in the form of an attachment which is clamped to the table of a drilling machine is shown in Fig. 27. The drill bushing is in line with the axis of the machine spindle, so that holes may be drilled as in the case of an ordinary jig, and there is a compound table with slides at right angles, which are operated by the usual screw and ball-crank combination. These screws are merely employed for making approximate settings; the actual locations which are depended upon to secure accurate spacing of the holes are made by means of micrometer heads and standard distance bars. The work-table is adjusted until both micrometers read zero against stops on the table which act as the micrometer anvils, and in this

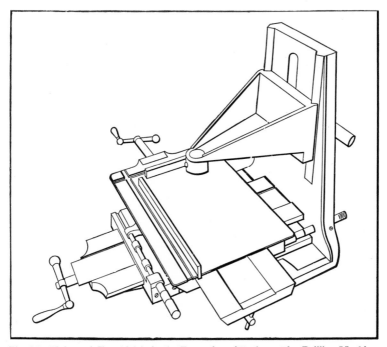

Fig. 27. Universal Jig which is in the Form of an Attachment for Drilling Machine

position the center of the drill bushing is located over the intersection of the guide strips on the work-table. The work is clamped against these guides, and in starting to locate the first hole, the two table slides are manipulated so that an approximate setting is secured, after which the distance bars and micrometer heads are used to obtain the final location in the manner to which reference has already been made. The arm which supports the drill bushing should be set to bring the bushing as close to the work as possible. It is possible to use this equip-

ment to locate any number of holes in the work in the desired
relation to each other, as the table slides may be manipulated
and final settings made with the micrometer heads and distance bars, so that each hole is located in the proper relation
to the preceding hole.   Clamps are provided to lock the table
in each position before the drilling operation is started.

The distance bars are supported by bushings held in
V-shaped seats, which support them at the proper height to
line up properly between the micrometer spindles and stops on
the table which come in contact with the micrometer spindles

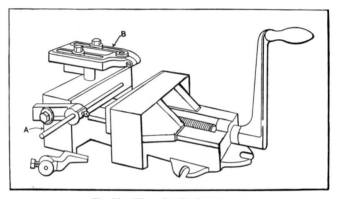

Fig. 28.   Vise with Jig Attachment

when the table is set in the zero position.   Johansson or other
gages may be used in place of the distance bars, if so desired.

Jig Attachments for Drilling in Vises. — The machine vises
such as are used for milling or planing operations may be used
for drilling when they are provided with attachments for holding drill bushings or locating stops.   There are now on the
market vises furnished with jig attachments ready for use.
One of these vises is illustrated in Fig. 28, where it will be seen
that a stop *A* may be used to locate the work while the bracket
B holds the bushing which guides the drill.

As a simple illustration of the principle involved in using
a jig of this type, reference is made to Fig. 29, in which the
part being machined is a round collar.   This collar *A* is gripped
against a vee in the solid jaw, and the bracket containing the

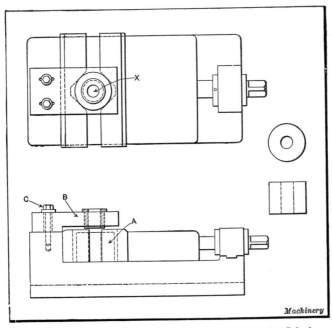

Fig. 29. Vise equipped with Jig Attachment and V-blocks for Gripping Cylindrical Part

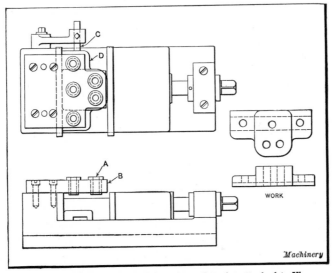

Fig. 30. Drilling Several Holes with a Templet attached to Vise

bushing B is adjusted to the correct position for guiding the drill into the work. It is clamped in place on the solid jaw by means of bolts C. To operate the jig, the movable jaw is opened and a piece of work inserted in the V-block; then it is only necessary to tighten the jaws and proceed to drill. In this way, duplicate parts are obtained without an elaborate jig. By using suitable plates in these jigs, many odd-shaped pieces can be drilled, of which Fig. 30 is a typical example. The method of using this plate is shown by the illustration. Bushings A are placed in the plate B at the proper location to guide the drills into the work. The plate is screwed on top of the vise, the stop C is adjusted to the proper location, and the work D placed in the vise against the stop, after which the holes are drilled.

This jig construction adapted to drilling holes on an angle is illustrated in Fig. 31. In this case, a swivel vise is fitted with a plate A set at the proper angle in relation to the base B. Then by swinging the vise up to the proper angle, the parts may be drilled in duplicate as in the previous case cited. That there are infinite possibilities in the fitting of vises with bushing plates, when these are intelligently used, will be readily seen by considering the methods of drilling illustrated in Fig. 32. This illustrates a swivel vise used as an indexing jig, and where extreme speed or accuracy is not required it works out very satisfactorily. The first drilling is done with the vise in the position illustrated. The subsequent drilling is accomplished by tilting the swivel vise to the right and left the desired number of degrees.

Another example of drilling in a vise is shown in Fig. 33, a number of holes being drilled around a circle. The work is gripped between the jaws in the vise proper and a bushing plate is located by pins A and B in the vise. By sliding the vise to various positions the holes are drilled in the usual manner. This bushing plate is removable for taking out the work.

The vises here illustrated are not always the most economical means of handling work, but they are often the best that the extent of the job will warrant. They must not be confused with more elaborate jigs and fixtures which, although vises

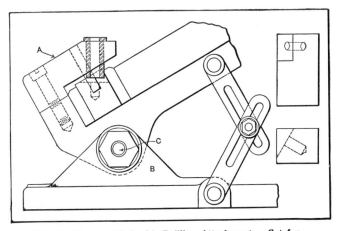

Fig. 31. Vise provided with Drilling Attachment — Set for
Drilling at an Angle

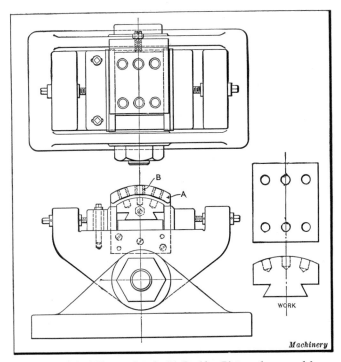

Fig. 32. Swivel Vise equipped with Bushing Plate and arranged for
Angular Drilling

in principle, are special in construction. Not all shops can afford the costly design that the manufacture of guns or automobiles will warrant. They must compromise on the cheaper and less effective equipment that can be adapted quickly to a wide range of work, and the machine vise, as shown in the foregoing, can be made a universal fixture within its limits.

Multiple Drilling Jig of Reversible Type. — The drilling of the spoke holes in the hubs of motorcycles is illustrated in Fig. 34.

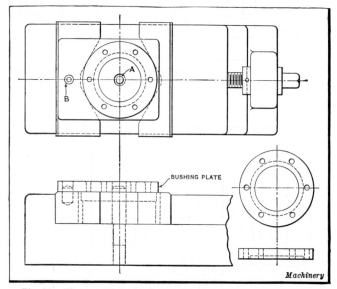

Fig. 33. Vise provided with Removable Bushing Plate for Drilling Holes on a Circle

These hubs are made of low carbon steel and the end flanges through which the holes are drilled are $\frac{1}{8}$ inch thick. Through each flange, sixteen No. 25 holes are drilled at a slight angle so that the direction of the drilling is along the lines of a cone. The distance between the holes is about one-half inch.

The spindles of the multiple-spindle drilling machine in which the work is done are guided in their inclination by a steel ring supported from the head of the machine. The jig is of the swiveling type, permitting the holes in one end of the hub to be drilled, after which the work-holding part of

Fig. 34. Swiveling Drill Jig for Motorcycle Hubs

the jig is swiveled 180 degrees and the holes in the opposite end are drilled. The drilling is performed by running the head and drills down to the work, which on account of the inclination of the spindles is the only way possible.

In order that the work may be quickly inserted and removed, the jig is made in halves. As the illustration shows, these halves are hinged at the left and held together for the drilling by a latch that appears at the right of the illustration. The drill bushings are located in the faces of the halves of the jig. After the holes in one flange of the hub have been drilled, the steel plate that takes the thrust is removed from beneath

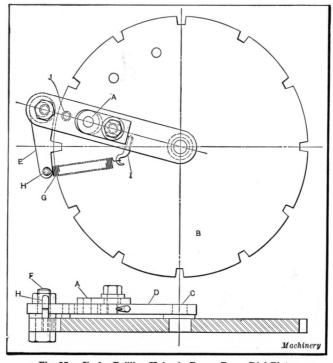

Fig. 35. Jig for Drilling Holes in Power Press Dial Plates

the work. Then by withdrawing the index-pin at the left, the working part of the jig can be turned 180 degrees to present the other face of the hub to the drills. The heavy stud on which the jig swivels is directly behind the work, and, therefore, not visible in the illustration. The index-pin is inserted, the thrust plate is replaced, and the drilling of the hub is completed. The hubs, each having 32 holes — 16 in each end — are drilled at the rate of 300 per ten-hour day.

Jig for Drilling Power Press Dial Plates. — The jig shown in Fig. 35 is used for drilling dial plates of the form employed on automatic feed mechanisms for power presses. These dial plates have the center hole bored and the notches milled to suit the locating plungers on the power presses, but the holes had to be drilled later because they are located with reference to the particular presses on which the dials are used. Before

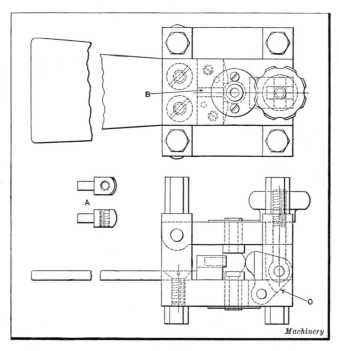

Fig. 36. Jig in which a Single Screw tightens both Clamp and Hinged Cover

using the drill jig it was necessary to make center punches to fit the punch-blocks on the different power presses and also to fit bushing *A* in the jig. Each dial plate *B* was then put on its bed and the press was set in the usual way, care being taken to have the locking device fit properly in one of the notches. The center punch was then mounted in the punch-block and one prick-punch mark was made on the dial in the proper relation to one of the notches. The dial plate was next placed on the table of a drill press and the center punch was set in the chuck in the drill spindle so that the prick-punch mark on the dial could be lined up with the spindle. The plate was then strapped to the table and stud C driven into the center hole. The top of the stud C is machined to fit the pivot hole in the arm D of the jig.

The next step consisted of lining up the bushing A of the fixture with the center punch in the drill spindle. It will be noted that the bushing is made adjustable relative to the center C about which the arm swings, so that it may be set in the required position before clamping the binding bolt. The bushing is located in the proper relation to the notches in the dial plate by means of the locking pawl E, and the eccentric screw F adjusts the position of the pawl relative to the arm D of the jig. The pawl is held in the proper notch in the dial by the spring G which is mounted on the pins H and I; and stud J is used to hold the arm of the fixture true with the face of the dial plate. It will be evident that after this setting has been made, the bushing A is located directly over the center punch mark which was made on the dial plate while the prick-punch was mounted in the punch-block of the power press. The hole can now be drilled in the dial plate, after which successive holes are drilled by simply swinging the dial around the pivot C and locking it for drilling each hole by dropping the pawl E into successive notches in the dial plate.

Duplex Clamping Arrangement on Drill Jig. — The jig shown in Fig. 36 is used for drilling and tapping stud A, which is made from $\frac{1}{4}$- by $\frac{1}{4}$-inch cold-drawn steel. The end of the stud enters hole B in the locating block, and this hole is milled to provide clearance for the head of the stud. The work rests on the drill bushing which is slightly counterbored to provide clearance for the tap. The most interesting feature of the jig is that the cover and clamping mechanism are both secured by the same knob; clamp C holds the stud securely in place when the knob is screwed down, and the same operation tightens the cover. It will be readily seen that this principle could be employed on jigs and fixtures used for holding a great variety of parts.

CHAPTER VIII

BORING JIGS

Boring jigs are generally used for machining holes where accuracy of alignment and size are particularly essential, and also for holes of large sizes where drilling would be out of the question. Two or more holes in the same line are also, as a rule, finished with the aid of boring jigs. The boring operation is performed by boring bars having inserted cutters of various kinds, and boring jigs are almost always used in connection with this kind of boring tool, although boring operations may be satisfactorily accomplished with three- or four-lipped drills and reamers. The reamers may be made solid, although most frequently shell reamers mounted on a bar and guided by bushings are used. The majority of holes produced in boring jigs, whether drilled or bored out, are required to be of such accuracy that they are reamed out in the last operation.

The boring-bars are usually guided by two bushings, one on each side of the bored hole, and located as close as possible to each end of the hole being bored. The bar is rotated and simultaneously fed through the work, or the work with its jig is fed over the rotating bar. Boring jigs may be used either in regular boring lathes, in horizontal boring and drilling machines, or in radial drills.

The jig body is made either in one solid piece or composed of several members, the same as in drill jigs. The strain on boring jigs is usually heavy, which necessitates a very rigidly designed body with ribbed and braced walls and members, so as to allow the least possible spring. As boring jigs when in operation must be securely fastened to the machine table, means must also be provided in convenient and accessible places for clamping the jig without appreciably springing it.

The places in the jig where the bushings are located should be provided with plenty of metal so as to give the bushings a substantial bearing in the jig body. Smaller jigs should be provided with a tongue or lip on the surface which is clamped to the machine table; this permits the operator to quickly locate the jig in the right position. As an alternative, finished lugs locating against a parallel or square may be provided. It is frequently advantageous to have small sized boring jigs provided with feet so that they can be used on a regular drill-

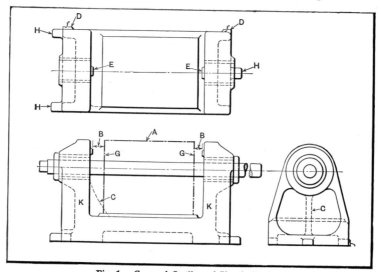

Fig. 1. General Outline of Simple Boring Jig

press table in cases where holes to be bored out are to be opened up with a drill piercing the solid metal. It is both easier and cheaper to do this rough drilling in a drill press.

The guide bushings, of the same type as the bushings for drill jigs, are made either of cast iron or steel and ground to fit the boring-bar, which is also ground. The bushings should be made rather long to insure good bearing.

Boring Jig of Simple Design. — The most common type of boring jig for small and medium size work is shown in Fig. 1. In this engraving, *A* represents the work which is held down by straps or clamps. In many instances when the work is provided with bolt and screw holes before being bored, these holes are used for clamping the work to the jig. In some cases it is important that the work be attached to the jig in the same way as it is fastened to its component part in the machine for which it is made, and also that it be located in a similar way. If the work is located by V-slides when in use on the machine, it is preferable to locate it by V's in the jig. In other cases the locating arrangement for the work in the machine where it is to be used may be a tongue, a key, a dowel pin, a finished pad, etc. The same arrangement would then be used for locating it in the jig. In Fig. 1 enough clearance is left at B, at both ends, to allow for variations in the casting and to provide space for the chips; also, if the hole is to be reamed out, and the reamer be too large to go through the lining bushing, then the space left provides room for inserting the reamer and mounting it on the bar. In nearly all cases of boring, a facing operation of the bosses in the work has also to be carried out and provisions must be made in the jig to permit the insertion of facing tools.

A great deal of metal may be saved in designing heavy jigs by removing superfluous metal from those parts where it does not materially add to the strength of the jig. In Fig. 1, for instance, the jig can be cored out in the bottom and in the side standards as indicated without weakening the jig to any appreciable extent. The rib C may be added when necessary, and when it does not interfere with the work to be finished in the jig. It will be seen that extended bosses are carried out to provide long bearings for the bushings. The bosses may be made tapering, as shown, providing practically the same stiffness as a cylindrical boss containing considerably more metal. Finished bosses should be located at suitable places to facilitate the laying out and the making of the jig, as shown at D. The finished faces of these bosses are also of advantage when locating the jig against a parallel, when it is not provided with a tongue for locating purposes.

In some cases bosses are placed where measurements may be taken from the finished face to certain faces of the work, in which case the finished bosses, of course, must stand in a certain relation to the locating point; such bosses are indicated at E, from which measurements B can be taken to surfaces G on the work. The three lugs H are provided for clamping purposes, the jig being clamped in three places only to avoid unnecessary springing action. If the jig is in constant use, it would be advisable to have special clamping arrangements as component parts of the jig for clamping it to the table, thereby avoiding loss of time in finding suitable clamps.

The walls or standards K of large jigs of this type are frequently made in loose pieces and secured and doweled in place. In such a case, the most important thing is to fasten these

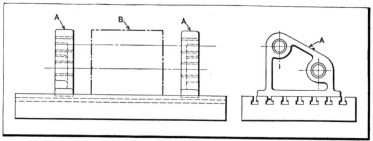

Fig. 2.   Simple Design of Adjustable Boring Jig

members firmly to the base, preventing shifting by tongues, keys, or dowels. It is evident that, when the standards are made loose, it is easier to finish the pad of the base, and this is of importance, particularly when difficult locating arrangements are planed or milled in the base; the patternmaker's and the molder's work is also simplified. As a rule the standards are screwed to the base permanently and then the bushing holes are bored. In some cases, however, it may be easier to first bore the hole in a loose part, and then attach it to the main body.

Adjustable Boring Jigs. — When boring jigs are designed for machine parts of a similar design but of different dimensions, arrangements are often made to make one jig take various sizes. In such a case, one or both standards may have to be moved, and extra pads are provided on the face. This shifting of the standards will take care of different lengths of work. Should the work differ in height, a blocking piece may be made. Sometimes special loose brackets m?y be more suitable for replacing the regular standards for shorter work. If there is a long distance between two bearings of the work, a third standard may be placed in between the two outside ones, if the design of the bored work permits; this may then be used for shorter work together with one of the end standards. In Fig. 2 is shown an adjustable boring jig. Here the jig consists of two parts A mounted on a common baseplate or large table provided with T-slots. The work B is located between the standards. A number of different standards suitable for different pieces of

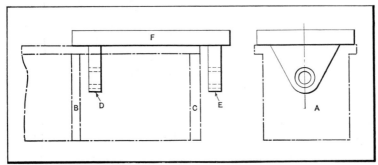

Fig. 3. Jig located on and supported by the Work

work may be used on the same baseplate. The jigs or standards are held down on the baseplate by screws or bolts, and generally located by a tongue entering the upper part of the T-slots.

Boring Jig supported on Work. — Boring jigs are frequently made which are located and supported on the work. Fig. 3 shows such a jig. The work A, which in this case represents some kind of a machine bed, has two holes bored through the walls B and C. This jig may guide the bar properly if there be but one guide bushing at E, but it is better if it can be arranged to carry down the jig member D as indicated to give support for the bar near the wall B. It may sometimes be more convenient to have two separate jigs located from the same surfaces on the top or sides. In other cases it may be better to have the members D and E screwed in place instead

13 J

of being solid with F, and in some cases adjustable. Of course, these variations in design depend upon the conditions involved, but the principles remain the same. The jig or jigs are held to the machine on which they are used by clamping arrangements of suitable type.

Jigs for Supporting Bar on One Side of Hole Only. — The type of boring jigs previously described supports the bar in two or more places, and the cutting tools are placed at certain predetermined distances from the ends of the bars, depending upon the shape and size of the work. Sometimes it may prove necessary, however, to have a cutting tool inserted just at the end of the bar. For example, a boring jig may consist of

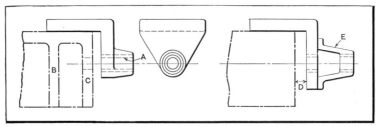

Fig. 4.   Examples of Guiding Arrangements where no Support is obtainable on One Side of Hole to be bored

simply one bracket as shown at the left in Fig. 4. A very long bearing A is then provided so as to guide the bar true. The arrangement shown at the right in Fig. 4 is sometimes used to insure a long bearing for the bar. A special bracket E is mounted on the jig and bored out at the same time as the jig proper is machined. This provides, in effect, two bearings. In these cases bars with a cutting tool at the end are used. There are several reasons why a boring jig of this kind may be required. For instance, there is a wall B immediately back of the wall C in which the hole is to be bored. Other obstacles may be in the way to prevent placing a bearing on one side of the hole to be finished. Instead of having a space D between the jig and the work, the jig can oftentimes be brought up close to the work and clamped to it from the bushing side.

Each of the different holes in boring jigs has, of course, its own outfit of boring-bars, reamers, and facing tools. In making

the jig it must be considered whether it will be used continu-
ously and what degree of accuracy will be required. When
extreme accuracy is required there should be a bar provided
with cutting tools for each operation to be performed. It is
cheaper, of course, to use the same bar as far as possible for
different operations, and ordinarily, satisfactory results are
obtained in this way. It is desirable to have bushings fitting

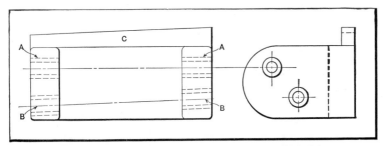

Fig. 5.   Jig for Boring Holes located at an Angle to Each Other

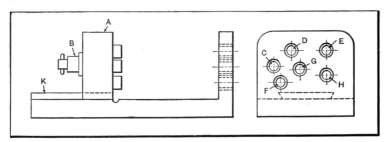

Fig. 6.   Diagram illustrating Principle of Multiple-bar Boring Jig

each bar, but often this expense can be reduced by using the
same bushings for bars having the same diameter.

   When Holes are not Parallel. — It sometimes happens that
one or more holes form an angle with the axis of other holes in
the work to be bored. In the jig shown in Fig. 5, the bushings *A*
guide one bar for boring one hole and the bushings *B* the bar
for boring another hole, the axis of which is at an angle with
the axis of the first hole in the horizontal plane. Then an
angle-plate *C* can be made in such a manner that if the jig is
placed with the tapered side of plate *C* against a parallel, the
hole *B* will be parallel with the spindle. This arrangement

may not be necessary when universal joints are used between
the spindle and the bar.

Jigs for Multiple Boring. — As a rule but one hole is bored
out at a time, owing to the fact that machines for boring
generally have but one spindle. Several holes, however, could
be bored out in a large-size multiple-spindle drill, in which
case the jigs naturally ought to be designed somewhat stronger.
Another method of designing jigs for boring two or more holes

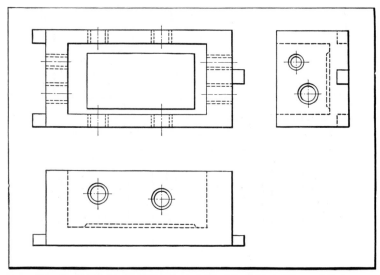

Fig. 7.   Jig for Boring Holes through Work both from Sides and Ends

at the same time is illustrated in Fig. 6, the outlines only being
shown in this illustration. The gear-box A contains the main
driving gear which is mounted on a shaft B which, in turn, is
driven by the spindle of the machine. The gear on shaft B
drives the gears and shafts connected with the boring bars
passing through the bushings C, D, E, F, G, and H. The gears
are proportioned according to the speed required for each bar,
which in turn is determined by the sizes of the holes. The
housing or gear-box A slides on a dovetail slide K. A particularly good fit should be provided, and the gear-box can be fed
along in relation to the work either by table or spindle feed. If

boring operations are to be performed in two directions, a jig on the lines indicated in Fig. 7 is designed. This jig may be mounted on a special revolving table permitting the work and the jig to be turned and indexed so as to save resetting and readjusting the work and jig when once placed in position on the machine.

The foregoing outline of boring jigs illustrates only the fundamental principles involved, it being considered more important to state the fundamental principles in this connection than to describe complicated designs of tools in which the application of such principles may be more or less obscure or hidden.

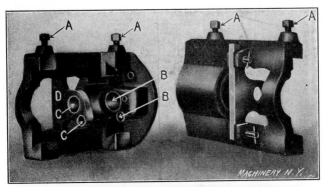

Fig. 8. Example of Small Boring Jig, with Removable Leaf for Holding Guide Bushings

Boring Jig Designs. — In Fig. 8 are shown two views of a small jig supported directly on the work to be bored. This jig is used for boring out a cross-slide carriage, and is located on the work by the dovetail slide and held in place by the two set-screws A. The two bushings B are driven into the solid part of the jig and the two corresponding bushings C are placed in the loose leaf D which is removed when the jig is placed in position on, or removed from, the work. The two set-screws A do not bear directly on the side of the carriage, but are provided with brass or steel shoes. The leaf D cannot be attached permanently to the jig and simply swung out of the way when the jig is located on the work, because it could not be swung in place after the jig is applied on account of the small clearance in the cross-slide carriage. The leaf is therefore made loose, which is an objectionable feature, but lugs have been carried up on the casting on both sides of the leaf as shown, to give good support; these lugs are carefully finished to fit the leaf, and the latter is located and held in place by ground plugs.

In Fig. 9 is shown a boring jig which receives the work *A* between two uprights. The work in this case is the tailstock of a lathe where two holes *B* and *C* are to be bored out. The bottom surface of the tailstock is finished before boring, and is located on the finished bottom of the jig by means of a key

Fig. 9.　Common Type of Medium-size Boring Jig

and keyway. The keyway is cut in the jig and is a little wider than the key in the work, and the set-screws *D* bring the key against one side of the keyway, that side being in accurate relation to the hole *B* to be bored in the tailstock. Longitudinally the work is located by a stop-pin, against which it is brought up by a set-screw from the opposite side. The tailstock is held to the jig by bolts *E* exactly as it is held on the lathe bed.

The placing of the set-screws *D* at different heights is one of the features of the jig; this makes it possible for the jig to take tailstocks of various heights for different sizes of lathes, raising blocks being used for the smaller sizes. The raising blocks are located exactly as the tailstock itself, so that the work placed on them will come in the same relative position to the uprights of the jig whether the work rests directly on the jig bottom or on the raising pieces. The two finished strips *F* are provided for facilitating the making of the jig, and the lugs *G* for the clamping down of the jig to the boring machine. The jig, however, can also be clamped to the boring machine table as shown in the illustration. At *H* is a liberal clearance between the work and jig, allowing ample room for the inserting of facing cutters, reamers, and boring tools. Ribs are provided for strengthening the jig, as shown.

Fig. 10. Large-size Boring Jig made from a Solid Casting

Fig. 10 shows a large-size boring jig made from a solid casting. In this case the work to be bored out is the head of a lathe. It is located and clamped to the jig in a way similar to that mentioned in the case of the tailstock; clamping it to the jig in the same way that it is fastened to the lathe bed insures that the effects of possible spring will be less noticeable. Opinions differ as to whether it is good practice to make up a jig of the size shown in one piece, the distance between the standards *A* and *B* being from four to five feet, or whether it would be better to make loose members located on a baseplate. With loose members there is no assurance that the standards are located correctly in relation to each other or to the work to be bored, and it involves more or less work to get the jig in order. The jig in Fig. 10 does not need to be as heavy as would be inferred from the illustration, because a large portion of the bottom can be cored out.

Four-part Boring Jig. — The boring jig illustrated in Fig. 11 consists of four parts; the upright members *A*, *B*, and *C*, and the baseplate *D*, which latter may be used for all jigs of similar construction. This type of boring jig is used only for very large work. In the case illustrated, large lathe heads are to be bored. The work is located on the baseplate between the two members *A* and *C*. The member *B* is only used when the distance be-

Fig. 11. Boring Jig consisting of Baseplate and Separate Removable
Uprights carrying the Guide Bushings

tween *A* and *C* is very long, so that an auxiliary support for the boring-bar is required, or when some obstacle prevents the bar from passing through the work from one of the outside members to the other. As a rule these members are located on the baseplate by a tongue fitting into one of the slots as shown at *E*. The members are brought as close as possible to the work, sufficient space, of course, being permitted for the cutting tools to be inserted. The standards are cored out and ribbed and lugs provided so as to give the bearing bushings long and substantial support. Good results will be obtained with this type of jigs provided they are carefully set up on the baseplate. At F in the member B is shown a boss; this is provided with a tapped hole for a hook or eye-bolt to facilitate moving the jig member by an overhead crane. The other members have tapped hole on the top for the same purpose.

Alignment of Jig when Holes are at an Angle. — In Fig. 12 is shown a boring jig for boring out the top frame A for adial drills. The design of the jig is simple, but effective; the hole

Fig. 12. Jig having Wedge-shaped Locating Piece for Boring Holes at an Angle

B is parallel with the finished side C of the jig and is bored out after the jig has been brought up square against a parallel and strapped to the machine table. The hole D is bored at an angle with the hole B, and the setting of the jig for the boring out of this hole is facilitated by providing a wedge-shaped piece E of such an angle that the jig will be set in the proper position when moved up against the wedge. If universal joints are used for connecting the boring-bar with the driving spindle, the setting of the work at an angle could be omitted, although it is preferable even when using universal joints to have the boring-bars as nearly as possible in line with the spindle. This eliminates a great deal of the eccentric stress, especially when taking a heavy cut with coarse feed.

Using Work to Guide Boring-bar. — Boring operations are sometimes carried out using parts of the machine itself as guiding means for the boring-bars, and in some instances it is very essential that boring operations be performed in this way in order to obtain perfect alignment. In Fig. 13 is shown a machine bed with the headstock solid with the bed. In the top view is shown a method for boring out a hole at *B* by the use of two jigs *C* and *D* which are located on the V's of the machine and held down by hook-bolts. If the hole *B* only passes through the part *E* of the head this would be the preferable way of

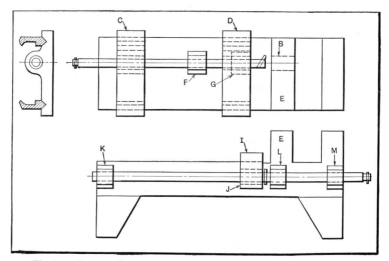

Fig. 13.   Example illustrating Use of Work as a Guide for the Boring-bar

boring it. In some instances, however, the hole *B* may be required to be in alignment with the holes in a carriage or in a bracket as at *F* and *G*. These holes, of course, can then be used to great advantage as guiding means. Should the holes be too large to fit the boring-bar, cast-iron bushings can be made to fit the holes and the bar. The front elevation in Fig. 13 shows how a cross-slide carriage and apron *I*, which has a hole *J* in line with the holes in bearings *K*, *L*, and *M*, and travels between *K* and *L*, can be bored out by using the brackets *K*, *L*. and *M* to guide the boring-bar. By keying the traveling part *I* close to the bracket during the boring operation, as illustrated, accurate results will be obtained. It is evident that two of the bearings could be bored out by using the finished bearing and the traveling part *I* as guiding means. Arrangements of this kind usually save expensive tools, and often give better results.

Fig. 14. Combined Drilling and Boring Jig used with a Horizontal Drilling and Boring Machine

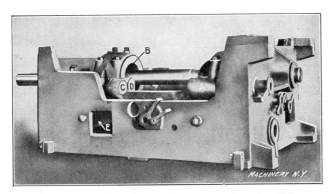

Fig. 15. Another View of the Jig in Fig. 14 — Note that Holes are drilled or bored from all Sides

Combination Drill and Boring Jig. — Jigs for performing both drilling and boring operations are frequently used to great advantage. Combination jigs are sometimes used, however, when the operations can be more easily performed in two separate jigs. For some classes of work it is advisable to have a jig for the boring alone; the bored holes are then used for locating the work in a separate drill jig. In other cases it may be better to do the drilling first and locate the work for the boring operations from the drilled holes. The designer should decide which method would be preferable, considering the time required and the accuracy of the work. It is impossible to give any definite rules for this work; but it may be said that combination jigs should be used only when the drilled and bored holes have nearly the same diameters. As a general rule, when the holes are of widely different diameters, two jigs are preferable. For example, if a few holes of small diameter for holding a collar or bracket were located around a large bored hole, and were drilled with the same jig used for the large hole, the jig, when used on a small drill press, would be entirely too heavy to manipulate. It is likely that in such a case a small separate drill jig could be attached directly to the work. In many other cases, however, it will prove a distinct saving to combine the boring and drilling jig in one.

In Figs. 14 and 15 is shown a combination drill and boring jig of large size. The work consists of a headstock for a lathe with a number of holes to be drilled. The large holes B, Fig. 15, at both ends of the headstock are cored as usual, and allow the boring bar to enter for taking the roughing cut. The holes at C and D are opened up by drills previous to the boring operation. As there is considerable distance between the end of the headstock and the uprights of the jig, long bushings are used to give the tools a good bearing close to the work. Both the drilling and boring operations may be performed on a horizontal boring and drilling machine. As the horizontal boring and drilling machines usually have adjustments in all directions, the only moving of the jig necessary is to turn it around for drilling the holes on the opposite sides.

CHAPTER IX

MILLING AND PLANING FIXTURES

Milling machines are now used for so many different purposes that the fixtures used for holding parts to be milled differ considerably in form and size, and there are several distinct types. The simplest form of milling fixture is represented by the type which simply holds and locates a single piece for a milling operation. Then there are multiple or gang fixtures for holding a row of duplicate castings or forgings. This type may be intended either for machines having a straight-line feeding movement or a circular motion, as in the case of machines designed for "continuous milling." Other milling fixtures, which often are more complicated in design than the work-holding fixtures, are arranged to hold the work in different positions either for milling surfaces which are at an angle, or for milling at various points around a circular part. The path followed by the milling cutter is also controlled by some fixtures, especially in connection with profile milling; or the fixture may be constructed to give the work a rotary feeding movement as when milling a curved slot or groove on a cylindrical part. Some idea of the variation in different types may be obtained from the designs illustrated in this chapter.

Care should be taken to design milling and other fixtures in such a way that the parts to be machined will be properly located, and so that the operator who uses the tools cannot get the work in wrong and thus spoil the parts. The fixture should be easily loaded and unloaded, and it should be as open as possible, to make cleaning easy and to prevent pockets for chips. Hardened steel seats should be ground parallel with the base after assembling, to obtain the best results. To bring the cost as low as possible, the tool parts should be standardized wherever practicable. The bodies and bases of fixtures should be made of cast iron and kept in stock in various sizes to meet the requirements of the shop whenever this is practicable. Clamping cams, dowel pins, bolts, and screws should be made up in large quantity, and steel seat blocks, straps and other steel parts should be made of standard stock sizes, if possible, to prevent unnecessary machining.

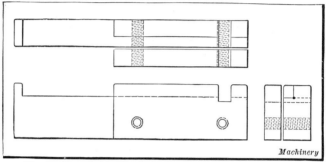

Fig. 1. Detachable Vise Jaws for Use in cutting off Bar Stock

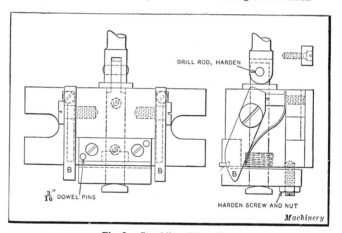

Fig. 2. Straddle-milling Fixture

Detachable Jaws for Vise. — The cheapest kind of milling fixture that can be built is a pair of detachable vise jaws, as shown in Fig. 1. These jaws are made of cold-rolled steel and casehardened. They can be removed from the vise quickly and replaced by other jaws. It is advisable, however, to use vise jaws only where great accuracy is not required, such as when cutting to length or milling clearance cuts. The jaws here shown are used for cutting off pieces from a bar of stock, which is pushed up against the stop and then cut off to the desired length.

Fixture for Milling to Given Length. — When accuracy in length is essential, a fixture like the one shown in Fig. 2 can be used to advantage. The part to be machined is cut to the approximate length in vise jaws or with a power hacksaw and then straddle-milled in the fixture. Here it is located between the two pawls B and clamped in place by the strap and cam. On the arbor shown in Fig. 3 are mounted two steel disks A about $\frac{1}{4}$ inch larger in diameter than the two side milling cutters.

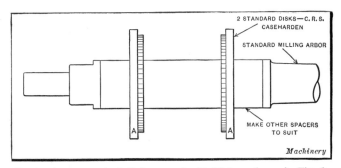

Fig. 3. Arrangement of Cutters used with Fixture shown in Fig. 2

When the fixture is fed underneath the arbor, these disks depress the pawls and give clear passage for the cutters. On the same arbor can be mounted other cutters to suit the work. This arbor should never be taken down, as it is important that the distance between the straddle-mills be kept constant; the cutters should be ground on the arbor.

Duplex Fixture. — The milling fixture shown in Fig. 4 is made for machining two parts in one operation. On the cast-iron base is mounted a double seat block and the seats are ground after assembling. The parts to be milled are clamped in place by cam binders at each end and two straps. By using set-screws in the straps, accuracy in making the cams is not necessary, and wear on the cam faces can be taken up by these adjusting screws.

Adjustable Fixture for Angular Work. — Occasionally in every line of manufacture there are parts which are simple in appearance, but difficult to machine. Fig. 5 shows a part of a belt shifter used on an automatic machine, the makers of which use eight different shaped pieces of this kind. The stock is flat and one-half inch thick. If the sides of the slots were perpendicular, the manufacture of these pieces would be very simple, but the sides are not perpendicular, and the angles they form with the bottom differ with each different shaped piece. As a result, these pieces are difficult to manufacture without the proper form of fixture.

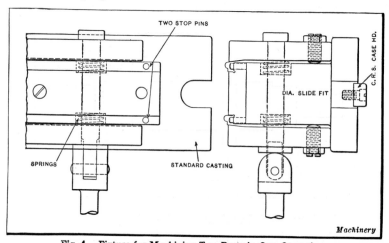

Fig. 4.   **Fixture for Machining Two Parts in One Operation**

The fixture shown in Figs. 6 to 8 consists of two parts *A* and *B*, which are clamped together, when in the proper position, by bolts passing through holes in the lower casting *A* and slots in the upper casting *B*. A tongue planed in the bottom of the base *A* fits a slot in the milling machine table, to which the base is bolted. The upper part *B* is turned to fit the lower part so that no gib is required. The parts to be milled are held in place by a set-screw, which is not shown. Each shape has its own number, and these numbers are stamped upon the top surface of the base *A*. The upper part of the fixture can move in either direction from the center, so that by placing

Fig. 5. Belt Shifter Parts held in Adjustable Fixture shown in Figs. 6 to 8, inclusive

Fig. 6. Milling Steps *D* and *E* of the Part shown in Fig. 5

the locating pin *C* in the proper hole, as shown by the number, the fixture can be quickly set for machining any shape. Fig. 6 shows the different size cutters milling projections *D* and *E*, Fig. 5; in Fig. 7, the central slot *F*, Fig. 5, is being cut. Fig. 8

14 J

Fig. 7.   Milling Central Slot in Belt Shifter Part

Fig. 8.   Position of Fixture for Cutting Angular Side of End Slot

shows how the angular slots may be finished. This type of fixture can be used for all kinds of angles, as holes can be placed where desired from zero to its full capacity.

Fixture arranged for Lateral and Angular Adjustment. — A fixture designed for milling the sides of the block shown in Fig. 9 is illustrated by the plan view, Fig. 10. Three operations are involved; the parallel sides A are milled by means of the straddle cutters and the two sides B and C are then milled in two subsequent operations. These three operations are all performed without requiring more than one setting of the work. The block is cut off from bar stock, and drilled and counterbored to receive two fillister-head screws which hold it in place on the machine of which it forms a part. These holes are also utilized for holding the block in position on the fixture.

The milling fixture consists of an upper plate A which is pivoted on the stud B. This stud is mounted in the cross-slide C which operates on the base D. The plate A is provided with two tapped steel bushings which are a forced fit in holes drilled and counterbored for the purpose. These bushings receive the two screws which

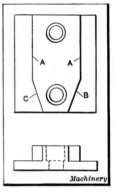

Fig. 9. Piece which is milled on Sides A, B, and C

secure the work in position on the fixture, their purpose being to prevent the rapid wear of the threads which would take place if they were tapped directly into the cast iron. The fixture is shown in the illustration set in position for milling the parallel sides A of the work. There are two tapered pins E and F which are used for locating the work in the required position. For milling the parallel sides of the work, the pin F is inserted in the hole N to locate the cross-slide C in the required position. Similarly the pin E is located in the central hole to locate the swivel plate A. These pins are merely used to locate the fixture, the bolts G and H being provided to secure it in the required position. When the fixture is set for milling the angular side C of the work, the pin E is inserted in the hole

J and pin *F* in the hole *O*. This sets the swivel plate *A* at the required angle and also locates the cross-slide *C* at the required distance off center to enable the work to be milled by the outer edge of the cutter. After this operation has been completed the swivel plate *A* is swung over to enable the pin *E* to enter the hole *K*. Similarly the cross-slide *C* is moved so that the pin *F* will enter the hole *M*. This brings the work in posi-

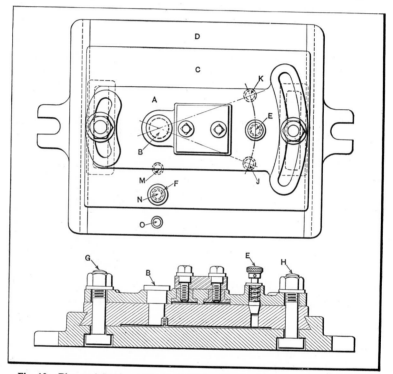

Fig. 10. Plan and Sectional Views of Milling Fixture for Piece shown in Fig. 9

tion to enable the angular side *B* to be milled by the outer edge of the other cutter on the arbor.

Lever-operated Fixture for Milling Oil-groove in Bushing. — Figs. 11 and 12 show a special milling fixture designed to hold the brass bushing *A* while milling the oil-groove *B*. The fixture with the bushing in place may be seen in Fig. 11. The detailed construction of the fixture, however, will be more clearly understood by referring to Fig. 12. The fixture consists of a base *C* which carries a slide *D*, set at an angle of about 30 degrees with the base. The V-block *E* supports the work, which is held between the angle-plates *F* and *G*. Plate *F* forms a stop for the work, while plate *G* is milled to make provision for the insertion of the wedge *H*. The hand-lever *J* is more clearly shown in Fig. 11. To operate this fixture, which may be used on any milling machine, the cutter *K* is placed in the horizontal spindle of the machine, and the fixture set up facing it. The method of holding the bushing during the machining of the groove is apparent from the illustrations, which show it seated in the V-block and held firmly between the angle-

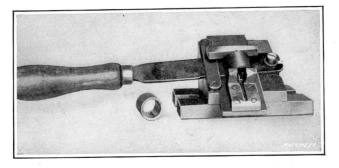

Fig. 11. Fixture for Holding Bushings when Milling Oil-groove

plates by the wedge. After the wedge has been driven into place, the cutter is fed into the work to the required depth, and slide *D* is operated by means of hand-lever *J* advancing the bushing until the proper length of groove has been milled.

This fixture could no doubt be greatly improved upon by the addition of better means of clamping the work, and could also be made to handle a wider range of work by the addition of suitable stops for controlling the length of the cut. However, for the particular work for which the fixture was designed, this was not thought necessary, as the quantity of pieces to be machined did not warrant it.

Indexing Milling Fixture for Roller Separator. — The bronze roller separators seen in Fig. 13 form part of the roller bearing of a gun mount upon which the carriage turns when training the gun or adjusting it horizontally. These separators have twenty-four holes, and opposite holes must be in alignment and in a radial position, as otherwise there will be a creeping action of the rollers relative to their bearing rings or tracks. A milling machine equipped with a simple type of indexing fixture is used for this work. The base A of the fixture is bolted to the machine table and the upper part B is free to revolve. This revolving member has accurately spaced holes which are engaged by indexing plunger C. After the holes have been

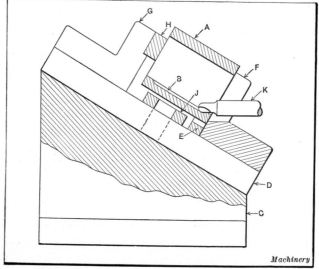

Fig. 12. Detail View of Milling Fixture shown in Fig. 11

drilled and reamed, they are counterbored by the use of suitable tools. The separator rings are located on the fixture by means of the central bore.

Indexing Fixture for Milling Clutches. — The design and construction of a special form of fixture used for cutting the clutches on transmission drive pinions and sliding gears is shown in Fig. 14. This fixture consists of a frame A into which the spindle B is fitted. The spindle is designed to serve as a collet chuck on the upper end and is arranged to carry the large index plate C at its lower end. The index plate has a series of holes E drilled in it at a convenient angle to receive the handle *D*. To turn the spindle, it is merely necessary to withdraw the spring-supported locking bolt seen at the right-hand side of the base, by means of the small lever provided for that purpose, and move the index plate around by means of the handle *D* which passes through an elongated slot.

Fig. 13. Fixture for Drilling, Reaming, and Counterboring Holes in Roller Bearing Separator Rings

The method of chucking the pinion shaft *G* is clearly shown and will need little description to make it clear to any mechanic. It will be seen that a small collar *H* rests in a hole at the bottom of the spindle; this collar receives the downward thrust of the work and also serves the purpose of locating the lower end of the work to bring it exactly perpendicular. In using this fixture it is customary to put a sheet-metal washer between the lower face of the pinion and the top surface of the chuck ring *I* in order to keep chips and oil from running down into the dividing-head.

When milling the clutch gear *J*, the split collet is replaced by the expansion chuck *K*. The body of this chuck fits into the spindle and is locked in position by the chucking ring *I*. The work is held on this chuck by expanding it by means of the taper-headed screw *L*, which is turned by a square key.

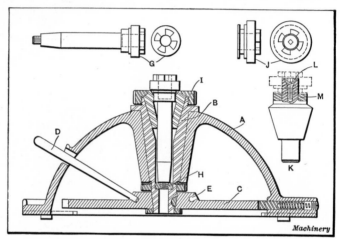

Fig. 14.   Cross-sectional View of Fixture for Milling Clutches and Details of Work-holding Arbors

The hardened steel collar *M* is fitted on the chuck to provide a good bearing surface and resist wear. The clutch gear is shown in position on the chuck by dotted lines.

Eight cuts are required to complete the milling operations on one of these clutch gears, and consequently it is necessary to use an eight-point index plate. After setting to bring the cutter to the required depth, the milling machine saddle is moved in until one edge of the cutter registers with a point 0.010 inch to the left of the center; four cuts are then made, completing one side of the clutch teeth. To mill the other side of the teeth, the milling machine saddle is moved out until the other side of the cutter registers with a point 0.010 inch to the right of the center. The head is then indexed $\frac{1}{8}$ revolution to mill the side of the first tooth, and then $\frac{1}{4}$ revolution for taking each of the three remaining cuts. The clutch teeth are cut a little off center in order to give the clutches the required amount of clearance.

The ideas embodied in the design of this special fixture may suggest other uses for a tool of this kind where it is required to perform milling, drilling, and other operations on work for which the regular milling machine dividing-head is not suitable.

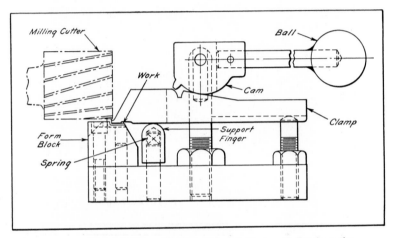

Fig. 15. Milling Fixture with Cam-Actuated Clamp. A Tooth on the Cam moves the Clamp to the Right or Left when the Handle is Raised or Lowered.

Milling Fixture with Cam-Actuated Clamping Device.—Work can be clamped with one quick stroke in the milling fixture shown in Fig. 15 by a cam-actuated clamping device. The work-piece is shown secured between the clamp and the form block, ready for the milling operation. It will be noted that the cam is provided with a handle having a ball on one end. At the completion of the cut, the handle is raised to a vertical position. This causes a tooth on the under side of the cam to enter a notch in the top of the clamp, thus moving the clamp away from the form block and permitting the part to be unloaded from the fixture.

The clamp is held in contact with the cam by a spring-loaded support finger which slides up and down on a dowel-pin. When another part has been placed on the form block, the ball is again lowered to the position shown. The tooth provides a positive engagement between cam and clamp, moving the clamp to the left over the part. The cam surfaces then force the clamp down on the part, holding it securely during the milling operation. The weight of the ball prevents the part from working loose due to chatter or vibration.

Fig. 16.   Fixture for Rough-milling a Circular Slot in Sight-bar

Radial Milling Fixtures. — Radial fixtures are so called because they are used for machining parts to a given radius. In general, the work-holding part of the fixture is either pivoted or is guided by a curved track so that it is given a circular motion when in use. Some ingenious radial fixtures used for machining the sight-bars of naval gun mounts, at the plant of the Mead-Morrison Mfg. Co., East Boston, Mass., will be described. The radial or circular surface of the sight-bar must be so nearly perfect that the sight may be operated through its complete range of adjustments without any binding action and without perceptible lost motion between the moving parts. The curved surfaces of the sight-bar and of the bearing in the sight-bar bracket must be exactly concentric with the axis of the pivot about which the sight moves in elevation. These and other exacting requirements make this a very interesting, although difficult, part to produce on an interchangeable basis, and it was necessary to design special radius milling fixtures.

Radial Fixture for Rough-milling Slot. — The slot which is milled in one side of the sight-bar is rough-milled as illustrated

Fig. 17. Fixture for Milling Curved Slot in Sight-bar Bracket

in Fig. 16. This is the type of fixture which has a curved track that causes the work-holding member to follow a circular path as the work feeds past the cutter. The sight-bar A is held on a movable part which has a slot B in the rear side of the same radius as the slot to be milled. A block C, which is free to swivel and is pivoted to a stationary part of the machine, engages slot B. The cross-feed screw in the knee is removed, and as the table is fed in a lengthwise direction, a slot is milled to the same radius as the slot B in the fixture. A weight is attached to the saddle of the machine by means of a wire cable which is connected at D. The object of using a weight is to hold block C in contact with the slot on one side, and thus by eliminating all play it is possible to secure a higher degree of accuracy. A two-lipped end-mill is used for this operation. The slot is milled 0.8 inch wide and $1\frac{5}{8}$ inch deep.

Another radial fixture of the general type just described is

Fig. 18. Radial Milling Fixture used for Different Operations on Sight-bar

shown in Fig. 17. This fixture is for the bronze bracket through which the sight-bar slides when being elevated or lowered. It has a curved slot which must be milled to the same radius as the sight-bar to avoid any cramping or binding action. A finished surface on the bracket A is clamped against a top plate or bridge B of the fixture, and it is further located by a plug C at the right. The base of the fixture fits between curved tracks or guiding strips D. At one end of the fixture a transverse slot is formed, and this is engaged by a block pivoted to a nut through which the feed-screw passes. The feed-screw is connected by gearing E with the regular feed-rod of the machine, and as the movable section of the fixture is fed along, a slot is milled to the same radius as the tracks.

Pivoted Type of Radial Fixture. — The curved sides of the sight-bar and also the beveled surfaces along one edge are milled by means of a radial fixture of the type shown in Fig. 18. This general style of fixture is used extensively in connection with other operations on the sighting mechanism. It has a very heavy base casting A, which is bolted to the table of the machine. The sight-bar B is held on the swinging part C of the fixture, which is pivoted at D. At the work-holding end of the swinging member there is a swiveling nut through which passes a feed-screw. This feed-screw is connected by gearing located at the end of the table with the regular feed-screw of the machine, the nut in the milling machine having been removed; consequently, when a sight-bar is being milled, the part C of the fixture is given a circular movement about the pivot D as the power feed traverses it from one end of its swing to the other. The illustration shows the machine milling the beveled edges on the top of the sight-bar. When the sides are being milled, the cutter shown at E is used. After one side has been milled, the stops F are transferred to the opposite side so that they will not interfere with the cutter. The gage used for testing the radius of the inner surface forms part of the fixture, and consists of a bar G which is free to slide through a block H. This block is also free to turn about the same pivot which is used for the swinging part of the fixture. The radius of the sight-bar is tested by bringing the gage point into contact with it and then noting the position of the end of bar G relative to the outer surface of block H. When the end of the bar and the surface of the block are exactly in the same plane, as indicated by tests made with a dial gage, the work is correct.

The sight-bar is located in the fixture by the finished face of the head, which also serves as a common locating point for many other operations. There is considerable overhang of the fixture relative to the machine table, and in order to avoid sag, the overhanging part is counterbalanced by a heavy weight attached to one end of the wire cable J which passes over pulleys fastened to the ceiling.

Fig. 19.   Radial Indexing Fixture for Cutting Gear Teeth in Sight-bar

Radial Fixture for Gear-cutting Operation. — The sight-bar
and the other parts of the sight mechanism which are attached
to it are elevated or lowered through a pinion which engages
teeth cut on one side of the sight-bar. These teeth must be
very accurately spaced; in fact, the total tolerance or allowable error in the fifty-five teeth of the sight-bar is only 0.0005
inch. The fixture used for milling these gear teeth is illustrated
in Fig. 19. The gear teeth on the sight-bar do not form a rack,
but rather the segment of a gear, since the pitch line is an arc;
therefore, the radial type of fixture is employed. The base A
is bolted to the machine table, and the swinging part B is
pivoted at the rear end. Beneath this swinging part there is
a segment of a worm-wheel, and meshing with it a worm carried by the shaft of the indexing mechanism. The indexing
crank C connects with this worm-shaft through spur gearing.
The sight-bar is clamped to an adapter plate, which is replaced by
another adapter when the same fixture is used for milling operations on the yoke. The sight-bar is located in part by the finished
surface of the head, as is the case in the other operations.

As it would be difficult, if not impossible, to construct a
large fixture of this kind and eliminate all measurable error,
the original inaccuracy is eliminated as far as possible in order
to reduce the error in spacing the teeth to a minimum. The
method of compensating for this original error is as follows:
When indexing the fixture a distance equivalent to one tooth
space, crank C is turned one revolution or until its spring-pin
again comes around into mesh with the hole in the disk shown.
Since there are 55 teeth in the sight-bar, and as the total original
error was a few thousandths inch large, this error is compensated for by turning the indexing disk D backward an amount
equivalent to $\frac{1}{55}$ of the original error. There are really two
indexing movements, therefore, for each tooth space, the same
as in compound indexing. A gear tooth caliper of the vernier
type is used for testing the tooth thickness; the spacing is
verified by placing pins between the gear teeth at each end of
the segment, and also at intermediate points, and then measuring the distance between the pins by using a vernier caliper.
The counterbalancing weights are also used in conjunction

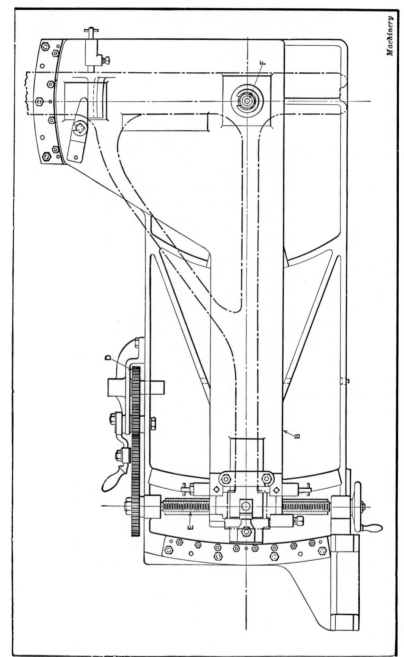

Machinery

Fig. 20. Plan View of Radial Milling Fixture provided with Hand- and Power-operated Feeding Movement — Shape of Work is indicated by Dash-and-dotted Lines

with this fixture, the attached cables E and F passing over pulleys above. These weights not only counterbalance the overhanging parts of the heavy fixture, but also make it easier to elevate the knee for feeding the cutter down past the work.

Radial Fixture having Hand- and Power-operated Feed. — The yoke of the sight mechanism is a cast-steel member which carries the telescopes at its forward end and is attached at the

Fig. 21. Fixture for Milling Curved Openings in Bronze Recoil Liners

rear to the sight-bar. There are some radial milling operations on the rear end of the yoke. The curved surfaces at the end of the yoke are milled to the required radius by a type of fixture which, in many respects, is similar to the radial designs already referred to in connection with the sight-bar. The base of the fixture (see Fig. 20) is bolted to the table of a column-and-knee type of milling machine, and the upper part B is free to swing about a pivot located at the required radial distance. One radial milling operation is that of form-milling the worm-gear segment in which worm teeth are cut later to mesh with a worm which enables the yoke to be adjusted horizontally. Several

15 J

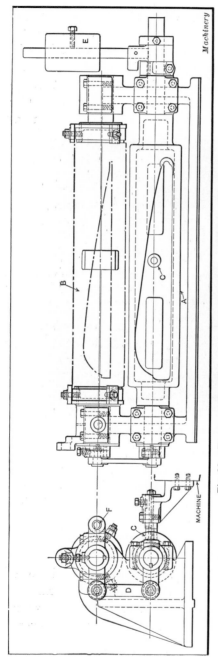

Fig. 22. Front and End Elevations of Milling Fixture for Recoil Liners

other curved surfaces are also milled with the same fixture. The swinging member of the fixture is provided with both a hand-operated and an automatic feeding movement. The latter is derived from the regular feed mechanism of the machine. The universally jointed shaft, originally designed to transmit feeding movements to the work-table, was disconnected and arranged to drive the feed-screw of the

fixture through a train of spur gearing. The universally jointed shaft drives gear D which, through the other spur gears shown, revolves a feed-screw E. This feed-screw passes through a swiveling nut connected with the swinging part B of the fixture which is pivoted at F. The yoke is indicated by the heavy dot-and-dash lines.

Profile Milling Fixture for Recoil Cylinder Liner. — An unusual type of milling fixture, and one which proved very effective for a contour milling operation on the bronze liners of recoil cylinders, is illustrated in Figs. 21 and 22. The former illustration shows the fixture set up on a milling machine. This fixture has a master sleeve or former A in which there is an opening corresponding to the one to be milled in the recoil cylinder sleeve B. A roller C, mounted upon a bracket secured to the front of the machine, engages the opening in the former. The

Fig. 23. Fixture for Routing Oil-grooves on Two Bushings at One Time

master former and the recoil liner are caused to turn in unison by a link D which, as clearly shown by the end view, Fig. 22, is connected to the ends of extension arms on the former and work-holding shafts. When milling the lower edge of the opening, which is the operation shown in Fig. 21, the weight E is swung over to the right, so that it tends to hold the former firmly in contact with roller C. When the machine table is fed in a lengthwise direction for milling this edge, the master former and liner do not have any turning movement, since the lower edge of the opening is straight. For milling the upper or curved side, weight E is swung over to the left, and then the curved part of the opening in the master former is held securely against the roller; therefore, when the milling machine table is fed in a lengthwise direction, the former and liner turn in unison as the curved section of the opening is milled. Two lugs on the hub of the weight lever alternately engage a stop as the lever is turned from one position to the other, and in this way either the lower or upper sides in the master former are held against the roller C. The liner has a similar opening on the opposite side, which is milled by simply connecting the upper end of link D with the opposite end F of the double extension arm (see end view, Fig. 22).

Duplex Fixture for Routing Oil-grooves. — A duplex type of fixture used for routing oil-grooves in bronze bushings is shown in Fig. 23. The routing operation is performed on two bushings simultaneously, and a drilling machine is used for the operation. The oil-grooves of the bushings, in this particular case, extend around about two-thirds of the circumference of the bushing and branch out into a Y-shape at each end. The horizontal spindle of the fixture is rotated for feeding the bushing past the routing tools, by handwheel A, which serves to revolve a worm meshing with wheel B. The axial movement of the fixture spindle is derived from cam grooves on each side of gear B. The shafts C and D carrying the rollers have rack teeth which engage the segment gears formed on the pivoted lever E. By swinging this lever in one direction or the other, the rollers are alternately engaged. When the left-hand roller is engaged with its cam groove, the left-hand branches of the Y-shaped oil-grooves on each bushing are milled, and when the right-hand roller is moved inward the right-hand branches of the oil-grooves are milled.

Planing Fixtures. — Fixtures for planing are as essential for interchangeable manufacturing as are drilling jigs or milling fixtures. Planing fixtures serve primarily the purpose of locating and holding the work, but they are often provided with setting pieces or templets which are used for setting the cutting tools so that the work is always machined in a certain relation to the locating means on the fixture itself. Some milling fixtures also have this tool-setting feature.

The strength of fixtures should be governed by the kind of

operation to be carried out on the work while in the fixture, whether planing, milling, slotting, etc., and how much stock is to be removed. A milling fixture, as a rule, must be made stronger than a planing fixture, because a milling cutter ordinarily takes a heavier cut than a planing tool. Many of the features often found on milling fixtures may be applied to planer fixtures with whatever change may be necessary on account of the particular operation required. As a rule, milling and planing fixtures are provided with a tongue or key in the base, for locating them on the machine table. Suitable lugs should also be provided for clamping the fixture to the platen.

The most commonly used fixture for planing, shaping, and milling is the vise. Standard vises are indispensable in planer or milling machine work or on the shaper, and by slight changes they can be used for a large variety of smaller pieces. The regular vise jaws are often replaced by false jaws, which may be fitted with locating pins and seats, and held to the vise the same as the regular jaws. Vises with false vise jaws are especially adapted for milling operations, but vises are not usually employed for long work, special fixtures being commonly used.

Planing Fixtures for Lathe Carriage Casting. — Assume that a set of planing fixtures for the piece shown in Fig. 24 is required. The work is a slide or carriage for a lathe. The finishing marks given on a number of the surfaces indicate where the work is to be finished. In the first place, it must be considered from which sides to locate, and *how* to locate and hold the work without springing it, and in what order the operations should be performed to best advantage. Fig. 25 shows a fixture for roughing out the ways on the bottom. The slide is located on three fixed locating points *A* and the sliding point *B*. This latter is adjustable in order to enable planing the slide as nearly as possible to uniform thickness. Sometimes, if the parts *A*, Fig. 24, bevel toward the ends, lugs *G* may be added; these can then be finished and used for locating purposes. The carriage, as shown in Fig. 25, is further located against the pins *C* in order to insure that the cross-slide of the carriage will be square with the bottom ways. The slide is brought up sidewise against the pin *D*, and then clamped down in convenient

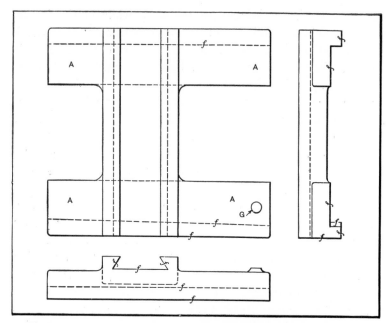

Fig. 24. Lathe Carriage Casting — An Example of Work illustrating Points in Planer Fixture Design

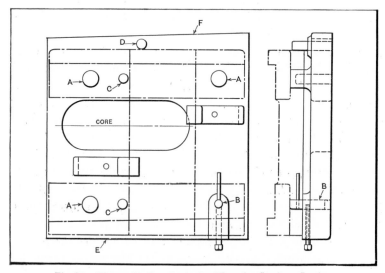

Fig. 25. Fixture for Rough-planing Ways for Carriage Casting

places, the clamps being placed as near the bearing points as possible to avoid springing. The reason for not having the locating point D on the opposite side is that this side must be finished at the same setting, as it is the front side of the carriage and is finished for receiving an apron.

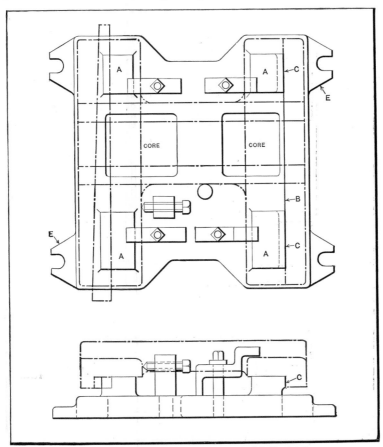

Fig. 26. Fixture for Planing Cross-slide Dovetail

The sides E and F of the fixture may be finished in a certain relation to the locating points and to each other, and side E may be made perfectly square with the locating points, so that, when brought up against a parallel on the machine table, the ways of the machined piece will be square with the ends. Side F may be finished on the same taper as required for a taper gib.

The fixture for the next operation is shown in Fig. 26. This fixture is made to receive the carriage and locate it by the now rough-finished ways; in this fixture, the cross-slide dovetail is planed. The slide rests on four finished pads A, and the straight side B of the ways in the slide brought up against the finished

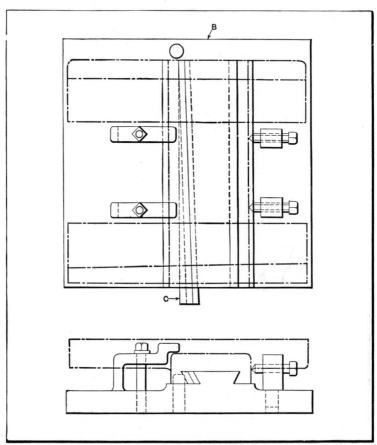

Fig. 27.   Fixture for Finish-planing Bottom Ways

surfaces C. If no other part is available for clamping the fixture on the machine table, lugs E are added. If there are no tapering surfaces, the fixture can be located on the machine table by a tongue or by placing a finished side against a parallel. The slide or dovetail is now roughed out and it is usually suffi‑ ciently accurate practice to finish it in the same setting, es pecially as slides must always be scraped and fitted to suit the machine on which they are to be used.

The next operation would be performed in the fixture illustrated in Fig. 27. The carriage is here located by the dovetail and by the pin B, and held by a gib C, or by straps and screws, as shown. It will be noticed that, with the given design, the straps and screws must be removed each time a new piece is inserted, which is an undesirable feature of the fixture. If parts A in Fig. 24 project out too far, so that a light finishing cut would cause springing, they are supported by sliding points or other adjustable locating means.

If the dovetail in the slide had simply been rough-finished in the fixture in Fig. 26, the finishing of the bottom ways could have been done in the fixture in Fig. 27, and then, after having finished the bottom ways in this fixture, the work could again have been located in the fixture in Fig. 26, and the dovetail finished; this might insure more accurate work in some cases.

In the case just described, the work requires three different fixtures to be completed. The number of fixtures to use in each case is entirely dependent upon the nature of the work. When there is a large amount of work of the same kind to be done, several fixtures of the same type are made up for the same piece, and when in use these fixtures are placed in a row on the table of the machine.

Gang-planing Fixtures. — It is very common in planer practice to locate a number of duplicate castings or forgings in a row extending lengthwise of the table and then plane them all at the same time. Gang planing is often done without a special fixture, by simply clamping the work directly upon the table, but fixtures make it possible to set up work more rapidly and accurately. Besides many pieces are of such a shape that a fixture is necessary in order to hold them in the correct position for planing. An example of work requiring a fixture is shown in Fig. 28. Twenty-three forgings are planed at one time and four cutting tools are used, two being held in the side heads while two are attached to the heads of the cross-rail. The forgings are located at right angles to the length of the planer table

Fig. 28.   Large Fixture for Holding Twenty-three Duplicate Forgings which are machined by Gang Planing

by the milled sides, one side of each bar being held against a
vertical surface on the fixture, as shown in the illustration.

Radial Planing Fixture. — A planer equipped with a special
radial fixture is shown in Fig. 29. An arm A is rigidly attached
to one of the planer housings and carries a shaft B which forms
the pivot for the swinging part C of the fixture. This swinging

Fig. 29.   An Example of a Radial Type of Planing Fixture

member has a slot on the rear side which is engaged by a pivoted
block which moves to and fro with the planer table; consequently, the sight-bar, which is held to the swinging member
in an upright position, follows a circular path and is planed to
a circular form, the radius of any surface being governed by the
horizontal distance from the cutting edge of the tool to the axis
of pivot B. This fixture is similar in principle to some of the
forms used in locomotive shops for planing the links of the valve-
operating mechanism.

CHAPTER X

ADJUSTABLE FIXTURES FOR TURRET LATHES AND VERTICAL BORING MILLS

When pieces of the same type, but of various sizes, are to be machined on the turret lathe or vertical boring mill, it is sometimes desirable to design the tools and fixtures in such a way that they can be adapted to handle the different pieces, thus avoiding the necessity of providing a separate tool or fixture for each piece. Naturally, when the production is large, such a procedure as this would be unprofitable, because the tools could only be used on one piece at a time, and a lot of pieces of one size might be held up for a considerable time waiting for a lot of another size to be machined. When, however, the work comes along in lots of from 100 to 200 pieces, a great saving in tool cost can be effected by the use of adjustable tools and fixtures, providing the design of the parts is such that it will permit of following this practice. Much depends upon the shape of the work to be held and its machining requirements.

There are instances when the desired results may be obtained by simple means, and there are other cases which require the application of considerable ingenuity in order to avoid complications in the design. Properly designed and carefully built tools and fixtures of the adjustable type are profitable investments on certain classes of work, and their advisability should be carefully considered when several pieces of the same general type are to be handled. The greatest forethought is necessary in designing fixtures of this kind, in order to make sure that every point for every piece has received proper consideration. There is probably no other type of fixture which requires so much care in its design, and for that reason the important points given herewith should be most carefully noted.

Important Points in Design. — 1. The number of pieces to be machined should be the first point considered, as this naturally has an effect on the design of the tools and fixtures.

2. The largest and smallest pieces in the group should be selected, and the machine on which the work is to be done should be determined according to the sizes of these pieces. If the variation in size is considerable, it may be economical to do a part of the work on one machine and the remainder on another, in which case the fixture should be so made that it can be adapted for use on both machines. There may even be cases when the range of sizes is so great that two or more fixtures may be necessary, one of which can be used on one machine and the other on a different one; or they can be made interchangeable, providing the speeds on both machines give range enough to handle the work. These points should be carefully considered.

3. The accuracy required in the finished work should be noted and care taken to provide means of upkeep on surfaces or locating points that are subject to wear. There may be occasional instances, on work requiring extreme accuracy, when it may be necessary to provide means of adjustment for truing up the fixture so that it will always run perfectly concentric with the spindle of the machine.

4. Rigidity in work-holding devices and tools should receive careful attention; and overhang from the spindle, turret, or cut-off slide should be kept down to a minimum, so that chatter will not result from lack of support. These points need more consideration when the tools and fixtures are to be used on the horizontal type of machine, than when a vertical machine is to be employed.

5. Clamping devices for adjustable fixtures should be laid out (by means of a piece of tracing paper) for each piece to be handled, so that there will be no chance of clamps being too long, too short, or improperly proportioned for some of the work. Errors are very likely to occur in this part of the design unless the greatest care is used; and there are also cases when the work varies in thickness as well as in diameter; therefore, this point must be carefully considered.

6. Provision for cleaning the fixture must be made, so that all locating points and surfaces will be readily accessible. If

several sizes of studs or locating rings are to be used, they must be so arranged that chips and dirt will not interfere with the proper location of the work. They must also be placed so that they can be easily replaced or removed.

7. The adjustments which are necessary to provide for handling various sizes of work should be carefully studied, and suitable provision should be made so that the changes from one setting to another will always be uniform, and variations in the work cannot occur due to errors in adjustment. If necessary, setting gages can be made for the various pieces to be handled, or a separate set of screws or other adjustable locating members can be made for each piece and properly stamped to avoid mistakes. The nature of the work has a great deal to do with the method used to secure uniform adjustments, and specific cases will be noted in following paragraphs.

8. Convenience and rapidity of operation should be given consideration, and provision should be made for setting up the work in as short a time as possible. The fixture should be so arranged that the work can only be set up in the correct way, and it should be as nearly "fool-proof" as possible.

9. The cost of the fixture should be kept down to the lowest figure that is consistent with good design, because the number of pieces to be machined is comparatively small. If the work for which the fixture is made is of such a nature that it is not likely to be changed, a little more latitude is permissible; but as changes in design are always possible, it is advisable not to make an elaborate fixture.

10. The safety of the operator should always be considered, and projecting lugs, set-screws, or other parts which might catch in his clothing should be eliminated from the design. Other points in design not mentioned in the foregoing will be specifically mentioned throughout this chapter; comments will be made, and faulty points criticized and discussed.

The three- or four-jawed chuck is perhaps the most frequently used of all the holding devices which are adjustable to take various sizes of work. There are also collets of numerous kinds, which are adjustable within certain limits, and step chucks for work of a little larger size. For handling work in the rough state, the three- or four-jawed chuck is adaptable to a great range of sizes, without any changes in the chuck

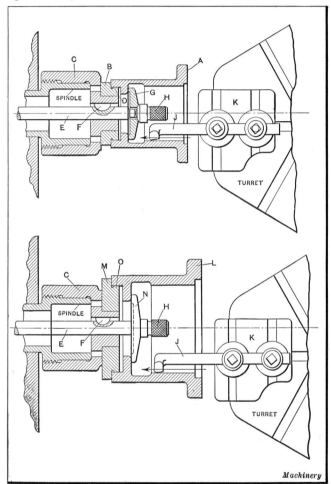

Fig. 1. Fixture for Holding Pot Castings on Horizontal Turret Lathe; Different Clamping Collars are provided for Different Sizes of Work

jaws; but collets and step chucks require a change in jaws, or a re-setting if much variation is found in the diameters of different pieces of work. The step chuck is more frequently used for partly finished work, while collets are used for both rough and finished pieces — principally for bar work or something of a similar character. When a round piece of work is to be made up in several sizes and is ot simple form, it may often be handled to good advantage in a set of soft jaws applied to a three-jawed universal chuck. These jaws are bored out on the machine to the exact diameter of the finished work, and when set up on the piece they present a good holding surface with sufficient accuracy for the ordinary run of commercial work.

Adjustable Fixture for Holding Castings of Different Diameters. — Fig. 1 shows at A and L the smallest and largest sizes of castings to be machined on a horizontal turret lathe; and there were two intermediate sizes which were also handled on the same fixtures. A special nose-piece C is screwed to the end of the spindle and has a hub at its forward end on which the locating ring B (upper view) is fixed. The finished portion of the work fits this ring at D and is drawn back against it by the collar G; the rod E passes through the spindle and is pulled back by means of a handwheel at the end, while the key F prevents it from turning. The forward end of the rod is threaded to receive the knurled finger-nut H which has a spherical bearing in the collar G to equalize the pressure. In setting up the work, the piece is placed on the locating ring, the collar G is slipped over the end of the rod E and the knurled nut H is rapidly screwed on with the fingers, after which the handwheel at the end of the spindle is used to tighten the collar. A long boring tool J is used to rough out the shouldered portion of the work and to bore the bearing, and it will be noted that although this tool has considerable overhang it is well set up in the tool-holder K, and given additional strength by the use of two toolposts.

The larger piece L, shown in the lower part of the illustration, is set up on the ring M locating on the surface O, which has been previously bored. A larger collar N is used for clamping this piece. With the exception of the locating ring and collar, all of the other parts of the holding device are the same as in the preceding instance. Additional rings and collars for the intermediate sizes make the fixture complete. It will be noted that there are two holes in the front of the nose-piece, which are so placed that a rod may be used to drive off the locating rings when changing over the fixture for another size of work. This fixture is simple and comparatively inexpensive,

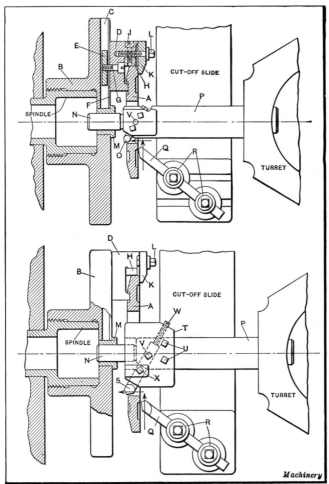

Fig. 2. Fixture for Holding Bevel-gear Blanks of Various Sizes

yet it is adapted for use on four pieces of work of different sizes and the changes required are of such a nature that they may be performed quickly so that there is very little loss of time. It may futher be noted that the boring tool is the same in

16 J

each case and that the adjustment for different diameters is obtained by the cross sliding movement of the turret.

Adjustable Fixture for Special Bevel-gear Blanks. — The work A shown in Fig. 2 is a special bevel-gear blank, and these gears are used in a great number of sizes on textile machinery. The pieces were held in the first setting by the interior and were machined on the side having the beveled surface and on the periphery; they were also partially under-cut along the edge of the rim in order to provide a clamping surface during the second setting. Extreme accuracy was required in the work, and yet there were so many sizes to be handled that the construction of separate fixtures was deemed inadvisable. A special faceplate B was, therefore, designed having three radial dovetail slots C (upper view) in its face; and a small portion F of each of these slots was left straight to assist in locating the movable jaws D. These jaws were made of steel and were radially adjustable to various diameters, being clamped in any desired position by means of the screws G and the dovetail shoes E. A number of sets of soft steel supplementary jaws H were drawn back into a seat on the main jaws by the two screws J and were bored in place to the diameter of the outside of the gear, the main jaws being set in place to an approximation of the correct diameter in each instance.

The clamps K were drawn down upon the finished portion of the work by means of the screws L in the jaws. A bushing M was set in the center of the faceplate and used as a guide for the pilot N of the boring-bar P which was held in the turret. The tool O was used to bore the hole while the tool Q faced the unfinished portion of the gear blank, the latter tool being held in two toolposts R on the cut-off slide. In handling some of the larger gear blanks, a supplementary head T (lower view) was placed on the end of the boring-bar and held in place by the screws U on the flatted portion of the bar. This head gave good support to the tool S which was used for boring the larger sizes of gear blanks. This tool was held in place by the screws X and V, the latter passing through the hole provided for it in the bar. Fine adjustments were provided for in the backing-up screw W and the facing of the blank was accomplished by the same tool. This fixture took care of seven gear blanks of various sizes and gave very satisfactory results.

Adjustable Fixture with Means of Maintaining Accuracy. — A fixture which is somewhat out of the ordinary and which may be adjusted to handle several sizes of work A is shown in Fig. 3. As absolute concentricity is required in the finished surfaces of the work machined in this fixture, it is essential for the fixture to be arranged in such a way that it can be trued up if it becomes inaccurate through misuse or neglect. The

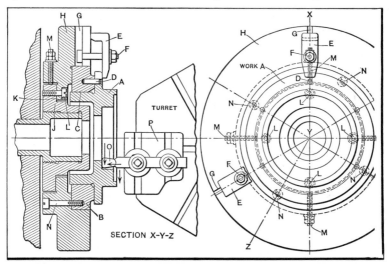

Fig. 3. Fixture in which Provision is made to Compensate for Inaccuracy resulting from Misuse or Neglect

cast-iron nose-piece J is screwed to the spindle in the usual manner and the supplementary casting H is bolted to it with the four bolts L. The holes in this piece are slightly larger than the bolts so that small adjustments may be made. The flanged portion of the supplementary casting carries four headless set-screws at M, by means of which the ring can be trued up, and check-nuts are provided to secure a permanent setting of the fixture. The locating rings C are made in several sizes to take the various pieces that are machined in this fixture, and each of these rings is furnished with a driving pin D which enters one of the bolt holes in the work.

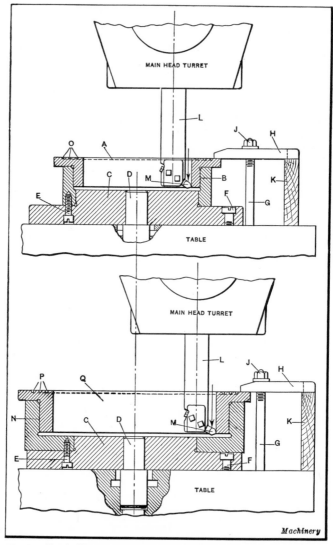

Fig. 4. Simple Fixture for Holding Three Sizes of Steel Flanges, while
boring, facing, and cutting Packing Grooves

The screws N are set into the ring from the rear and are
located in different places for the various rings. The fixture
has three T-slots G in order that the clamps E may be conveniently adjustable by means of the T-bolts F which enter

these slots. The boring and shoulder work performed on the piece is accomplished by the shovel-nosed tool O which is mounted in the tool-holder P on the turret. This is an example of a fixture designed for standard work of various sizes coming through in small lots, and which requires extreme accuracy in machining. The fixture is a compact design and it is built close in to the spindle so that, although the fixture itself is heavy, there is so little overhang that the weight is of small importance.

Adjustable Fixtures for the Vertical Boring Mill. — The table of a vertical boring mill is so arranged that it may be used either as a faceplate or as a chuck with provision for clamping in the T-slots when necessary. This is a distinct advantage in many kinds of work and especially so where a number of pieces of similar construction and different sizes are to be handled. Fig. 4 shows a simple fixture for handling three sizes of steel flanges A. The base C of the fixture is made of cast iron and is centered by a plug D in the table hole; and it is fastened down to the table by means of the screws F which enter shoes in the T-slots. In the upper illustration, the work A has been previously turned, faced and partially under-cut to provide for clamping, and it is held during the first setting by means of jaws on the inside of the flange.

On the second setting (shown in the upper illustration) the operations performed consist of boring the hole, facing the flange as far as the clamps, and cutting the packing grooves O. The locating ring B is slipped on the finished portion of the base and is drawn down by the screws E. The clamps H are supported at the outer end by the wooden blocks K, and are drawn down upon the work by nuts and washers J through the medium of the T-bolts G which are adjustable radially in the table slots. The boring-bar L is used for boring the interior of the flange with the tool M, while the side head (not shown) faces the flange and cuts the packing groove. The lower illustration shows the fixture adapted for holding the largest piece Q which it handles. In this case, the ring N is made of somewhat different shape so that it will locate properly on the

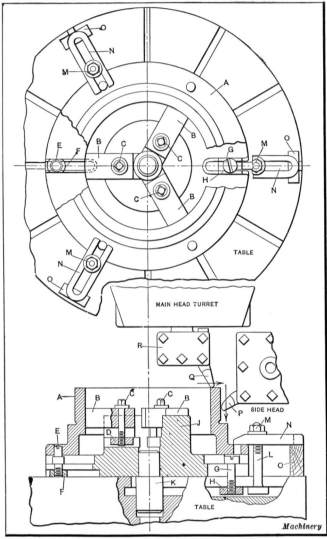

Fig. 5. Method of holding Three Sizes of Work which has been bored and faced and has had the Holes drilled in Flange

finished portion of the base C. All other portions of the fixture are the same as in the preceding instance, the clamps H being moved outward in the T-slots a sufficient amount to take care of the work of larger diameter. The tools for boring, facing, and cutting the packing grooves P are also the same.

Fixture with Adjustable Driver and Soft Internal Jaws. — The work A shown in Fig. 5 is made in three sizes, the largest of which is illustrated. These pieces have been previously bored and faced, and the flange holes have been drilled in a jig. The base J of the fixture is made of cast iron and is centered on the table by means of the plug K. It is held down by three screws G which enter shoes H in the table T-slots, and it should be noticed that the slots in the fixture permit the T-slots L to be moved inward to take care of work of smaller diameters. It is obvious that the screws G must either be moved inward when this is done, or else they can be placed at the extreme inner position and kept there at all times. The driving pin E is also arranged in a T-slot cut in the fixture, so that it can be moved radially to a position corresponding with the bolt holes; and the shoe F makes it secure in whatever position it may be placed.

Instead of using a locating ring, three soft jaws B are set in slots in the fixture base, and these may be clamped in place by means of the screws C which draw up on the shoes D in the T-slots. After clamping them in an approximately correct position, they are turned to the size of the interior of the casting. Attention is called to the fact that the outside portion of the hub in the base casting J is finished in order to facilitate calipering when turning the jaws. The clamps N are supported at their outer end by wooden blocks O and are drawn down on the flanged portion of the work by the nuts M. Radial adjustment of the clamps is obtained in the manner previously mentioned. The tools Q and P in the tool-holder R and the side head, respectively, are used for facing and turning the outside diameter of the work. Adjustments for diameters are obviously obtained by setting the machine slide. This fixture may be made up at little cost, is easily adjustable and will take care of a great range of sizes. In addition to this, the accuracy obtained by its use leaves nothing to be desired.

Adjustable Fixture for a Cast-iron Bracket. — The work A shown in Fig. 6 is a cast-iron bracket which has previously been machined along the face D and has had the tongued por-

tion cut approximately central with the cored hole at Y.   Four
holes have also been jig-drilled at J.   Two sizes of these brackets
were made several times each year in lots of ten or twelve, so
that the expense of a complete fixture for machining each piece

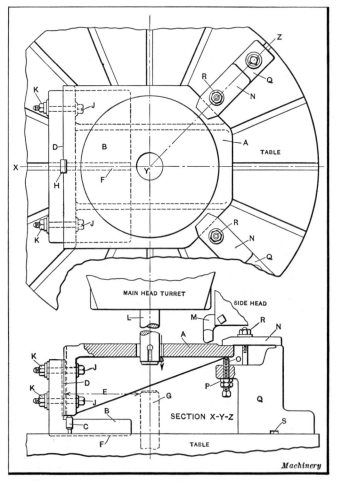

Fig. 6.   Inexpensive Fixture for Holding Two Sizes of Brackets

would have been excessive in view of the number of pieces
produced.   The following equipment proved satisfactory: An
angle-plate B is tongued on the under side F to fit one of the
table T-slots and is held down by screws (not shown).   The

distance E for the two sizes of brackets is easily determined by placing a stud G in the center hole of the table and locating the angle-plate B from it. The bracket is placed in position on the angle-plate so that the tongue H fits into the groove,

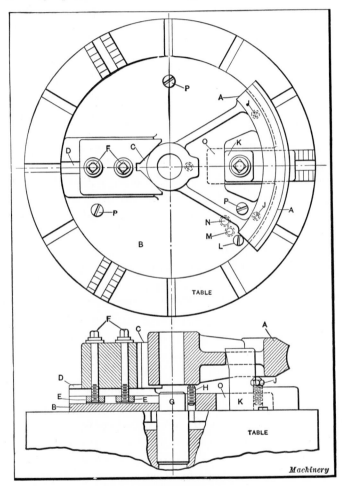

Fig. 7. Adjustable Fixture for Holding Three Sizes of Bronze Worm-gear Sectors

and the bolts J are passed through the holes in the bracket and tightened by the nuts at K.

A little freedom is allowed in the bolt holes and the finished edge of the bracket rests on the pins C. Two special jaws Q are fixed in position on the table but may be adjusted radially when necessary to bring them into the correct position for the other size of bracket. The jaws are provided with set-screws O which are adjusted to support the overhanging end of the bracket, after which they are locked by the check-nuts at P. The jaws are keyed at S to the sub-jaws of the table; and the clamps N are used on the unfinished portion of the bracket, being tightened by the nuts at R so that the surface to be machined is clear of interferences. The boring-bar L is used to bore the hole and the side-head tool M faces the pad. This is another example of a table being used with a faceplate having adjustable moving parts on it.

Adjustable Fixture for a Bronze Worm-gear Sector. — The fixture shown in Fig. 7 was designed to handle three sizes of the bronze worm-gear sectors A. The base B of the fixture is centered on the table by means of the stud G in the center hole, and it is clamped securely by means of three screws P which enter shoes in the table T-slots. An adjustable V-block C is mounted on a finished pad and tongued on the under side to fit the slot D. All the jaws on the table chuck are removed and a special jaw K is substituted for one of them. This jaw is slightly under-cut on its face to assist in holding down the work, and at the same time it forces the hub of the casting up into the vee locating block. A slot O is cut in the base of the fixture in order to allow the necessary movement for this jaw. The hub rests on a headless set-screw H which is tapped into the base, and two other adjusting screws are provided at J. These are adjusted by means of a wrench after the jaw has been tightened. The set-screw H, however, remains set after it has been adjusted to suit the particular piece which is being machined. A driving screw at L takes the thrust of the cut and may be removed and placed in either of the holes M or N when used for the other pieces. In setting the V-block for another diameter of hub, it is only necessary to loosen the screws F and move the block radially to the desired position. The jaw K is readily set to size while the screws J and L are placed in holes provided for them.

CHAPTER XI

THE FLOATING PRINCIPLE AS APPLIED TO FIXTURE WORK

There are many instances in the design and construction of fixtures for machine tool equipment work that require application of the floating principle in order to make them thoroughly efficient. When thin castings are to be handled, the application frequently takes the form of a system of floating clamps, which are arranged in such a way that pressure sufficient to hold the work can be applied without danger of distorting it. It may also be necessary to have the locating points so designed that they too will float to a certain extent so as to adapt themselves to varying conditions. The latter application may be necessary when rough castings are to be machined, so that inequalities in the work will not affect the location in the jig or fixture. Abnormal or extraordinary conditions sometimes require the application of the floating principle to the location of work which has two or more finished surfaces in different planes.

The nature of the castings for which the fixtures are designed has a strong influence on their construction, and the type of machine tools on which they are to be used is also a prominent factor in the design. The accuracy required in the finished product, and the number of pieces to be machined, must also be considered in connection with the design.

Fixtures of this kind may be adapted for work on various kinds of machine tools, such as drill presses, milling machines, lathes (turret and engine types), boring mills, or grinding machines. All of these require fixtures of somewhat different construction, according to the machines on which they are to be used, and the purpose for which they are intended.

It is practically impossible to cite examples of every kind of device to which the floating principle can be applied, but typical designs will be described so that the various devices shown may be applied to a wide range of work.

It is well to state that in connection with the application of the floating principle, the greatest care must be used in the design in order to make sure that it is correctly applied, as it is quite possible to obtain a "float" in some portion of a device or tool, which, being of faulty construction, will not produce the results desired.

Important Points in the Application of the Floating Principle. — In order to obtain the most satisfactory results in its application, a few points are here noted which are worthy of attention.

1. As applied to clamping or holding methods, the greatest care must be used in order to make sure that the floating action is not constrained in any one direction, but will operate equally well and with uniform pressure on the required area. Frictional resistance may at times be sufficient in cases of this kind to cause imperfect work by reason of unequal pressures on the work itself. When the clamping action is applied to a rough surface, still greater care must be used in this regard, and the amount of float must be so proportioned that it will take care of a considerable variation in the castings or forgings. When a great number of pieces are to be handled, several patterns are often used and these will be found to vary somewhat so that there are slight differences in the resulting castings. For this reason, due allowance must be made.

2. When applied to methods of locating the work, or as supporting points on which it rests, the construction must be such that it will not by any possibility cause distortion. If springs are used under supporting plugs which are afterward to be locked in position, the springs must be proportioned so that they will not be strong enough to cause any trouble by forcing the piece out of its true position. Also when supports are placed against finished surfaces they should be so arranged that they will not injure them. In locating a piece of work from two previously machined surfaces which are in different planes, the float-action must be very carefully studied, so that the contacts are positively assured, and no tilting of the work will

result. There are occasional instances which require the location of a piece of work from a previously machined surface, in connection with a threaded portion by which it must be clamped. In a case of this kind, the "float" must be made so that it will

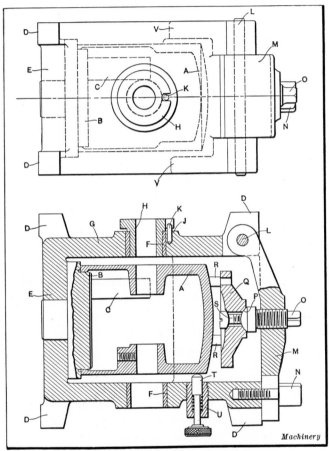

Fig. 1. Piston Drill Jig having Floating Clamps

take care of a possible lack of concentricity between the thread and the other finished surfaces and at the same time provide means of equalizing variations in the alignment of the thread.

3. Locking devices for floating members must be so arranged that the members can be positively locked or clamped without causing any change in their positions. A turning

action such as might be caused by the end of a screw against a locating point is often sufficient to throw the work out of its correct position. The interposing of shoes between screws and floating members will prevent any trouble of this kind.

Other points in construction and design will be noted in connection with the examples to be described.

Piston Drill Jig with Floating Clamps. — A very good example of a drill jig which is provided with a floating clamp to work on a rough surface is shown in Fig. 1, the work being a piston casting A which has been previously machined at B. The body of the jig G is of semi-box section and is provided with feet D on which it may be rested, both during the loading and when under the drill. A hardened and ground steel stud E is let into the casting at one end and serves as a locating point for the machined interior of the piston B. A stud C is further provided to give the correct location to the wrist-pin bosses.

As the end of the piston is of spherical shape and in the rough state also, it is necessary to provide a means of clamping which will so adjust itself to the inequalities of the casting that an equal pressure will be obtained so that there will be no tendency to tilt the work. A heavy latch M is pivoted on the pin L and is slotted at the other end to allow the passage of the thumb-screw N which is used to clamp it in position. A special screw O is threaded into the latch, and is ball-ended at P so that it has a spherical bearing against the floating clamp Q. The screw S keeps it in position, but it will be noted that clearance is provided to allow for the floating movement around the body of the screw. Three pins R are set 120 degrees apart in the face of the floating clamp so that a firm three-point bearing is assured. In order to assist in supporting the work under the pressure of the drill, two spring-pins T are provided, these being set in the form of a vee near the front end of the piston. They are encased in a screw bushing U and are locked in position by means of set-screws, not shown, after they have been allowed to spring up against the piston casting. (In order to avoid confusion in the drawing, one of these pins is shown at an angle of 45 degrees from its actual position.)

The steel liner bushings F are provided in the body of the casting so that the main bushings, which are of the removable type as shown at H, may not produce too much wear in the jig body itself. A slot is provided in the head of the bushing so that the pin K will prevent it from turning under the twist-

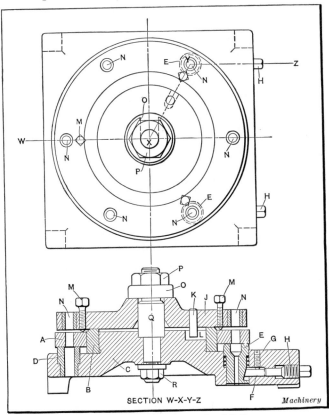

Fig. 2. Drill Jig for Rough Steel Collar

ing action of the drill. It should be noted that in the construction of the spring-pins which are used to help support the casting, the springs themselves should be very light so that they will not force the piston out of its true position, determined by the locating stud.

Drill Jig for a Rough Collar. — The steel adjusting collar A which is shown in Fig. 2 has been previously bored, but no other work has been done upon it, the sides being left in their natural forged shape. Six holes are to be drilled around the rim, as shown at N, and it will be seen that some care is necessary in the locating and clamping arrangements so that the resulting holes will be parallel with the axis of the collar. The jig body C is of cast iron, and is provided with a hardened and ground steel locating collar B on which the previously machined interior of the ring is located. The ring is placed on this steel collar resting against the single steel bushing D which is inserted in the body of the jig. Two other bushings E are arranged 120 degrees apart, and are provided with very light coil springs which force them up against the under side of the ring. The shoes F are then set up against the angular cut on these bushings by means of the screws H. The small set-screws G bear against the flattened side of the shoes and prevent them from turning. It will be noted that the angular cut on the body of the bushings is such as to prevent them from pushing down under the pressure of the drill.

The bushing plate J is located on the stud Q and is prevented from turning by the pin K which fits the slot L in the body of the jig. Six bushings N are set into the plate at equal intervals. A nut P and a C-washer O provide for ready removal of the plate and draw it down solidly on the top of the locating ring B. The three pointed screws M are set into the work slightly to prevent any change in its location. It is well to note that it would have cost no more to machine one side of the work while it was being bored, thus obviating the necessity of the floating locating bushings.

Drill Jig with Floating Bushings and Locating Vees. — A somewhat peculiar condition is shown in Fig. 3, the work A being a bellcrank of ordinary construction such as is used in large quantities in automobile work. There are some instances on work of this kind when a variation of $\frac{1}{32}$ inch or more in the center-to-center distances is not considered of extreme importance, but it is quite important to have the holes as near the center of the bosses as possible. In order to counteract variations in the castings and still obtain holes which are central on the bosses, it was necessary to adopt some sort of floating construction such as that shown in the illustration. A number of jigs of this kind are in use in a large automobile factory and their action is very satisfactory. In the instance shown the work is located on a stud *J* from the previously reamed hole in the hub. It should also be noted that both hubs and bosses have been faced to size previous to the drilling operation. A

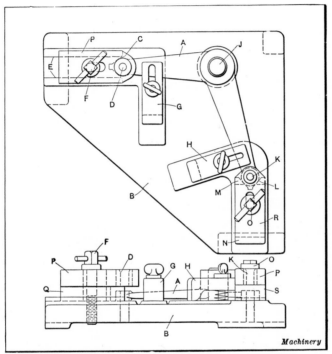

Fig. 3. Drill Jig with Floating Bushings and Locating Vees

sliding V-block *Q* is carefully fitted to the slot *E* in the body of the jig, and on it is mounted the bushing plate *P* in which the bushing *D* is carried. After the piece has been placed in position the sliding block is pushed forward by the operator until the vee *C* comes up against the boss on the casting and locates it. The thumb-screw *F* locks the block firmly in position, and the sliding clamp *G* holds the work. Another block *S* is also cut out in the form of a vee at *L*, but is not

17 J

tongued on its lower side to fit a slot, as in the other instance.
A bushing plate R is mounted on it with a bushing K at the
forward end.   The under side of the block has two narrow
bearing surfaces N and M and it is free to swivel in any direction required by the slightly varying positions of the boss.

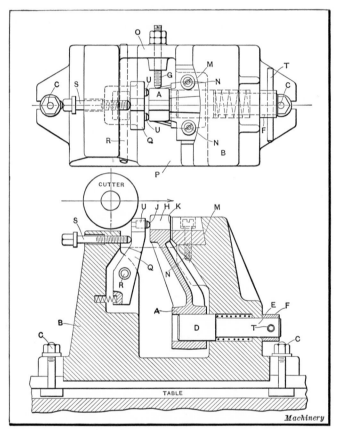

Fig. 4.   Milling Fixture with Floating Clamps and Locator

The thumb-screw O holds it in place after it has been located
by the operator.   The other clamp H is then used to hold the
piece firmly.   A drill jig of this kind is not suited to all classes
of work, but it proved satisfactory in this case; the floating
action gives excellent results when absolute accuracy in the
product is not required.

Milling Fixture with Floating Clamps and Locator. — In the design of milling fixtures a point which is of extreme importance is that of so arranging the various clamping devices that they will not produce undue strain or distortion. In addition to this, all members used must be of sufficiently heavy construction to avoid chatter. The work A as illustrated in Fig. 4 has been previously chucked and it is desired to mill the slot H at its upper end in a certain relation to the reamed hole. The two portions of the casting J and K are left rough, and as a consequence it becomes necessary to arrange the clamps and locating points so that they will equalize the inequalities of the casting. The body of the fixture B is cast iron and of somewhat heavy section, being tongued at its lower side to fit the slot in the table and held down in the usual manner by the T-bolts C at each end. The work is placed on the adjustable plunger D which is pulled back by the pin T passing through the outer end. A stop collar F is forced on the end of the shank E in order to prevent too great a movement of the plunger. The upper end of the work is swung over against the stop-screw G which is set in a boss in the rib O that ties the two sides of the fixture together. One of the rough sides K of the casting strikes against the rocker M which automatically adjusts itself to the variation in the casting. It will be noted that the fixture is bored out radially and slightly under-cut to fit this rocker, and that it is held in place by the screws N. The holes which these screws enter are slightly enlarged to permit the necessary movement. Two steel pins U bear against the other side of the rough casting, these pins being set in swinging floating clamp Q, the provision for float being supplied by an over-sized hole at R. The set-screw S bears against the center of this rocking clamp and gives the pressure necessary to hold the work. A small coil spring throws the clamp back out of the way when assembling or dissembling the work. The direction of the cut in machining the slot is such that the pressure comes against the solid body of the casting and not against the clamp. Clamping members which float are found on various designs of fixtures.

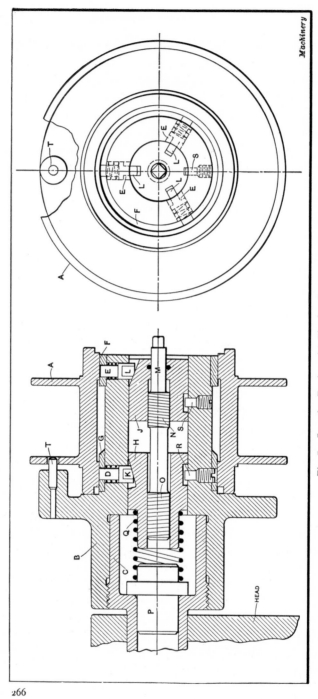

Fig. 5. Locating Device with Floating Pressure Compensator

Locating Device with Floating Pressure Compensator. —
The work A, shown in Fig. 5, has been partially machined in
a previous operation, and the flange has also been drilled so
that one of the holes can be used for driving purposes. The
machine to which this device is applied is a turret lathe of
the horizontal type, and the body B is screwed to the spindle
end C in the usual manner. The pin T is set into a boss in
the face of the fixture and acts as a driver in one of the flange
holes. Two steel rings F and G act as approximate locators
for the work when it is first placed on the fixture. Two cylindrical steel cams H and J are accurately ground to fit the
central hole in the fixture, and are operated by the rod M
which is threaded right- and left-hand, respectively, at N and
O. Each cam is milled to a 20-degree angle at K and L, three
of these slots being equally spaced around the periphery so
that their angular surfaces control the movement of the locating pins D and E. The coil springs return the pins to an in-
active position when released by the cams. A plug P is placed
in the spindle as shown in the illustration, for the purpose of
providing a seat for the coil spring Q which assists in the releasing of the pins after the machining has been done. The
two stop-pins R and S limit the movement of the cams and
take all the thrust of the twisting action of the operating
screw.

In this connection it is well to note that these stop-pins are
a nice fit in the cam slots, while the locating pins have a side
clearance in the angular slots of 0.010 inch so that there is no
possibility of trouble being caused by friction at these points.
Attention is further called to the fact that the action of the
cams is such that a true floating motion is produced when the
screw is operated so that all of the locating pins are set up
with an equal amount of pressure. A floating action of this
nature may be readily applied to holding fixtures for a great
variety of work.

**Chucking Fixture with Floating Clamps and Taper Locating
Plug.** — A somewhat unusual condition is shown in Fig. 6,
the work A being a special clutch flywheel which has been

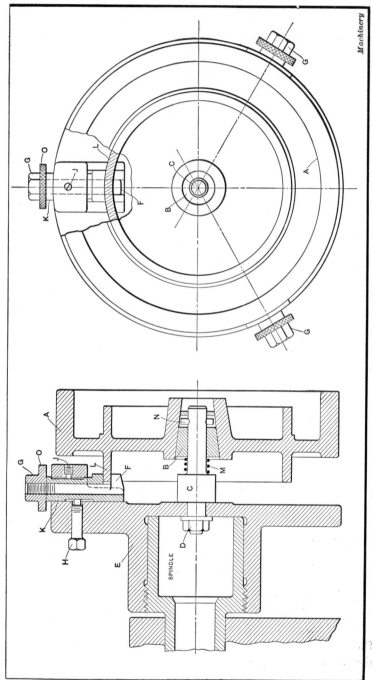

Fig. 6. Chucking Fixture with Floating Clamp and Taper Locating Plug

partially machined. In order to obtain concentricity of the various surfaces, it is necessary to locate the work from the taper in the hub. In order to compensate for slight variations between the taper and other finished surfaces, a tapered shell locating bushing B is centrally located on the stud C which is held in place in the faceplate fixture E by the nut and washer at D. A light coil spring M insures a perfect contact with the tapered surfaces, while a small pin N restrains the movement. As the outside of the work is to be finished during this setting, it is necessary to grip the casting in such a way that the clamps will not interfere with the cutting tools, nor cause distortion in the piece itself. With this end in view, the three lugs around the rim of the fixture are provided with shell bushings K, each of which is squared up at its inner end to form a jaw which is bored to a radius corresponding with the rim of the casting L. It is splined to receive a teat screw J which prevents it from turning, and it also gets a good bearing directly under the point where the work is held so that there is no danger of springing out of shape.

The bolts F pass through the shell bushings and are furnished with nuts G at their outer ends, the nuts having a knurled portion O which permits of rapid finger adjustment before the final tightening with a wrench. It will be seen that this construction automatically obtains a metal-to-metal contact with the thin flange of the casting without distorting it in the least, as the floating action of the bushings equalizes all variations and yet holds the work very firmly. After the clamps have been set up tightly, they are locked in position by the setscrews H at the rear of the fixture. This application of the floating principle may be adapted to many kinds of work, and the results obtained leave nothing to be desired. The machine for which this device was designed is a turret lathe of the horizontal type.

Two-jaw Chuck arranged with a Floating Jaw. — The work A, shown in Fig. 7, is a motorcycle flywheel which it was desired to machine in one setting complete. The machine to which the equipment was applied was a horizontal turret lathe. Several

lugs on the interior of the casting prevented the work from being held in a three-jaw chuck, on account of interferences with
the jaws. A two-jaw chuck was, therefore, utilized, and interferences thereby avoided. As the centering action of a chuck
of this type is very uncertain when used for holding work by
an interior surface of comparatively large diameter, some method
of locating was necessary which would at the same time center
the casting, and yet not cause trouble by interfering with the
lugs on the interior of the flywheel. (The lugs on the interior
of the casting are not shown in the illustration, in order to
avoid confusion.)

The chuck body *B* is screwed to the spindle *C* in the usual

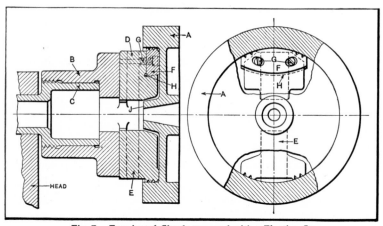

Fig. 7.   Two-jawed Chuck arranged with a Floating Jaw

manner and is provided with two special jaws, one of which, *E*,
is of plain design having two bearing surfaces on the inner rim
of the flywheel casting. The other, *D*, is grooved to fit the
chuck like the regular jaw, but is very much wider as it comes
above the face of the chuck. This portion is turned to a radius
at *H* and given an angle of 10 degrees at the same time in order
to counteract the lifting tendency which might cause trouble
when the jaws were tightened. The floating member or "rocker"
F is mounted on this jaw as shown in the illustration, and is
limited in its movement by the two screws *G* and the elongated
holes in the rocker. This construction gives a very good center-

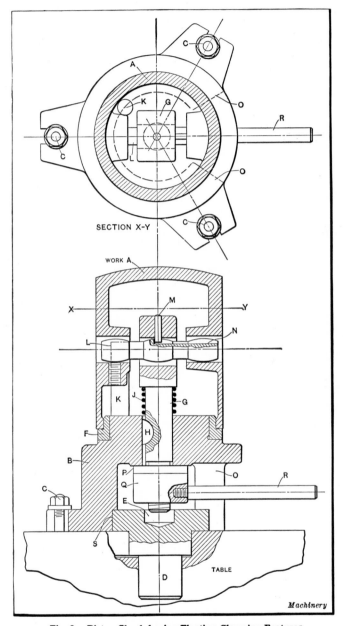

Fig. 8. Piston Chuck having Floating Clamping Features

ing action, and the rocker jaw has sufficient "float" to take care of variations in the casting.

Piston Chuck having Floating Clamping Features. — The work A, shown in Fig. 8, is a large automobile piston which has been bored and faced on the open end to a predetermined size and which is to be completed in this setting, concentric and square with the finished portion. Previous to this setting and after the boring and facing operation, the wrist-pin hole is rough-drilled in a jig in order to facilitate the holding of the work on the fixture.

The casting is located on a hardened and ground steel ring F which is forced on the body of the fixture B, and a small annular groove on the ring prevents trouble or errors in locating, which might be caused by the presence of chips or dirt on the locating surface. The body of the fixture is held in place on the table of the machine by the bolts C which enter the table T-slots, and it is centered on the table by the plug D which is forced into it at S. The clamping pin L is ball-ended, and has a spherical portion in the center also. It is slotted at N so that the pin M in the draw-bar G will enter the slot as it is passed through the wrist-pin holes, and bring up against the shoulder so as to center the clamping pin in the piston. A great deal of strain is taken by this clamping pin, and for this reason it is made of tool steel and spring tempered, so that there will be less chance of breakage.

The draw-bar G is also of tool steel, and it is keyed with a Woodruff key at H to prevent its turning, the key being a sliding fit in the body of the fixture. The lower end of the rod is threaded with a 4-pitch Acme thread, double, left-hand, to fit the operating nut Q, this latter being provided with a handle R which extends out through a cored opening O in the fixture. The permissible movement of this handle is sufficient to produce a vertical movement of $\frac{3}{16}$ inch of the draw-bar, which is ample for the purpose of clamping and releasing. A thrust collar P is interposed between the operating nut and the boss on the under side of the fixture, and a coil spring J keeps the rod up so that the clamping pin may be easily placed

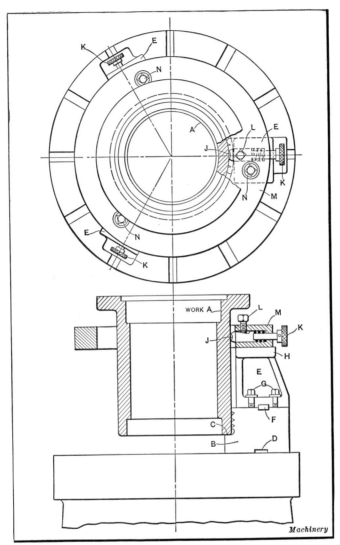

Fig. 9. Chuck Jaws with Floating Locating Points

in position. The pocket *E* in the upper end of the centering plug is for clearance only. A heavy pin *K* acts as a driver against one of the wrist-pin bosses, so that the draw-rod and pin are not called upon to perform this part of the work.

While this chucking device is very rapid in its operation, there is no tendency to tilt the piston or distort it in any way, as the floating action of the pin with its three-point bearing equalizes all pressures, and at the same time provides a very secure method of clamping the work.

Chuck Jaws with Floating Locating Points. — The work *A*, shown in Fig. 9, is to be bored, shouldered and faced complete in one setting, and on account of its length it was considered necessary to provide additional supporting points besides the jaw surfaces. A set of special jaws *B* is keyed to the sub-jaws in the table at *D*, each special jaw being shouldered at *C* to support the work.

The brackets *E* are tongued at *F* to fit the special jaws and are secured thereto by the screws *G*. These brackets act as a

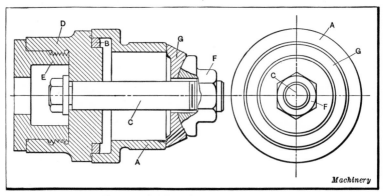

Fig. 10.   Grinding Fixture for Steel Collars

support for the steel floating ring *M* in which the three spring-pins *J* are placed. Elongated holes at points *N* allow the required floating action, the ring being clamped by the collar-head screws. The brackets on which the ring rests are provided with a shelf *H* which is offset slightly from the center so as to give the necessary width for the screws. In using the device, the screws *L* and *N* are loosened, and the work placed in the jaws, which are then tightened while the ring floats sufficiently to allow for variations. It will be noted that the pins, being spring-controlled, adapt themselves to the casting and are there locked by the screws *L*, after which the ring itself is clamped by the collar-head screws *N*.

Although the floating action of this device was satisfactory, the driving or gripping power was found insufficient to hold the work securely, and it became necessary to replace the spring-pins with square-head set-screws, cup-pointed, the ring being tapped out to receive them. The ring was then allowed to float while these screws were lightly set up on the work after which the clamping screws N were tightened. After this change in construction, the action of the mechanism was much improved, and the driving power was found sufficient.

Floating Clamping Ring on Grinding Fixture. — The work A shown in Fig. 10, is a steel casting which is to be ground on the two exterior surfaces. A nose-piece D is screwed to the end of the spindle E and is provided with a hardened and ground locating ring B on which the work locates. The stud C is forced into the nose-piece and is threaded on its outer end to receive a spherical nut F. The collar G is concaved to the same radius as the spherical portion of the nut so that it floats against the end of the work.

CHAPTER XII

APPLICATION OF THE THREE–POINT PRINCIPLE IN FIXTURES

The three-point principle is illustrated by a stool having three legs. Such a stool will be firmly supported even when placed upon an uneven surface, which is not the case if a stool having four legs is used. If a jig having four feet is placed upon the table of a machine, and there is a chip under one of the feet, this will cause the jig to rock when pressure is applied to the upper side; but if there were only three feet and these were located with one foot on a line mid-way between the two feet at the opposite end of the jig, a chip under one foot would not cause a rocking movement. The jig, however, would be tilted upward and, as explained in Chapter I, this might not be noticed by the operator. For this reason, four feet are generally considered preferable when they simply serve to support the jig or fixture. In the mechanical field, however, the principle of three-point support is applicable to many classes of work and its importance is understood and made use of in various kinds of machine and fixture work. In the automobile industry, alignment of the working parts is preserved by making the power plant a self-contained unit and having it supported on three points in order to equalize or neutralize the twisting action caused by the passage of the car over the more or less uneven surface of the road. If some provision of this kind were not made, distortion of the parts would result and they would consequently fail to operate properly.

In machine design, the three-point principle is utilized in numerous ways. Sometimes the bed of a lathe is supported on two points at one end of the machine while the other has a single swivel bearing or its equivalent. The machines provided with this feature are easily set up without danger of distortion or changes in the alignment. Some other types of machine tools also have a three-point support and this principle is applied to machine design in various ways to secure a solid support, to equalize strains, etc. Castings for various purposes are often made with three projecting lugs or bosses in order to gain a good bearing surface under all conditions. In the design of fixtures, the principle of three-point support is used in many ways, on both rough and finished work and on all varieties of machines. In this chapter we shall consider its application to fixtures for horizontal and vertical turret lathe work, and in order to make the matter as clear as possible, simple examples have been selected to illustrate the subject and to avoid complications.

Three-point Locating and Clamping Devices. — In applying the three-point principle for the location and support of rough castings or forgings, there are several important points to consider. To begin with, it is well to make sure that none of the points will strike against a fin or parting seam, or come against the portion of the work on which the piece number may be imprinted. If the work is to be located from two rough surfaces at right angles to each other, it must be remembered that, if three fixed points are used as locators on one side, the other points must be arranged so that only one is fixed, and two are adjustable to compensate for variations in the surfaces. When the work is shallow and is held in chuck jaws, this point may be neglected, as the work can rest on three points and be gripped by the jaws.

When a finished surface is used for centering a piece in a fixture, and it also rests on a finished surface, the three supporting points may be fixed. If the work is to be clamped as on a faceplate fixture, the clamps should be arranged so that they will draw the piece directly down or back upon the supports in order to avoid any chance of tilting or distortion. When a finished surface is used for centering the work and a rough one for end location, the points must be arranged the same as for handling rough castings, i.e., with two of them adjustable. It is often desirable on large work to locate the

piece on three strips instead of on a continuous surface in order
to facilitate assembling. When this is necessary, it is advisable
to make the strips in such a way that they can be readily
replaced when worn.

The supporting points should be so located that they can
be easily reached for cleaning, in order that locations will not
be affected by an accumulation of chips or dirt at important
points. Adjustable points should be so arranged that dirt and
chips will not clog the screws and thus make them difficult to
operate. This point in design should receive careful attention
when fixtures are designed for use on the vertical turret lathe
or vertical boring mill. On machines of the horizontal type,
less trouble is likely to be experienced in this respect, because
the chips do not tend to fall on the screws. In either case,
however, it is always well to provide against any trouble from
this source.

It is frequently desirable to insert hardened steel buttons of
uniform height in the jaw screw holes in order to raise a portion
of the work above the tops of the standard jaws, so that the
work can be faced or under-cut. These buttons form an excellent three-point support for the work in addition to performing
the function already mentioned. Short parallels cut from cold-
rolled steel may be used on a vertical turret lathe and are
somewhat cheaper than the buttons, but they are open to the
objection of becoming easily displaced and lost.

When it is necessary to arrange points to act as a vee on long
cylindrical surfaces, it is good practice to make them so that
they can be adjusted to take up wear. This can easily be done
by means of headless set-screws with check-nuts to lock them
securely in any position; and it is a better construction to
place one check-nut on the outside and another one inside,
than to have both nuts on one side of the fixture wall. The
construction of the fixture will not always permit of using this
method, but, when it will, very satisfactory results are obtained.

When the three-point support is applied to the fixture itself,
the clamp screws which hold the fixture in place on the table
should be arranged at the points where the supports are placed,

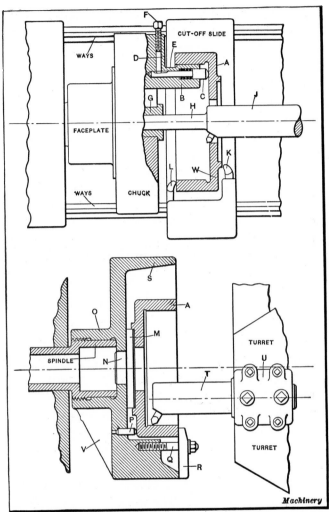

Fig. 1. Application of Three-point Principle in holding a Flywheel while performing Boring and Facing Operations

and any clamps for the work itself should be as near the same place as possible.

Three-point Support for Flywheel Fixture. — The fixture for the motor flywheel shown at *A* in the upper part of Fig. 1 has a three-point support. The flywheel is of such a diameter that a single supporting point in one of the chuck jaws would

18 J

not be sufficient to resist the pressure of the cutting action of the various tools used in machining. The work is held by the inside in the special jaws B which are relieved at E to permit the back-facing of the rim. The tools L and K, which are held in a special tool-block on the cut-off slide, are used for back-facing and finishing the pad; and other tools (not shown) in the turret face the portion W of the flywheel. The boring-bar J has a pilot H which enters the guide bushing G in the chuck to give greater accuracy and rigidity. Two of the jaws are provided with spring-pins C which are released and locked by the action of the screws F on the shoes D. The stop-pin in the third jaw is fixed in order to give positive longitudinal location of the work. Work of this kind is very frequently located on the three fixed ends of the jaws and gripped by the inside as shown, but when this is done there is always a chance of incorrect holding and possible slippage due to spring of the casting. Sometimes this results in the production of grooves or a wavy surface on the outside of the work.

In the second setting of the work a fixture is used and the point of location is the recess which has been machined in the first setting. This locates the piece on a plug M which is shouldered at N and fits a hole provided for it in the center of the fixture. The previously machined surface W rests on three pins P which are of uniform height and so arranged that they leave a slight clearance between the face of the plug M and the face of the shoulder on the work. The fixture body O is screwed to the spindle and its exterior forms a continuous ring S so as to make this surface clean and avoid danger to the operator through projecting lugs, etc. The work is drawn back against the pins P by means of the clamps R through the medium of the screws Q. Work of this kind is frequently held and drawn down upon a continuous finished surface instead of a series of pins. The disadvantage of a continuous surface is that dirt collects upon it and renders location uncertain unless great care is taken to keep the fixture clean.

Three-point Fixture for a Pot Casting. — The fixture shown at H in Fig. 2 was arranged to hold the casting A which is

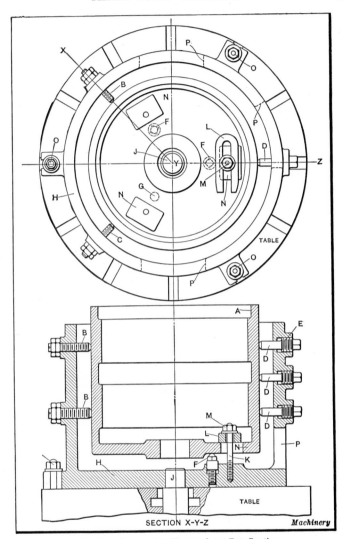

Fig. 2. Three-point Fixture for a Pot Casting

of large size, instead of using jaws, for the reason that better
supporting and driving facilities were required than could be
obtained by means of jaws. Large castings held in a fixture
require considerable clearance between the work and the fixture, because of the variation in size and also on account of the
finish allowance that is necessary. Care must, therefore, be

taken to see that the amount of clearance is ample to take
care of any condition which might be found. An inch of clearance all around is none too much on a large casting. The pot
fixture *H* is centrally located on the table by the plug *J* and
is fastened down by the T-bolts *O* in the table slots.

The set-screws at *B* and *C* serve as locating points for the
casting. There are two screws at *B* and one at *C*, the latter
being located midway vertically between the other two and
90 degrees from them. This is somewhat contrary to the usual
custom and in some cases might not be found desirable — for
example, when considerable dependence has to be placed on
the locating screws to assist in driving the work. In this case,
however, ample provision for driving is obtained. The work is
forced over against points *B* and *C* by the central set-screw *D*
of the three shown. When the casting has been brought up
snugly into place, the upper and lower screws *D* are also
tightened. Protection against chips is provided for in connection with these set-screws, no portion of the thread *E* being
exposed. The work rests on a fixed point *G* (shown in the
upper view) which acts as a positive stop. Two additional
points *F* are adjustable by means of a wrench, and their threads
are protected from dirt by a cylindrical portion above. The
openings *P* in the wall of the fixture allow access for the screws;
the U-clamps *L* draw it down upon the points by means of
the nuts and washers *M* on the studs *K*. The clamps *L* being
of U-section are readily removable without requiring the nuts
and washers to be taken off. The plan view shows only one
clamp in position in order to show this clearly.

**Two Methods of Obtaining a Three-point Support on a Hub
Casting.** — The work *A*, shown in the upper portion of Fig. 3,
is a hub casting of large size, and the method to be described
was first suggested in connection with the handling of this work.
The idea was abandoned, however, in favor of the method
shown at the lower part of the illustration. In the upper illustration, the jaws *C* are mounted on the raising blocks *E* and
tongued to them at *D*, while the raising blocks are tongued
and fastened to the sub-jaws of the table at *F*. Three hardened

points B are set in projections of the upper jaws and the work rests on these points. A supplementary casting G is centered on the table by means of the hollow plug M which also acts

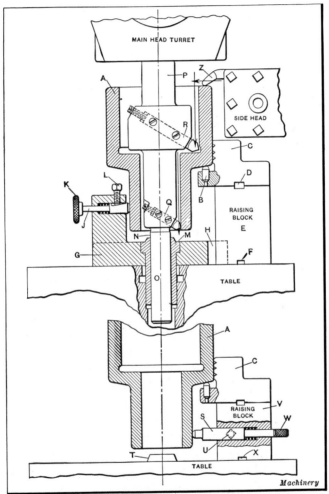

Fig. 3. Original and Improved Methods of holding Large Hub Casting by Three-point Support

as a guide for the boring-bar pilot O; and the upper part of this bushing is beveled as shown, but the edge of the hole is left sharp so that chips will not be drawn down with the bar and tend to destroy it together with the bushing. The base of the fixture is slotted at three points H to allow the necessary movement of the jaws; and there are three lugs midway between the jaws on the base, in which the spring-pins J are carried. After the work has been centered by the jaws, these pins are released and allowed to come into contact with the work; they are then locked by the set-screws L. The boring-bar P is of the multiple type, having two tools Q and R for the two inside diameters. The tool Z is carried in the upper part of the side head instead of the lower, in order to economize on the length of the boring-bar.

As the purpose of three supporting points J was simply to steady the work, it was thought that a simpler design would answer all purposes, and the previous method was therefore abandoned in favor of the one shown in the lower part of Fig. 3. In this case the bushing T is used directly in the center hole of the table and the boring-bar is made correspondingly shorter. The raising blocks V are also lower than in the previous case, and are keyed to the sub-jaws at X in the same manner. The construction of the jaws C is identical in both cases. Three spring plungers S with knurled ends W are inserted in the jaws and tightened in any desired position by the set-screws U. This method is much simpler than the other and possesses the added advantages of being both cheaper and more efficient.

Fixture having Three Clamping Jaws and Three Locating Pads. — The work illustrated at A in Fig. 4 has been partially bored and faced, and in the setting shown, it is necessary to work from the previously finished surfaces. The base casting E is slotted to receive the three steel locating jaws C on which the finished surface B locates. These jaws are held in place by the screws D and are carefully finished after being drawn into position. The base is centered by the plug F in the table hole G, and is held down by the screws Q in the lugs P, one of which is shown in the plan view. Three pads H are finished to support the flange and a driver J is inserted in one of these pads. The work is clamped by means of the hook-clamps K in order to keep the diameter of the fixture as small as possible; and a cap-screw L passes through the hook-clamp and enters the bushings *M* into which it is threaded. The hook-clamp is backed up by the lug *R* so that it will not become distorted when under strain. The boring-bar *N* in the

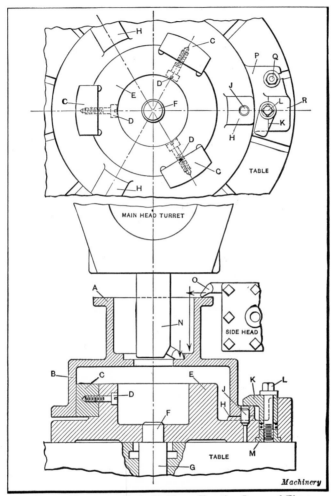

Fig. 4. Fixture provided with Three Clamping Jaws and Three Locating Pads

main-head turret, and the tool *O* in the side head, are indicated in order to show the method of machining.

Double Three-point Locating Device. — A somewhat peculiar arrangement is that shown in Fig. 5 for holding a piece of work

A by the interior cored surface. The base *B* is made of cast
˙ron and is centered on the table by means of the hollow plug *C*.
It is held down by screws *D* which enter shoes in the table

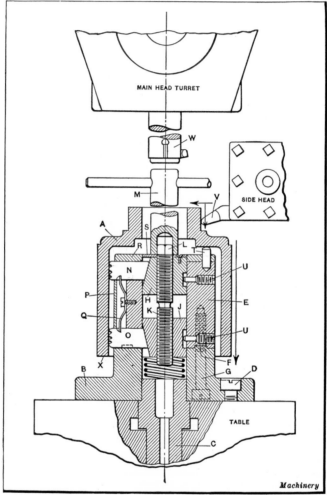

Fig. 5. Method of holding a Piece of Work by an Interior Cored Surface

T-slots. The upper portion of the fixture *E* fits a circular
tongue *F* on the base, to which it is fastened by the screws
G. The upper portion *E* is slotted to receive the jaws *N* and *O*,

and there are three pairs of jaws set 120 degrees apart. The upper portion of the fixture E is made separate in order to facilitate the machining of the slots. Two cylindrical cams H and J control the radial movements of the jaws by means of the screw K which is threaded with a coarse-pitch left-hand thread in the lower cam and a right-hand thread in the upper cam. The upper end of the rod is squared at L and is operated by a socket wrench M. In order to prevent the entry of chips and dirt into the mechanism, a felt washer S is fastened to the upper cam; and steel cover-plate R is placed on top of the fixture and held in place by screws. The hardened steel pin T strikes against the inner cored surface and locates the piece vertically. Slots are cut in the upper portion of the fixture E to allow the insertion of the flat springs Q which throw the jaws back into position upon withdrawing them from the work; and a sheet steel cover-plate P keeps the dirt out of these slots. The cams and screw are supported by the coil spring shown below the lower cam, and the action of the cams is limited by the screws U which enter slots in the cams. These screws also serve to prevent the revolution of the cams. A combination boring and reaming bar W is used for boring and reaming the hole while the outside surfaces are machined by various tools in the side head, one of these being shown at V.

In the construction of this device it will be noted that although six points or jaws are used for locating, the arrangement is such that they all bear against the inside of the casting with an equal amount of pressure, at the same time centering the work from the cored interior. As the right-and-left screw on the rod K is rotated, the two cams float vertically so that the pressure on the jaws is equalized. A device of this kind is useful in many instances when work is to be held from an internal cored surface.

CHAPTER XIII

SPECIAL JIG AND FIXTURE MECHANISMS

No single item influences the production rate to as great an extent as the design of jigs and fixtures. The saving of a few seconds clamping time means an increased production that offsets a high first cost. It is much easier for an operator to clamp his work by tightening one nut than the usual three, and, aside from the saving of time, he is expending less energy and works to better advantage to himself and his employer.

It is usually necessary to equalize the pressure in a jig before

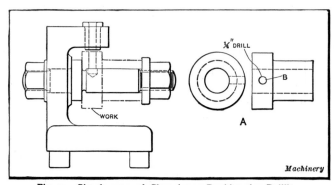

Fig. 1. Simple way of Clamping a Bushing for Drilling

applying the clamping pressure. When equalizing and clamping mechanisms are both operated by a single clamping operation, the danger of clamping before equalizing the pressure can be eliminated. Many object to the term "fool-proof," but the amount of work spoiled or sprung by careless clamping justifies care in designing jigs and fixtures that are at least "error-proof" in this respect.

The mechanisms described in this chapter are selected for their suggestive value, and only as much of the fixture is shown as is absolutely necessary. Great care should be used in selecting the mechanism desired, so that it meets the clamping or equalizing conditions of the work in hand. The examples shown are in many cases obtained from milling fixture designs, but the principles apply equally to drill jigs.

As an example in the choice of clamping mechanism, consider the piece A, Fig. 1. It is required to drill the hole B. A simple way of clamping this piece is illustrated in Fig. 1, using a hexagon nut and washer. The time required for running on and off the hexagon nut is saved in the design shown in Fig. 2, using a quarter-turn knob. Stud B has a flat milled on both sides of

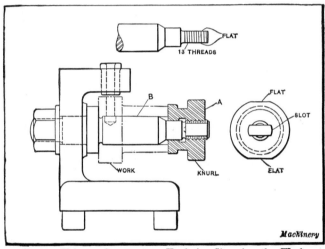

Fig. 2. Using a Quarter-turn Knob for Clamping the Work

its threaded portion. The slot in knob A slides on over this flat and a quarter turn clamps the work. If the variation in the length of the work is not too great, this makes a rapid clamping arrangement.

Fig. 3 shows another means of clamping the same piece, in which the variation in length of the work and the time required for turning the knob to match the flat on the stud has been considered. The slotted washer A and knob B are dropped over stud C; washer A is held against knob B, which can then be screwed up as freely as a solid knob. This can be used for a

variety of bushings of various lengths, the stud C being made to
suit the longest piece of work.

Clamps that have a tendency to draw the work down firmly
onto the rest-pins or stops are useful in all classes of fixtures.
Fig. 4 illustrates a simple means of accomplishing this. Care
should be taken to see that the stop is pivoted above the point A.
Another and more rigid device is illustrated in Fig. 5. The
plunger A, carried in plunger B, is forced down against the 45-de-
gree side of stop C, compressing spring D. A fixture that clamps
two clamps with a "down-and-in" pressure is illustrated in Fig. 6.

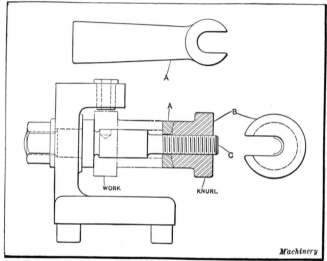

Fig. 3.   Means used for Clamping Bushing when the Work
Varies in Length

Slides B are equalized by strap C and ball-and-socket washers
D and E. This fixture is useful for milling and profiling, as the
clamps and stops are below the surface of the work. Fig. 7 shows
two down-and-in clamps equalized for holding a round piece of
bored work for a milling operation. Lever A is tapped to receive screw B, and the clamping pressure equalizes with lever C
by means of rod D. Levers A and C impart a down-and-in
pressure to plungers E. This fixture can be applied to flat work.

In the double movement clamp shown in Fig. 8, the clamp A is
carried by the hinge B, pivoted at C. Screw E gives clamp A

a down-and-in movement by means of a 45-degree taper on stud
D. The stud *D* is milled off at *F* to give the clamp sufficient
movement to remove the work. A mechanism for drawing down
both ends of two pieces, by means of a single nut, is illustrated in
Fig. 9. Each piece is clamped independently, thus making it
suitable for use on rough castings or forgings. Rod *A*, running
through the fixture, carries ball-and-socket washers at each end
and draws the end clamps *B* and *C* together. These clamps are
given a down-and-in movement against the 45-degree wedge
ends of rods *D* and *E*. The clamping thrust against rods *D* and
E imparts a downward movement to the inner clamps *G* and *H*,

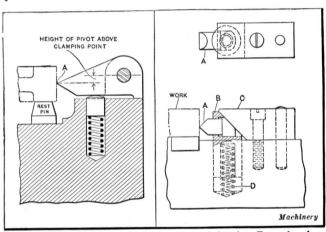

| Fig. 4. Simple means for Drawing the Work down Firmly onto the Locating Pins | Fig. 5. Another Example of Clamps Drawing the Work down Firmly onto the Locating Pins |

pulling the work down on the inner rest-pins. The clamps are
returned by means of plungers *K* and spring *J*.

The fixture illustrated in Fig. 10 shows a method of drawing
down two clamps and throwing the work against the stop-pin
by a single clamping operation. Tightening nut *A* clamps down
clamp *C* and pulls up rod *B* against the 45-degree tapered end
of rod *D*, giving a lateral movement against plunger *E*. Plunger
E is carried by the floating stud *G*. On the upper end of stud
G is a 15-degree taper that operates against plunger *H*. Plunger
E imparts, first, an upward movement to floating stud *G*, which,

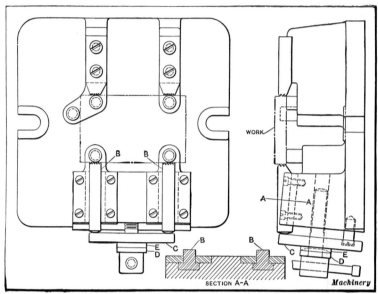

Fig. 6. Fixture with Arrangement for Clamping Two Clamps with a " Down-and-in " Pressure

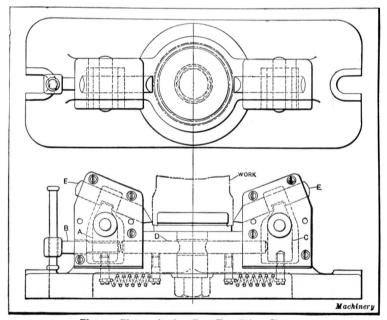

Fig. 7. Fixture having Two Equalizing Clamps

in turn, forces out plunger H and throws the work against stop-pin J; second, a downward pull on plunger K, drawing down the clamp L. Thus the work is thrown against the stop-pins before the final clamping pressure is applied. Clamps C and L are held up by spring plungers, not shown.

The clamping pressure on eight small washers is equalized, and the washers clamped with a down-and-in movement in the

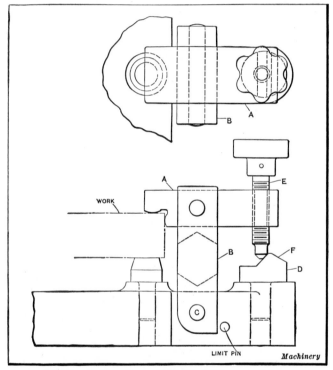

Fig. 8. Another Type of Double Movement Clamp

fixture shown in Fig. 11. Rod A clamps the equalizers B and C, which equalize the pressure against D and E on the one side, and F and G on the other. Clamps D, E, F, and G are given a downward pull by four plungers H, which also impart a downward pull on the inner clamps J, K, L, and M. The clamps are bored to receive the washers, and are returned to a normal position by the spring plungers N.

Fig. 12 illustrates a center clamp that gives a downward and outward thrust by means of the tapered ends of plate *A*, which is carried by plunger *B*. Plunger *C* wedges down the plunger *D*, which is tapped into plunger *B*. Plungers *B* and *D* are held up

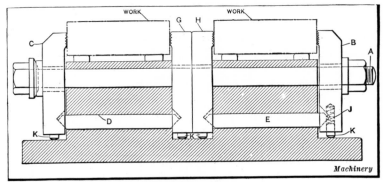

Fig. 9.   Mechanism for Drawing down Both ends of Two Pieces by a Single Nut

by a spring *E*. A small pin in plunger *D* allows a half turn of plunger *B*, so that the work may be lifted out.

In the fixture illustrated in Fig. 14, the work (two clutch shells) is equalized and clamped by a single movement of the handwheel

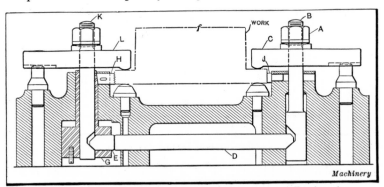

Fig. 10.   Method for Drawing down Two Clamps and Forcing the Work against the Stop-pin by a Single Clamping Operation

B, drawing out rod *C* against the collar *D*. The section *A–A* shows how this collar equalizes its thrust with plungers *E* and *F*. The collar *D* is free to slip to either side as required for equalizing. The plungers *E* and *F* draw in rods *G* and *H* through the medium of collars J and K. The strap M, held central by a small spring and plunger, equalizes the pull on the center clamp. All clamps are made to clear the work, when it is to be removed, by means of the lever L and the system of levers shown in the lower view.

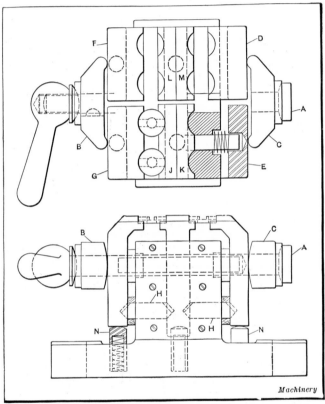

Fig. 11. Fixture for Equalizing the Clamping Pressure on Eight Small Washers

Figs. 13 and 15 illustrate a small double movement clamping mechanism for hand milling or profiling use. In Fig. 13, the clamping pressure against clamp A also pulls out plunger B, throwing up plunger C and throwing the work against stop E, by means of plunger D. Spring plunger G is used to return plunger D. In Fig. 15, the pull through clamp A on plunger B

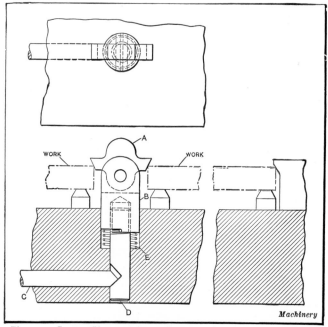

Fig. 12.   Center Clamp giving a Downward and Outward Thrust

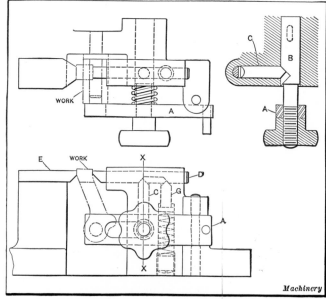

Fig. 13.   Small Double Movement Clamping Mechanism for Hand Milling or Profiling Machines

throws the work against the stop C, by means of plungers D and E.

In profiling or face milling fixtures, clamps on top of the work often interfere with the cutter. Fig. 16 illustrates a method of

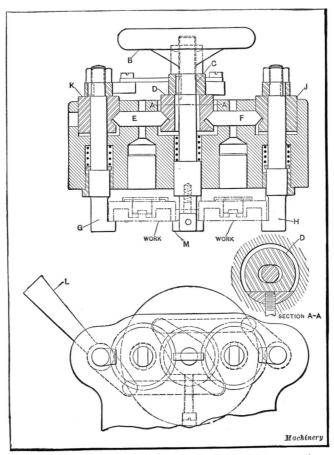

Fig. 14. An Equalized Clamping Arrangement making use of a Handwheel

holding this class of work by means of a flange at the bottom. Clamp A is operated by the wing-nut B and floats in slots to allow for any casting variation, and for hooking the projection on the clamp over the flange. The piece C is thrown over after the clamp is hooked over the flange. Care must be taken that the point X is below the pivot point of the piece C.

Fig. 17 illustrates part of a heavy milling fixture for clamping against the stop-plate A, by means of the two plungers B and C, by equalizing with the plunger D and sleeve E working against B and C with 45-degree wedge cuts. Projections on the work often prevent the use of plain clamps. Fig. 18 shows a resort

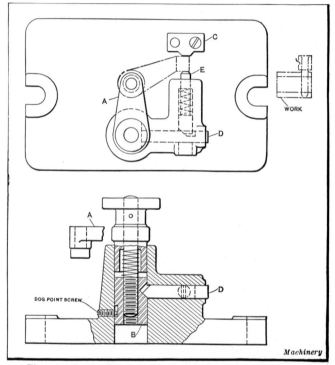

Fig. 15.   Another Double Movement Clamping Mechanism

to an unusual, but efficient, clamp to meet these conditions. The use of plungers A and B permits the clamp to be operated from the rear by means of a screw C and knob D. When work is long in proportion to its width or when the locating pins must be placed close together, as in the piece illustrated in Fig. 19, there is danger of it "cocking" or binding between one locating pin and the screw, if a plain screw is used to throw the work against the locating pins. The use of a roller instead of a screw prevents this. The roller A will turn until the work strikes both stop-pins. In the device illustrated, B and C are the fixed locating pins, and D, the clamp screw tapped into the bushing

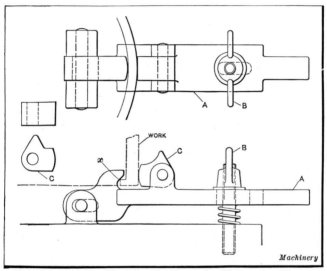

Fig. 16. Clamping Work by Holding it by Means of a Flange

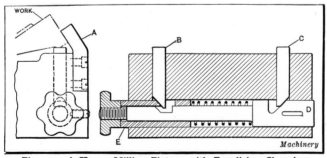

Fig. 17. A Heavy Milling Fixture with Equalizing Clamping Device

E operating the sliding plunger G. It is obvious that the work can be prevented from binding by using two equalizing plungers to throw it against the locating pins instead of a roller.

Fig. 20 shows the locating mechanism for a milling fixture in which two pieces are located by two plungers each, all operated

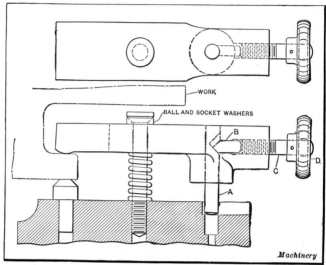

Fig. 18.   Special Type of Clamp used where Projections on the
Work Prevent the use of Plain Clamps

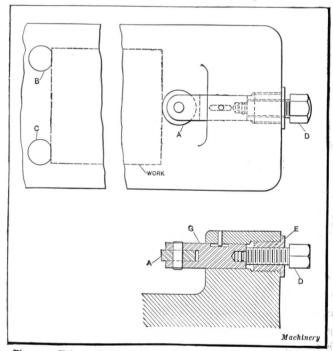

Fig. 19.   Using a Roller to Prevent Unequal Binding against the
Locating Pins

by a single clamping operation. Lever A draws out plunger B and throws in sleeve C, operating the plungers D and E. Plungers E are smaller in diameter than plungers D and permit of enough

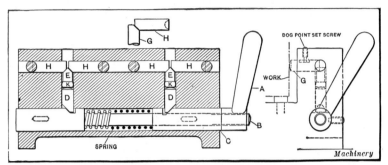

Fig. 20. Locating Mechanism where Two Pieces are Located and Clamped in a Single Operation

lateral movement to equalize plungers G through the auxiliary plungers H.

Fig. 21 represents a milling fixture with a quick-release feature. The particular work illustrated is milling a flat on a small bush-

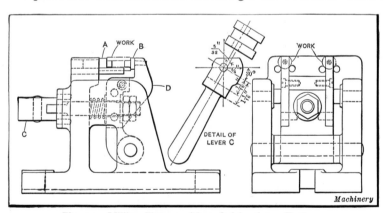

Fig. 21. Milling Fixture with a Quick-release Feature

ing made on the screw machine. The bushings are held on the pins A and B and clamped with the eccentric handle C, which draws in the hinged leaf D. Details of the quick-release lever are given.

Fig. 22 illustrates half of a fixture for milling a cylindrical concave surface on an unusual piece. The work is clamped against the pads A and B, on previously milled surfaces, by means of two differentially operated plungers C and D, similar to a previously described device. To prevent springing under cut, the work is backed up with the floating plunger E on the one side and F and G on the other. The plungers are operated by push-rods H and J. These push-rods are hand operated and are clamped by the bushing K and star knob L.

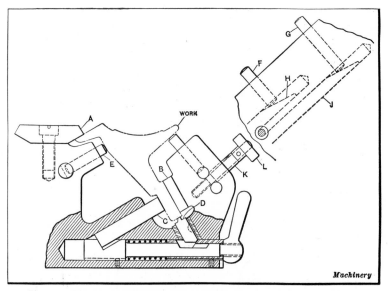

Fig. 22. Fixture for Milling a Concave Surface provided with Sliding Supports under the Milled Surface

Some occasions arise in which the 45-degree plungers do not permit of sufficient clamping movement. The mechanism in Fig. 23 was designed to overcome this objection. An unusually large movement of the clamp is required to clamp directly over the rest-pin. Rod A, operated by screw B, imparts movement to both plungers C and D. Plunger C pulls clamp E down and plunger D pushes up on clamp E through the plunger G. The wedge angle between plungers C and D should be less than that between plungers A and C. There is considerable friction in this mechanism.

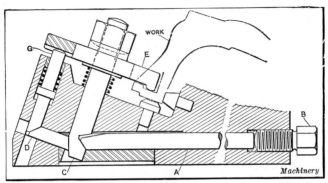

Fig. 23. Mechanism when an Unusually Large Movement of the Clamp is Required

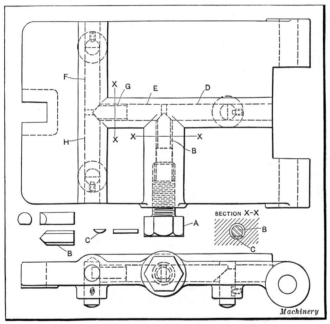

Fig. 24. Rigid Mechanism for Clamping at Three Points by Means of One Screw

A very rigid mechanism for clamping at three points, by means of one screw, is shown in Fig. 24. In this case, it is shown applied to a drill jig, but it is rigid enough to permit its use in milling or planing fixtures. In these cases, the clamping pins

become rest-pins and are subject to the thrust of the cut.   Screw
A thrusts against equalizing plunger B.   The details of this
plunger mechanism are illustrated in the engraving.   Plunger B
is of less diameter than the drilled hole and rests on the piece C.
This piece is cut from a rod of the same diameter as the hole
and is used to afford a flat base for plunger B to rest on and insure

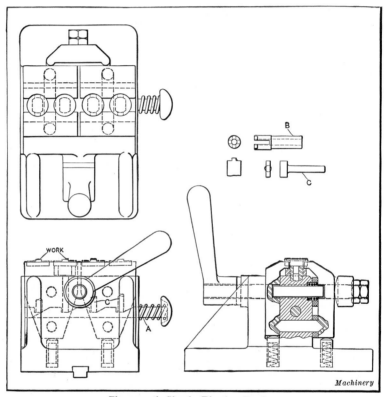

Fig. 25.   A Simple Ejecting Device

full contact of the wedge end against the plungers D and E.
Plunger G is a duplicate of B and equalizes the plungers F and H
by means of the same mechanism.

Considerable saving of time may be effected by the use of
ejectors.   Fig. 25 is an example of the use of an ejector.   Push-
rod A has four notches milled tapering on one end.   The pins

B are bored and slotted to receive the rods *C*. These rods are operated by the wedge cuts in push-rod *A*. The four pieces of work are ejected by pushing in rod *A*.

In work on Lincoln-type millers or on straddle-mill work, the return table movement must be long in order to eliminate the danger of the operator striking the cutters when unclamping or withdrawing the rear clamp. The necessity of the extra

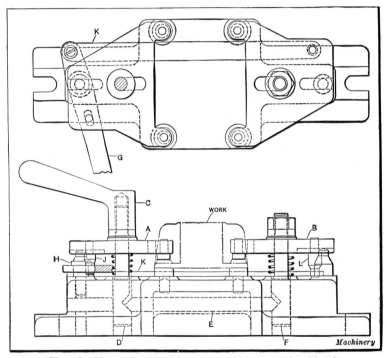

Fig. 26. Fixture Designed for use on Lincoln Milling Machine

long table return is done away with in the straddle-milling fixtures illustrated in Fig. 26. The clamps are operated entirely from the front of the fixture, thus making it unnecessary for the operator to reach in near the cutters. Clamps *A* and *B* are operated by the handle *C* through stud *D*, rod *E*, and stud *F*. The clamps are withdrawn by lever *G*, which is pivoted on stud *H* and operates clamp *A* by means of pin *J*. The strap *K* is connected to the other end of lever *G* and operates the rear clamp by pin *L*.

CHAPTER XIV

PROVIDING FOR UPKEEP IN DESIGNING JIGS AND FIXTURES

The importance of providing for upkeep in the design of the various types of fixtures used in manufactuiing work cannot be over-emphasized. In many cases provision for upkeep can be incorporated in the design without increasing the first cost of the fixture to any great extent, while in other instances considerable extra outlay may be necessary. Much depends upon the accuracy required in the finished product and the number of pieces which are to be machined. For example, in gun work, when great quantities of parts are to be produced, no expense is spared in making the fixtures in as durable a manner as possible, and in making provision for the replacement of worn locating points, etc. On machine tool work, however, discretion must be exercised, so that the expense of fixtures may be consistent with the required rate of production and accuracy of the work.

Many factors influence design in this regard. The size and general character of the work determine the type of machine on which the fixture is to be used, and, therefore, the need for stability and strength. The number of pieces to be machined is a factor which must be considered, for it is apparent that a small number does not require any special care to be taken in regard to the matter of upkeep. In drill jig work, the locating points, bushings, and feet may be made so that they can be readily replaced when abuse or wear of these parts tends to cause imperfect work. The probable necessity for replacements is naturally determined by the rate of production that is required. Jigs and fixtures are often handled roughly and they should be constructed to withstand such usage. Milling fixtures are frequently required to stand very heavy cutting so that great rigidity is an important feature in their construction. In the case of horizontal turret lathe fixtures or others which revolve about a fixed center, it may frequently be found desirable to make locating rings, points, or surfaces in such a way that adjustment can conveniently be made about this center.

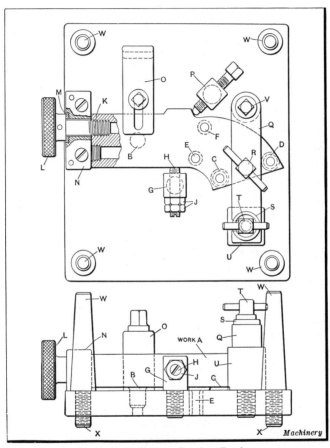

Fig. 1. Drill Jig for a Receiver Forging

Points Pertaining to Upkeep. — A few noteworthy points of construction are given herewith: 1. Location of the work. This is of primary importance and the various fixed points provided in the fixture should be made in such a way that they can either be readily replaced or adjusted, according to circumstances.   2. The number of pieces to be machined should receive proper consideration in the design, both in regard to cost of the fixture and in regard to probable necessity of replacements.   3. Weight and rigidity of the fixture.   This point is naturally somewhat dependent upon the class of work for which it is intended, and the convenience of handling.   4. Gibs. In the case of indexing or sliding fixtures, suitable provision should be made for adjustment by means of gibs or straps, in order that natural wear may be taken up.   5. Revolving fixtures.   Fixtures which revolve about a fixed center, if subjected to hard usage or if used for a great number of pieces, may be advantageously provided with means of adjustment about the center of revolution.   This is a refinement that is very infrequently used, and it is not necessary in the majority of cases unless extreme accuracy is required.   There are a few points in construction which are applicable principally to individual cases.   These will be referred to later.

Drill Jig for a Receiver Forging. — The work A, shown in Fig. 1, has been previously faced, milled and bored, and tapped at the end K, leaving four holes C, D, E, and F to be drilled on the jig shown in the illustration.   This type of jig is "built up" entirely from steel parts, a rectangular plate forming the base of the jig.   The work is laid down on the hardened pin B and the heads of the two jig bushings C and D which are ground to a uniform surface.   The threaded plug at K is provided with a knurled head L and draws the end of the receiver up against the steel block N which is screwed and doweled to the jig base. A thrust washer is provided at M and a slight float is allowed between the block and the plug.   The stud G is screwed into the plate and the set-screw H running through it forms an adjustable stop for the side of the receiver, check-nuts being provided at J.   After the work has been drawn up by the threaded plug at K, the set-screw in the stud P is used to push the work over against the point H.

The steel clamp O is slid into position and tightened, and the set-screw R in the swinging clamp Q at the other end of the work is brought to bear at that point.   The clamp Q is pivoted at *V*, and slotted at the other end where it is locked by an application of the screw and washer *T* and *S*, a steel stud *U* acting as a support for this end. The four legs of the jig *W* are made of hardened steel, screwed into the plate and pro-truding through the other side to act as a rest when placing the work in position. It will be noted in the construction of this jig that all parts are easily replaceable or adjustable for wear, and that al-though the jig is somewhat expensive in first cost, the provision for upkeep is ex-cellent. It is obvious that drilling is done *against* the clamps, so that these must necessarily be made some-what heavier than would be necessary if they were simply required for hold-ing the work.

Drilling and Reaming Jig. — The casting *A*, shown in Fig. 2, is part of an electrical machine, and has been previously turned and faced. It is required for this operation that the work be located by the previously turned and

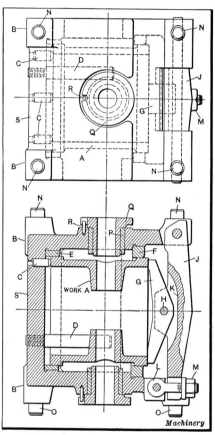

Fig. 2. Jig with Interchangeable Bushings for Different Tools used in Machining Cylindrical Part *A*

faced surfaces. The jig body in this instance is made of cast iron and is of box section, as shown at *S*; it is bored out to receive the two hardened and ground locating rings *E* and *F*. There are three pins *C* located 120 degrees apart, which act as stops for the end of the casting, the ends of the pins being rounded so that dirt or chips cannot lodge on them and cause faulty locating. The pin D simply acts as a stop for locating the internal bosses on the work; and feet are provided at B so that the jig casting can be set up on this end for loading purposes. A swinging clamp J is provided at the open end of the jig, and this clamp is provided with a rocker G which pivots on the pin H, slot K being cut for its reception.

A swinging clamp-screw is located at L, which works in the slot on the end of the clamp J, the nut and washer at M being used to draw it up firmly. An equalizing action is obtained in this manner on the swivel H, so that pressure is equally distributed on the end of the casting. As it was necessary during the machining of this piece to use several sizes of tools and to work from both sides of the casting, it was found advisable to use liner bushings P in order to prevent undue wear. These bushings are hardened and ground, and forced into position; and the slip bushings Q are slotted to receive the pin R to prevent them from turning. The steel studs N and O on opposite sides of the jig body are ground to a uniform surface and act as feet for the jig. In connection with this jig it is well to note that all parts subject to wear are readily replaceable, thus making the life of the jig almost indefinite.

Indexing Fixture for a Clutch Gear. — In every kind of indexing mechanism one of the chief points in design is to prevent variations in the spacing due to wear on the mechanism. The fixture shown in Fig. 3 is so arranged that wear on the indexing points is automatically taken up by the construction of the device, so that the provision made for its upkeep is excellent. In addition to this feature, the design is not very expensive and it may be made up at much less cost than many other kinds of indexing devices. The work A is a clutch gear, the clutch portion B of which is to be machined in this setting. As the work has been previously machined all over, it is necessary to work from the finished surfaces.

The body of the fixture G is of cast iron and it is provided with two machine steel keys at P; these keys locate the fixture on the table by means of the T-slots, and the hold-down bolts Q lock it securely in position. The revolving portion of the fixture F is also of cast iron and has a bearing all around on the base, while the central stud C is used as a locator for the work at its upper end, and holds the revolving portion down firmly by means of the nut and collar at H. The fitting at this point is such that the fixture may be revolved readily and yet is not free enough so that there is any lost motion. A liner bushing of hardened steel is ground to a nice fit on the central stud at E

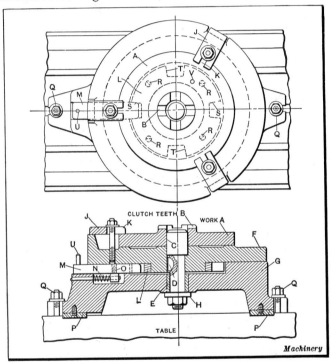

Fig. 3.   Indexing Fixture used for Milling Teeth in Clutch Gear

and will wear almost indefinitely, while an indexing ring L is forced on the revolving portion F of the fixture, and doweled in its correct position by the pin V and held in place by the four screws R. The work is held down firmly on the revolving portion by means of the three clamps J, these being slotted at K to facilitate rapid removal.

A steel index bolt M of rectangular section is carefully fitted to the slot in the body of the fixture, and beveled at its inner

20 J

end S so that it enters the angular slots S and T of the index ring. Clearance is allowed between the end of the bolt and the bottom of these slots so that wear is automatically taken care of. A stud O is screwed into the under side of the index bolt and a stiff coiled spring at N keeps the bolt firmly in position. The pin U is obviously used for drawing the bolt back and indexing the fixture. Points worthy of note in the construction of this fixture are the liner bushing at E, the steel locating ring L, and the automatic method of taking up wear by the angular lock bolt M.

Fixture with Inserted Jaws. — The work shown at A in Fig. 4 is a steel casting which has to be finished on the inside.

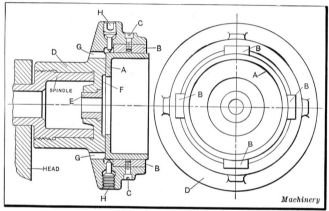

Fig. 4. Fixture provided with Interchangeable Jaws for Holding Different Sizes of Work

These castings are made in two sizes, one of which is 1 inch larger than the other. It was desired to use the same fixture for both pieces in order to avoid the expense of making two fixtures. (The larger piece of work is shown in the illustration.) For this purpose a fixture D was designed to be screwed to the end of the lathe spindle in the usual manner. There are four jaws B which rest in slots around the inside of the fixture, these jaws being drawn back into their seats by the screws C in order to be ground in place to the correct diameter. Beyond the ends of the jaws, the pointed hollow set-screws H are so placed that they will come opposite to the web portion of the casting.

By placing them in this manner it is evident that the entire width of the web will resist the strain of the screws so that they will not distort the work. Further than this, the screws *H* act as drivers, as they sink slightly into the work when set up. Two holes *G* are drilled at opposite sides of the fixture, these holes being utilized to force the work out of the jaws when removing it from the fixture.

A hardened and ground tool steel bushing *E* is placed in the fixture, and acts as a pilot for the cutter-head used in machining the work; and it will be noted that the surface *F* of the fixture is relieved to permit the passage of the tools through the work. In machining the smaller piece, it is only necessary

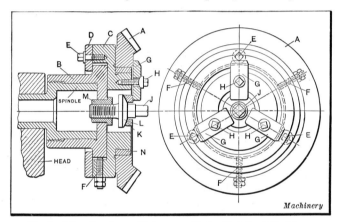

Fig. 5. Ring Bevel-gear Fixture provided with Adjustable Clamps

to remove the jaws *B* and hollow set-screws *H*, and substitute those suited for the smaller piece. Therefore, one fixture was found sufficient to handle both pieces and replacements were made easy by the construction. Adaptations of this type of fixture may be made for many varieties of work, when several pieces are to be handled, and it will be found both efficient and economical in upkeep.

Bevel-gear Fixture with Adjustable Features. — The work *A*, shown in Fig. 5, is a ring bevel-gear blank of heavy section, which has been partly machined. In this instance the fixture is really composed of two separate pieces, one of which, *B*, is screwed to the nose of the spindle while the other, *C*, is adjustable on the first piece. In the illustration, piece *C* is shown clamped firmly against the body *B* of the fixture by the steel clamping

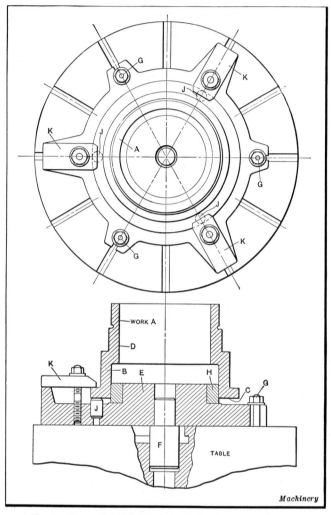

Fig. 6. Fixture for Holding the Partially Finished Casting *A*

ring *D* and the screws *E*, and it will further be noted that there is a slight clearance between the outside diameter of the body *B* and the inside of part *C*. Three set-screws *F* are equidistantly placed around the periphery of the ring C and these set-screws are furnished with check-nuts as shown. By loosening the collar D and manipulating set-screws F, the working portions of the fixture can be readily trued up when they become slightly out of true through use or abuse. A steel locating ring N is forced on the ring C and is ground to the size of the interior gear.

The method of clamping is somewhat out of the ordinary, consisting of the use of three clamps G and an operating screw J, and a floating collar K. The three clamps are placed 120 degrees apart and have slightly oversize holes through which the screws H pass. These screws have a ball surface on the under side of the collar corresponding to a similar depression in the clamps themselves. A steel bushing M is fitted to the body B of the fixture, and is threaded with a coarse pitch thread which corresponds to that on the operating screw J. After the clamps G have been swung into place on the ring gear, a few turns of the screw J sets all three of them with a uniform pressure through the medium of the spherical collar K which bears against their inner sides. Although a fixture of this kind is somewhat expensive in first cost, all the parts can be readily replaced at a minimum expense and the fixture may also be kept true with the center of rotation of the spindle with very little trouble.

Fixture for a Hub Casting. — The work A, shown in Fig. 6, is a hub casting which has been previously machined on the surfaces B, C, and D. The fixture E on which it is held for subsequent operations is made of cast iron; it is centered on the table by the plug F and held down by the screws G which enter the table T-slots. A steel locating ring H is forced on the body of the fixture and forms the point of location for the work. Three studs J are set 120 degrees apart in the base; and they are surface ground to the correct height to support the work. This arrangement makes locations positive regardless of chips or dirt. The clamps K hold the work down on the pins J. Features of this fixture are the ease of replacement of the locating rings and points, and freedom from trouble which might be caused by an accumulation of chips or dirt.

CHAPTER XV
ARC-WELDED JIGS AND FIXTURES

Radical changes in the methods of making jigs and fixtures have been introduced in many plants by the use of the arc-welding process. Usually only one fixture of a certain design is required, and the making of a pattern for a single casting for the frame of the fixture adds greatly to the expense.

The arc-welding process, by means of which the fixture is built up from steel plates and structural shapes, not only reduces the cost greatly, but often makes it possible to build the entire fixture in the time required for making the pattern alone; and frequently the cost of the welded fixture body is less than the cost of the pattern, thus saving the entire cost of the foundry work.

There is still another advantage derived through the use of welded jigs and fixtures. Because of the low cost of arc-welded construction, it is frequently economical to build jigs and fixtures for small-lot production, whereas with cast fixtures, the cost of the casting would make the fixture-cost prohibitive, unless the production were large enough to warrant the expense.

Tests for Warpage or Distortion and Vibration. — The Westinghouse Electric & Mfg. Co. has found that the time required for making jigs and fixtures can be considerably shortened by the use of arc welding, a process that the company has been using with satisfactory results for several years. A thorough investigation as to the reliability and accuracy of arc-welded construction was carried on by the company before it was decided to use this process extensively for jigs.

Several jigs and fixtures were fabricated and tested for inaccuracies such as warpage, distortion, vibration, etc.

This testing has been carried on for several years by periodically checking the fixtures constructed when the welded construction was first adopted. In no case was any serious disadvantage found. In fact, the maintenance cost of the jigs and fixtures thus produced has been less than for those of cast construction.

As time is a very important factor in supplying jigs and fixtures for manufacturing purposes, it is found advisable to handle the welding work in the tool department. Complete construction of all jigs, fixtures, and machine tools is under the jurisdiction of the tool-room, which is responsible for all operations from the selection of raw material to the completion of the job.

Welded Jigs and Fixtures Cost Less than the Cast Type. — It is interesting to note that an arc-welded jig body or the frame of a machine can be delivered to the machining department in about the same time that it would take to make a pattern for casting the same part. In many cases the cost of the base or machine tool part is about the same as the cost of the pattern. The cost of welded jigs and fixtures, as compared with the cost of making the same parts from castings, has been thoroughly checked several times. In all cases, the investigations have shown that the welded structures are about 25 per cent less expensive. Fewer operations and reduction in the weight of the material needed for welded construction are responsible for the lower cost.

Jigs and fixtures must be designed for welded construction in order to keep the cost as low as possible. The design must lend itself to standard structural steel shapes and plates. A designer must know this method or type of construction so that he can take advantage of all its possibilities without losing any of the qualities desired.

Arc-Welded Jig is Light and Strong. —The welded jigs and fixtures are more desirable than cast-iron ones, owing to the fact that they are lighter and, at the same time, of at least equal strength. Thinner material can be used for welded parts, as the materials used are of uniform strength; whereas, in the case of castings, a large factor of safety

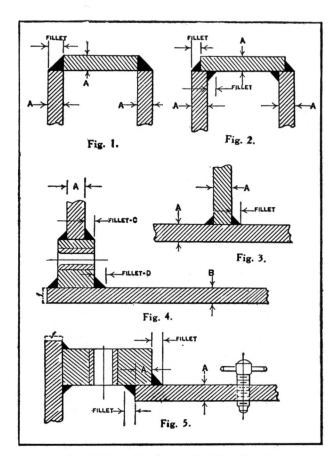

Fig. 1.

Fig. 2.

Fig. 3.

Fig. 4.

Fig. 5.

Fig. 1.—Plate thickness A 1/4 to 3/8 inch; fillet size same as thickness A, rod size 5/32 inch; thickness A 7/16 to 1/2 inch; fillet size same as thickness A, rod size 3/16 inch.

Fig. 2.—Thickness A 9/16 to 1 inch; fillet size 3/8 inch, rod size 3/16 inch; thickness A 1 1/16 inch up; fillet size 1/2 inch, rod size 3/16 inch.

Figs. 3, 4, and 5.—Thickness A (or A and B, Fig. 4) 1/4 to 3/8 inch; fillet size 1/4 inch, rod size 5/32 inch; thickness A 7/16 to 1 inch; fillet size 3/8 inch, rod size 3/16 inch; thickness A 1 1/16 inch up; fillet size 1/2 inch, rod size 3/16 inch.

Fillet sizes are determined by the thinner of the two adjoining sections. Where extra strength is required, use heavier fillets. The allowable stress under shocks is 5000 pounds per square inch.

must be allowed to cover casting irregularities and possible flaws. The arc-welded jig may be stronger, because it is possible to place the steel where the working stress demands strength.

On the line of work referred to here, only one or a few jigs of one type are made, so that if castings were employed, a pattern would only be used once, or, at the most, only a few times. Naturally, under such conditions, the pattern shop will not produce a pattern designed to reduce the required machining operations to a minimum. Hubs and bosses will generally be cast solid, or with an extra amount of stock, in order to lessen patternmaking difficulties. This extra material is lost and must be removed in the machine shop, all of which means additional expense. In the case of a fabricated jig, or fixture, no more allowance for finish is made than is necessary for cleaning up the surface. As a rule, this is 1/8 inch or less, except for very large work, in which case an allowance of 1/4 inch is made for finishing.

Establishing Standards for Welded Construction. — The Westinghouse Electric & Mfg. Co. has had considerable experience on welded construction in the manufacture of some of its standard products. As the company has trained welders and welding supervisors, it was not difficult to set up a standard of design for jigs, fixtures, or other welded parts.

The lay-out of the jig or fixture is made without any reference to welding. The designer makes a separate sketch which indicates how the welding is to be done. This gives complete information for manufacturing the jig. The welding sketch gives, in detail, the various sizes of material that are to be used, and also indicates the amount or size of the welding fillet or bead. (See diagrams, Figs. 1 to 5, and data given below them.) With the work laid out in this manner, there is no misunderstanding between the shop and designing department.

Materials Used. — The material used is hot-rolled steel, which is comparatively inexpensive. When good wearing surfaces are necessary, they are made from tool steel, hardened and attached to the jig by means of screws, bolts, or in the case of bushings, by pressing the parts into machined holes. In cases where chips are likely to become embedded in the feet of jigs or fixtures, it was found advisable to make the feet of a low grade of tool steel, heat-treated, and welded to the jig. When the jig is annealed to remove all strains, these feet are drawn to a scleroscope hardness of 45 to 50. The feet thus provided are much harder than the ordinary cast-iron feet, and yet are soft enough to be machined.

The parts required in the construction of jigs and fixtures are cut from bar stock by saws and from plates by means of oxy-acetylene cutting machines. Different types of these machines permit any shape or size of part to be cut that may be required. All large holes are produced before the parts are assembled in a jig.

Assembling, Welding, and Annealing. — Various parts of a jig body or other tool are assembled by a mechanic, who squares them up properly and clamps them in place, after which they are tack-welded sufficiently to hold the parts together. It is desirable that the man doing such work be well versed in welded construction. Only sufficient welding is done at this time to insure holding the parts in place. After this, a welder joins all the parts securely by welding. Thus, the cost of welding is kept at a minimum.

In order to remove all strains and to prevent any distortion, all jigs and fixtures are annealed. This is done by heating them in a furnace to a temperature of about 1000 degrees F. and then allowing them to cool in the air. The practice in one plant is to normalize arc-welded jigs, fixtures, etc., by heating to about 1300 degrees F. and allowing them to cool in order to relieve all strains set up by welding together rolled plates, shapes, or whatever types of sections are used.

Sand-Blasting and Painting. — In order to maintain the appearance of the jigs and fixtures, it was found desirable to sand-blast all fabricated parts after annealing. This removes any loose particles or scale, and prepares the sur-

Fig. 6. Drill Jigs of Arc-welded Construction are Now
Regularly Used by Many Manufacturers

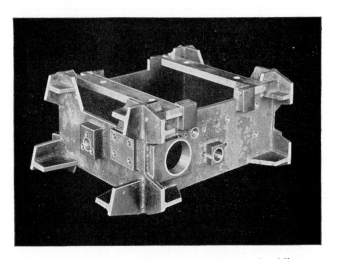

Fig. 7. Jig Made by Welding Steel Plates, Avoiding an
Expensive Pattern and Core-box

face for painting. All the parts are spray-painted before any machining is done. The machining of jigs and fixtures of this type is no different from the methods used in machining cast jigs, except that less material is removed. The machining time is about 10 per cent less for welded jigs than for those of cast construction.

Standard Shapes for Welded Jigs and Fixtures. — It is important for manufacturers in the metal-working industries to consider carefully the best and quickest methods for making their jigs, fixtures, and gages. Yet accuracy must not be sacrificed for speed, and in many cases must be of an even higher degree than was previously required. That arc welding is a successful answer to this tool-making problem has been demonstrated by the Brown & Sharpe Mfg. Co.

It is not enough, however, to apply arc welding to the construction of tool equipment of conventional design. The designs and methods of construction formerly employed in making such equipment of cast iron must be discarded. The welded jigs, fixtures, gages, and similar tool equipment must be designed with a view to making the best possible use of structural steel in all its various forms. The adaptability of standard plates, angle-irons, and shapes that are readily available and easily welded together must be kept in mind. The four corner posts of the box-type jig shown in Fig. 6 are made from angle-irons. This jig shows the facility with which bushings, clamps, and locating blocks can be assembled in almost any position by arc welding. Standard bushings, clamps, screws, and other available accessories must all be used to the best advantage.

When welded construction is employed, the plates for jigs can be readily cut to size with an oxy-acetylene torch, which can be employed to cut holes in the jig walls or base as well. The cutting torch can also be used for cutting large holes in bosses to approximately the rough-finished size before finish-boring. Small bosses can be chucked and drilled before being welded to the jig or fixture frame.

The jig shown in Fig. 7 is obviously of a somewhat complicated design, especially from the patternmaker's point of

Fig. 8. Properly Designed Arc-welded Jigs are Lighter
and Stronger than Cast-iron Jigs

view. Constructing this jig of steel plates assembled by simple arc-welding operations eliminated an expensive pattern and core-box job.

The advantages of the greater strength of steel over cast iron are readily visualized by referring to the design of the welded steel jig shown in Fig. 8. The comparatively slender corner posts of this jig will withstand considerable abuse and would not be broken off should the fixture be accidentally dropped, as would probably be the case with cast iron.

Jigs and Fixtures Can be Changed to Suit Changes in Product. — Pieces can be removed from or added to welded jigs to suit changes in the product or manufacturing methods. For example, changes can be made on the ends of clamps by welding on or cutting off pieces as required, thus eliminating time-consuming milling operations. Milling fixtures for present-day speeds and feeds must have rugged bases and heavy clamps with quick-acting handles. Almost any kind of clamp or handle can be cut to shape with the torch and assembled by welding. The clamps can be hardened in the regular way or the clamping points can be hard-surfaced and ground to shape.

Good construction should never be sacrificed for appearance. Good-looking tools can be made, nevertheless, by the arc-welding method. Sand blasting and painting improve their appearance, but are not necessary. Naturally, it requires a little more time to machine steel than it does cast iron, but the additional time should not exceed 5 per cent. This may be offset if the designer, in laying out the tool, will provide small blocks for squaring purposes, so that the machine work will be confined to small areas instead of large surfaces.

Examples Showing Flexibility of Design. — "How large a jig can be made by arc welding?" The jig for drilling milling machine stands, shown in Fig. 9, is larger than any ordinarily required in the average machine shop.

Fig. 10 illustrates a jig made by arc welding, which, with the construction details shown, would be impracticable to cast. This illustration shows how strips and angle-irons can be put in where they are most needed for rigidity. Patterns with tie pieces of this kind could not be drawn out of the molding sand; hence, such designs could not be made by casting. If redesigned to permit casting, the tool would have to be made much heavier.

In Fig. 11 is shown a box type of drill jig for a gear-case in which the center distances are held to close limits and the accuracy of the holes, with respect to size and alignment, must meet the requirements for roller bearings.

In Fig. 12 is shown a jig of the flat plate and angle-iron type, which can be made up quickly to meet any small-job requirement. From an examination of the arc-welded jigs illustrated, it is evident that the machining requirements have been reduced to a minimum; also the jigs can be made strong and still be light in weight. Where weight is required in present-day milling fixtures, it can be obtained by arc-welding in steel blocks to give extra strength with the necessary weight.

Fig. 11. Box Type Jig of Welded Construction for Drilling Gear-case

Fig. 10. Jig of Welded Construction that would be Difficult to Produce by Casting

Fig. 9. Arc-welded Jig of Large Size Employed in Drilling Milling Machine Stands

Fig. 12. Jig Constructed of Flat Plate and
Angle-irons Assembled by Arc Welding

The design of a production tool depends largely on the accuracy required; this is generally determined by the tool designer. The tool must be so constructed that these limits can be readily maintained, thus assuring accurate machine parts. The production, or the number of pieces made in a year, will also have a direct bearing on the design of the tool. For example, a tool that is used for only a few hundred pieces a year would probably have ordinary clamps and clamp-screws for holding the work, whereas one used for several thousand pieces should have such features as quick-acting clamps, air-operated locking or holding devices, etc. The fixtures should have hardened wear-resisting surfaces.

In order to make the greatest saving possible in tool cost, the structural steel shapes now available on the market should be employed, as they can be readily arc-welded. A good bead weld usually possesses sufficient strength to withstand the average requirements of this work. All arc-welded tools should be heated to about 1300 degrees F., before machining, to relieve any strains set up in the plates and angle-irons by the welding operation. Small pads or spots, such as shown at *A*, Fig. 9, and at *B*, Fig. 12, should be placed at advantageous points to eliminate unnecessary machining of large surfaces.

CHAPTER XVI

JIGS OF THE AUTOMATIC TYPE

Jigs and fixtures that automatically locate and clamp the work are used for some classes of automotive work or wherever production warrants the use of such special equipment. Some examples from the cylinder department of an automobile plant will be described. These jigs automatically locate and clamp the work, and when the operation is over, the clamps automatically release. One fixture even turns over to remove chips from the cylinder, ready for the next operation.

Three machines in a battery of four vertical multiple-spindle machines are equipped with automatic locating and clamping jigs. The four machines, as well as a dumping table between the third and fourth machines, are unloaded simultaneously by the movement of a single lever. As the operator completes the movement of this lever, the tilting table and all the machines, with the exception of the first, are loaded simultaneously with new cylinder blocks.

The dumping table removes all chips from the valve guide holes prior to the final operation on these holes. The first machine of the group spot-faces the surface around the valve holes accurately to height as determined by means of a dial indicator attached to the drill head. The second machine rough-bores the sixteen valve throats at one time. The third machine drills the valve guide holes, and the fourth machine reams the throats and guide holes.

The cylinder blocks are pushed into the first machine of the group from the conveyor seen in Fig. 1. As the cylinder enters the jig, its bottom surfaces pass over two rapidly revolving wire brushes, which thoroughly remove all the oil and grease left from a preceding tapping operation.

Fig. 1. Wire Brushes Facilitate Locating of Cylinder Blocks by Removing Oil and Grease Left from a Previous Operation

Previously, the oil and grease interfered with convenient locating of the work in the jig. These wire brushes are driven by a small motor on the floor adjacent to the conveyor. They revolve in the opposite direction to that in which the cylinder is pushed.

How Cylinders are Loaded Simultaneously. — Simultaneous loading of the second, third, and fourth machines and the dumping table is effected by means of a bar *A*, Figs. 2, 3, and 5, which extends the length of the installation, sliding through bearings in the different jigs. This bar is fitted with a number of spring-actuated fingers *B*, Figs. 3 and 5, which fold in when they meet obstructions during the travel of the bar toward the left, and spring out as soon as the obstruction has been passed. Thus, when all the operations have been performed by this group of machines and the dumping table, the operator turns crank-handle *C*, Fig. 2, and draws bar *A* to the left a distance somewhat greater than the length of the cylinder blocks. As the fingers *B*

Fig. 2. Operator's Station from which Three Machines and a
Dumping Table are Loaded Simultaneously with Cylinder Blocks

on bar *A* pass the cylinders, they fold in, and when they
reach the ends of the different cylinder blocks, they spring
outward again. The operator then turns crank *C* in the
reverse direction, thus moving bar *A*, and with it all the
cylinders in the four machines and on the dumping table,
toward the right. In this manner, five cylinder blocks are
advanced simultaneously to the next operation.

Locating the Cylinders Automatically. —The cylinder blocks
are located and clamped manually in the jig of the first
machine, but these functions are performed automatically
in the remaining machines. As the cylinder blocks enter
the jigs of the latter machines, they are roughly located

Fig. 3.   Dumping Table which Automatically Pours All Chips
out of the Valve Guide Holes and Throats in Cylinder Blocks

lengthwise by the spring-actuated fingers on sliding bar A.
Flat bars running the length of the jigs locate the castings
roughly from front to back.   In the second and third machines, the cylinder blocks are held above accurate seating
blocks by flat bars such as seen at D, Fig. 2, which are provided at both the front and back of the jig.   In the fourth
machine, transverse flat bars E, Fig. 7, hold the casting
above the accurate seating surfaces.

When the operator removes his hand from crank C,
Fig. 2, he immediately places it on the lever F and moves
it to the right.   This causes the second, third, and fourth
machines and the dumping table to start their operating
cycles simultaneously.   As each drill head comes down, the
flat bars D, Fig. 2, and E, Fig. 7, on which the cylinders
have been resting are lowered to permit the cylinders to
seat themselves on hardened and ground blocks and to enable dowel-pins, such as seen at G, Fig. 7, to enter previously reamed holes in the cylinder castings.

Fig. 4. Milling Operation in which the Cylinder is Automatically Located and Clamped as the Machine Table Feeds Downward

Lowering of bars D, Fig. 2, and E, Fig. 7, is accomplished by releasing a weight at the back of each machine, such as shown at H, Fig. 7. This weight is held on a lever connected by a wire rope to the drill head of the machine. The other end of the weighted lever is mounted on an eccentric shaft J which extends to the front of the jig. This shaft is connected through links to a second similar shaft K at the opposite end of the jig. When weight H is released, these shafts are forced to make a partial revolution to permit lowering the studs to which flat bars E, Fig. 7, and D, Fig. 2, are attached. As this happens, the cylinder blocks seat themselves over the dowel-pins.

The clamping of the cylinder blocks in the jigs takes

Fig. 5. The Cylinder Blocks are Automatically Loaded and Unloaded by Means of a Long Bar with Spring Fingers

place automatically as weights W, Figs. 2 and 5, are released upon the rapid downward movement of the drill
heads. These weights are mounted on levers attached to
the drill heads through links. The weighted levers actuate
shafts having eccentric ends, as seen at L, Fig. 2, which
engage slots cut across the vertical shanks of flat clamps.
When the weights are released, they cause the eccentric
shafts to swivel and the clamps are forced down on top of
the cylinder blocks to hold them securely for the operation.
Each weight is approximately 30 pounds. The clamps are
lifted from the cylinder blocks automatically as the drill
heads return to the upper position and raise the weighted
levers. Similarly, the cylinders are lifted from the dowel-
pins and accurate seating blocks as the weight at the rear
of each jig is raised.

Jig Designed to Shift the Cylinder Blocks Transversely. —
The fourth machine of this group requires a movement of

Fig. 6. Four Equalizing Clamps Grip Two Cylinder Blocks as the Table of the Machine Tilts the Work into Line with the Boring-bars

the cylinder blocks from front to back, in order to bring the valve throat and guide holes over the pilot bushings that guide the reamers. At the end of the operation, the cylinder block is shifted in the reverse direction for unloading. These transverse movements are obtained by means of two swinging arms M, Fig. 7, which are mounted on a shaft actuated by an air cylinder. The air cylinder is controlled by a valve N, Fig. 2, at the right-hand end of the second machine. Rack teeth on the air piston-rod engage a pinion on the same shaft as the arms and cause a partial revolution of arms M.

In addition to handle F which starts the second, third and fourth machines, there is a handle O, Fig. 5, that starts

Fig. 7. Jig Equipment that Enables the Cylinder to be Located
Accurately on Dowel-pins and Blocks

the fourth machine. All the machines can be stopped during operation by depressing lever *P,* Fig. 2, and they can also be stopped individually by means of handle *O,* Fig. 5.

Operation of the Dumping Table. — Fig. 3 shows the dumping table partially raised from the position it occupies as the cylinder is loaded on it. When the table has been completely dumped, all the valve holes in the cylinder block are pointed downward, the casting being actually turned through about 90 degrees. This allows all chips to slide out of the holes freely. When the table falls into the dumped position, it strikes a wood buffer fitted with rubber pads to deaden the noise.

The tilting of the table is actuated by the drill head of the fourth machine, to which it is attached by rod *Q.* When the drill head travels downward, this rod causes shaft *R* to turn in its bearings and tip over the table. Structural arms *S,* which are fastened to the back of the table, hold

Fig. 8. View Showing Raised or Loading Position of the Tilting
Table Used on the Cylinder Boring Machine Illustrated in Fig. 6

the cylinder block to it.   The table is fitted with conveyor
rollers to facilitate loading and unloading.

Milling Ends of Crankshaft Bearings. — All the crankshaft
bearings in the cylinder block are milled simultaneously on
the ends by the machine shown in Fig. 4.   This machine is
equipped with ten cutters mounted on a spindle that extends through the table and into the bearings of uprights
at both ends of the machine.   The operation is performed
by feeding the table downward to bring the cylinder block
to the cutters.

When the cylinder block is pushed into this machine,
lever A is thrown toward the back so as to locate the block
roughly in a lengthwise position.   The approximate sidewise location is obtained as the block is slid between ways

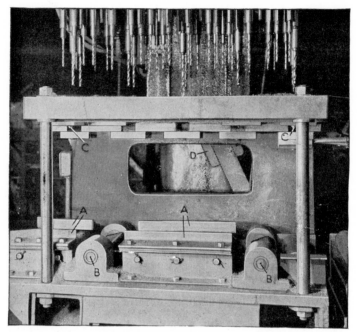

Fig. 9. Large-diameter Shafts with a Flat Surface are Used to Clamp the Cylinder Blocks in This Jig

in head *B*. With the table in the loading position as shown, the cylinder block rests on two bars *C* at the front and back of the machine, which hold it above accurate seating blocks and dowel-pins. When the table and head *B* feed downward for the operation, bars *C* tilt downward, allowing the cylinder to seat itself on the hardened and ground blocks and the dowel-pins to enter reamed holes in the casting.

At the same time weighted levers *D* are released, permitting eccentric shafts to swivel and force large flat clamps down on top of the block in the manner illustrated in Fig. 2. Upon the completion of this operation, the weighted levers *D*, Fig. 4, are pulled upward as shaft *E* revolves, thus releasing the two clamps, and bars *C* are again forced upward to raise the cylinder block from the locating dowels and seating blocks.

Fixture for Cylinder Boring Machine. —Four cylinders are bored simultaneously in each of two blocks by the machine shown in Fig. 6. Owing to the fact that the boring spindles of this machine are at an angle, and that the table of the machine tilts to bring the cylinder blocks in line with the boring spindles, it was necessary to provide the jig with a clamping means entirely different from those so far described. As will be seen from Fig. 8, the table of the machine is fitted with conveyor rollers. It is held horizontally for loading and unloading by means of cable A. Braces, as shown at B, locate the cylinder blocks roughly from front to back and prevent them from sliding off when the table is tilted. Handle C moves to bring stops into position for locating the blocks lengthwise. When the head of the machine feeds downward, and the table tilts, the cylinder blocks automatically seat themselves on hardened and ground surfaces and dowel-pins enter reamed holes in the castings to locate them accurately. Simultaneously, links D, which are hinged to the upper ends of braces E, move downward and allow the weighted levers F to fall. The movement of these levers results in four equalizing clamps G being gripped firmly on top of the cylinder blocks. After an operation, when the boring head returns upward, links D lift levers F and release the clamps.

Jig that Clamps from the Bottom. — Fig. 9 shows a simple clamping means which has been applied to a jig used in a multiple drilling operation. As the cylinder block is pushed into the jig from the left, it is located roughly sidewise by angle-irons A. Rough lengthwise location is obtained by means of a simple over-running latch, which is raised by hand. Accurate location of the work both sidewise and lengthwise is effected automatically when the drill head of the machine feeds down. At that time, weights mounted on levers attached to the back ends of shafts B cause the shafts to swivel and bring up a large-diameter section at the middle of the shafts. These large sections of the shafts lift the cylinder blocks firmly against hardened and ground blocks attached to the top plate of the jig. Just before the clamping action occurs, dowel-pins enter reamed holes in the cylinder block, such as seen at C, to in-

Fig. 10. Jig Equipped with Five Weights that Automatically
Locate and Lock the Cylinder Head for Drilling

sure accurate positioning of the work. The weight that
moves the right-hand shaft *B* may be seen at *D*. Upon the
upward movement of the drill head, wire cables attached
to the weighted levers and to the drill head pull up the
weights and swivel shafts *B* in the reverse direction. This
releases the block for unloading. When it is pushed from
the jig, brushes remove the chips.

Jig that Automatically Raises, Locates, and Clamps Cylinder
Heads. — An unusual jig employed in drilling cylinder heads
is shown in the open or loading position in Fig. 10 and in
the closed or drilling position in Fig. 11. From the first
of these illustrations, it will be seen that the casting is
placed in the jig with the combustion chambers upward.
Two adjusting screws *A* roughly locate the casting lengthwise, and it is approximately positioned sidewise by means

Fig. 11. Cylinder Head Jig, Illustrated in Fig. 10, Shown Locked in the Upright or Drilling Position

of two spring plungers *B*. As the table moves toward the drills, the slack developed in the cable *C* at each end of the jig permits weights *D* to drop down and swivel arms *E* from the position shown in Fig. 10 into the position seen in Fig. 11. Weight *F*, Fig. 10, falls forward at the same time and, through an eccentric shaft that engages shank *G*, closes two fingers *H* on the rib between the two central combustion chambers. In this way, the cylinder head is located for the job. Weights *J* also drop forward as arms *E* reach the vertical position and close pins *L* over the ends of arms *E*, as shown in Fig. 11, so as to securely lock the arms upright. When the table of the machine moves away from the drills at the end of the operation, the different weights are returned to the positions shown in Fig. 10, and the various moving parts of the jig operate in the reverse manner to that described.

CHAPTER XVII

DESIGN OF UNIVERSAL DRILL JIGS

In the design of drill jigs, the main points to be considered by the designer are speed of operation, accuracy, tool cost, and interchangeability. These points are more or less opposed to one another; that is, if the designer stresses speed of operation, he may have to compromise on the other factors. In considering a design, the designer more or less subconsciously weighs the various factors against one another and decides upon a solution that seems to produce a happy medium. The solution, however, may be influenced to some extent by prevailing business conditions, shop facilities, etc. Granted that the factors are extremely variable, it is possible to so analyze them as to find a definite governing principle. A procedure may thus be established that will make it unnecessary to go over all the factors involved every time a drill jig is to be designed. Jigs designed according to such a procedure will be developed uniformly in conformance with an established tool policy, and in the long run, will make it possible to realize a substantial saving in costs.

The design of the top plates and adapters for so-called "universal" drill jigs is especially adapted to standardization. This chapter will deal with fundamentals. Concrete examples will be given in an effort to illustrate the points clearly.

It should be kept in mind that the design procedure suggested here may not apply in every line of manufacture. The main point is, however, that some design procedure *can* be established which will be best suited to a given line of manufacturing.

What Are Universal Drill Jigs?—There are a number of companies manufacturing universal drill jigs. The term

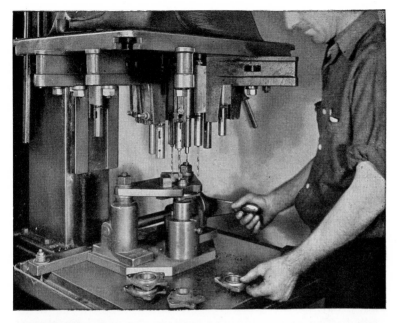

Fig. 1. Typical Designs of Universal Drill Jigs.

"universal" may be applied to any jig which is either adjustable, or adaptable to more than one drilling job. Some examples have previously been illustrated (see page 183). The commonly used type featured in this chapter is universal to the extent that the main body and operating mechanism can be used for a number of operations by changing the bushing plate (top plate) and adapter. Typical examples are shown in Fig. 1.

The construction of these universal jigs is quite simple. The top plate is secured to two vertical posts. These two posts are raised and lowered through a lever arm, the top plate maintaining a horizontal position at all times. The piece to be drilled is placed under the top plate, on the adapter, and the top plate is then lowered, clamping the work in position. After the drilling operation, the top plate is raised and the work removed, completing the cycle.

There is generally a locking device connected with the lever arm. This device maintains the clamping pressure and prevents the work from shaking loose while being drilled. The main difference between the various makes of universal jigs is in the construction of the locking device.

A typical top-plate blank is shown in Fig. 2. It consists simply of a steel plate with two holes drilled and reamed in it to accommodate the posts of the jig. Plates can be produced cheaply by flame-cutting them out of boiler plate and drilling the post holes in a simple drill jig. Fig. 3 shows a representative adapter blank. A commercial punch-holder —that is, the upper half of a postless die set—makes a satisfactory and inexpensive adapter blank.

The use of universal drill jigs can be justified because of the following advantages: (a) speed of operation; (b) interchangeability; (c) saving in tool cost; (d) saving in design cost; (e) saving in time-study cost. To further clarify these potential advantages, let us analyze each one.

Speed of Operation with Universal Drill Jigs.— Speed of operation is the greatest advantage of the universal drill jig. With a properly designed top plate and adapter, this type of jig is fast in operation because, first, it is operated by a simple motion of a lever handle. This eliminates the use of wrenches, C-washers, locking bars, and other work-securing devices that have to be handled.

Second, the operator goes through the same motions to drill any part. It is a well known fact that if an operator performs a highly repetitive operation day after day, he will involuntarily establish a smoothness of motion which results in increased efficiency. The universal drill jig makes it possible to drill a dissimilar line of parts as if they were all practically alike.

Third, the universal drill jig can be secured to the table of the drill press. This eliminates the necessity of positioning the jig relative to the drills for every drilling operation. In the case of single-purpose drill jigs, it is not possible to secure the drill jig to the drill table, because most jigs of that type have to be handled. The elimination of the need of positioning is particularly advantageous in multiple drilling, because it would be more difficult to position a number of bushings to the drills than it is to position just one.

An indirect advantage of securing the universal drill jig to the table is that the drills will enter the bushings practically without touching. This results in longer drill and bushing life. With single-purpose drill jigs, which must be positioned relative to the drills, there is almost invariably a noticeable chatter as the drills enter the bushings. This dulls the lips of the drill and subjects the bushing to severe wear.

Fourth, in ordinary shop practice where single-purpose drill jigs are used, it will be noted that most of the drill jigs have to be turned over for loading and unloading. The reason for this is that it is easier to turn the jig over, lay the work in the jig, and secure it in place than it would be to reach under the jig and have to hold the work in place while securing it. In the case of the universal drill jig, the work is always laid on the adapter and the bushing plate clamped down on the work. This eliminates the necessity of turning the drill jig over.

Fifth, in most instances, the top plate and the adapter of the universal jig can be so designed that it is unnecessary

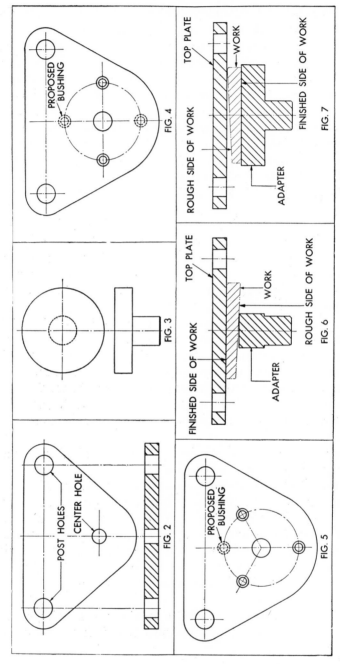

Figs. 2 to 7. Examples of Top-plates and Adapters for Universal Jigs.

to clean the chips from the locating surfaces. This important advantage can be realized without sacrificing accuracy. This is not generally true with single-purpose drill jigs. The ways and means of eliminating chip cleaning through proper design will be explained later in this article.

Interchangeability of Universal Drill Jigs.— The purpose of interchangeability in drill jigs is to maintain a minimum tool inventory. The most desirable condition is to have a line of tools that will operate at maximum efficiency, with a minimum investment. It should be kept in mind that this ideal is not always achieved by having a minimum number of jigs in stock. The smallest possible number of jigs to cover any given line may result in decreased efficiency of operation.

Interchangeability in universal drill jigs is obtained in three ways: First, the main body and operating mechanism can be used with a variety of top plates and adapters. It is generally less expensive to make a top plate and adapter for a universal jig than it is to make a single-purpose drill jig which will be *equivalent* to the universal jig in *speed of operation*.

Second, a top plate can be used for drilling more than one part by changing the work locators. In case the work locator must be made an integral part of the top plate, and therefore is not removable, the top plate can be turned over and the other side used. This turning over of the top plate is made possible by the use of headless drill bushings. The purpose of the head on the ordinary drill bushing is to prevent the drill from pushing the drill bushing through the bushing plate. In the universal jig, this is avoided by securing the drill jig to the drill-press table, so as to align the drills and bushings perfectly. This aspect of interchangeability can be best attained if the design is made with this objective in mind. Fig. 4 gives an idea of the range that can be covered by a top plate by simply changing work locators.

The third possibility of providing interchangeability in the top plate is in the addition of more bushings or in using only a few of the bushings in the plate. This phase of interchangeability can easily be overdone. There are disadvantages which may be incurred by having each plate perforated with bushings.

An analysis of the cost of making top plates will generally show that the greatest item of expense is the precision-boring of the holes to hold the drill bushings. The cost of the material for the top plate is a minor consideration. The ideal is to have the smallest number of precision-bored holes possible to cover any given line of parts without handicapping the efficiency of any one operation.

As an illustration, suppose there is a top plate in stock that has two holes bushed for a 3/8-inch drill, spaced 6 inches apart. A new top plate is required for four holes of the same size, equally spaced on a 6-inch bolt circle. In this case, one would add two holes to the plate and save the cost of precision-boring and bushing the other two holes. (See Fig. 4.)

In another case, we may save the boring of one hole. Suppose there is a top plate in stock which has three equally spaced bushings on a 6-inch bolt circle. A jig is required with two bushed holes of the same drill size, spaced 6 inches apart. One hole could be bored and the cost of boring and bushing the other saved. (See Fig. 5.) This clearly illustrates the possibility of interchangeability.

Tool and Design Costs Saved by Using Universal Drill Jigs.— Top plates for universal drill jigs are similar to a certain extent. Because of this similarity, an inexpensive drill jig and a boring fixture can be made which will greatly facilitate the producing of top plates. In this way, it is possible to tool up to make tools. Almost every manufacturing plant is continually producing new drill jigs. By using the tools suggested later in this article, the top plates can be made efficiently. This saving would not generally be possible in the case of single-purpose drill jigs.

The cost of designing top plates and adapters for universal drill jigs should not be so great as that of single-purpose jigs because of (1) standardization of design; (2) standardization of tool drawings; and (3) easy check on interchangeability.

Standardization of design has already been referred to. Standardization of tool drawings enables all superfluous details to be omitted in a tool drawing for universal drill jigs. This is possible because of the similarity of all top plates. The only details necessary are those of bushing size and location, and position of work locators.

The checking up of all existing single-purpose jigs before designing a new jig is a discouraging job. In the case of universal drill jigs, a master sheet showing the number of bushings, size, and spacing will make such checking a matter of only a few moments. A chart of this nature would not function for single-purpose drill jigs, because the mechanical construction of single-purpose jigs allows little interchangeability.

Savings in Time-Study Cost.— An indirect advantage of universal drill jigs is that there is a possible saving in time-study costs. In the time study of drilling operations, there are two main factors—handling time and drilling time. The actual drilling time in almost any case can be accurately calculated, knowing the size of the hole, depth, and the material to be drilled. It is the handling time on single-purpose tools, which cannot be accurately estimated, that necessitates individual time studies.

In the case of universal drill jigs, the operator goes through practically the same motions for almost any piece to be drilled, as previously stated. When universal drill jigs are used, it should be possible to set rates accurately, without individual time studies, by establishing a small chart of handling times and calculating the drilling time.

Where are Universal Drill Jigs Used to Best Advantage?— At first thought, one would be likely to discuss this point from the standpoint of single or multiple drilling, or interchangeability, or some similar phase of operation. The real answer is quite simple. The ratio between the drilling time and the handling time determines where universal drill jigs can be used to best advantage. In the operation of any drill jig, the actual drilling time is the same. The difference in operation between various types of jigs would be all in the material-handling time.

For example, suppose that, in a given line of manufacturing, small, short holes are being drilled in cast iron. If, by using universal drill jigs, 50 per cent of the handling time can be saved, it may be possible that 30 per cent of the total operation time will be saved, because the drilling time is a comparatively short element. The other extreme is where deep holes in tough material are being drilled. If, by using universal drill jigs, 50 per cent of the handling time can be saved, only 5 per cent, perhaps, of the total operation time will be saved, because in this case, the actual drilling consumes a greater amount of time, as compared with the total operation time.

As can be seen, the ratio between the handling time and the drilling time is the real issue. This does not mean that the use of universal drill jigs for drilling deep holes in hard materials cannot be justified. The main point is that the use of universal drill jigs for drilling short holes in soft materials pays greater dividends. The speed of handling is the greatest advantage of the universal drill jig, and it is entirely possible that the use of a universal drill jig as a single-purpose tool can be justified, if used for highly repetitive work.

Design Practice as Applied to Universal Jigs.—Before going into an explanation of design procedure, it is best to make clear just what factors of the universal jig are not subject to the judgment and decisions of the designer. The mechanical operating characteristics of the universal jig cannot be controlled by the designer. For example, (1) the drill bushings will always be in the top plate; (2) the work is always clamped between the top plate and the adapter through the medium of a lever arm; and (3) the fundamental motions that the operator will go through are already established.

In stating that the mechanical operating characteristics are out of the control of the designer, it should not be assumed that almost any design of top plate and adapter will operate satisfactorily. The few factors that are dependent on the decision of the designer will result in a pronounced effect in the operation of the jig. It should always be kept in mind that the inefficiency of a haphazard design of top plate and adapter will not be obvious until a really efficient design is produced to serve as a contrast.

Now as to the elements that the designer does control. The real issue confronting the designer is: "How shall the work be located?" On this one point hinges all the potential advantages of the universal jig. The method the designer selects to locate the work will affect speed of operation, interchangeability, and tool cost.

The Location of the Work in Universal Drill Jigs. — An analysis of the fundamentals of work location will show that there are three principal methods to be considered. They are: (1) establishment of a plane; (2) concentric location; (3) radial location. These terms are rather vague, and require explanation. Each presents a separate problem, and every designing job should be studied with this in mind.

Establishing the plane of the work means to clamp the work in the jig so that the finished face of the work will assume a true horizontal position. At first sight, one might think that any work clamped between the top plate and the adapter would be forced into a horizontal position. However, under certain conditions this is not true.

In order to illustrate this point, assume that there is a piece of work that has only one side surfaced, the machined side, therefore, not being truly parallel with the rough side. It is obvious that, with such a piece of work, both sides cannot assume a bearing in the jig. Unless certain precautions are taken, the drilled holes may not be perpendicular to the finished side of the work. If the holes drilled are to serve as clearance holes, this will probably not matter. However, if the drilled holes are to be tapped, any variation from the perpendicular would be objectionable.

In Fig. 6 is shown the method of establishing a true horizontal plane when the finished side of the work is up. An adapter of small area is used, very little pressure being required to insure the work coming "home" against the top plate. In Fig. 7 is shown the method of establishing a true horizontal position when the finished side of the work is down. An adapter of large area is used; as may be seen from the drawing, no amount of pressure would cause the work to bear fully against the top plate. A simple rule to remember is that, if the finished side of the work is up, a small-area adapter should be used; if the finished side of the work is down, a large area adapter should be used.

Locating Work Concentrically.—By "concentric location" is meant the securing of the work in the jig so that the center hole in the top plate is concentric with a circular edge of the work. This edge can be either internal or external. For example, if a round hole in the work is to serve as the locating means, some sort of machined plug must be provided in the universal jig which will enter the round hole of the work and thus provide a concentric location.

If an external cylindrical surface of the work is to serve as a locating means, some sort of machined surface must be provided in the jig which will fit over the outside of the work and thus provide a concentric location.

In concentric location of work, there are only four possible conditions that can occur: (1) concentric internal location from top plate; (2) concentric internal location from adapter; (3) concentric external location from top plate; and (4) concentric external location from adapter. Some form of concentric location will be required for the majority of work.

Examples are shown to suggest design procedure for each of the four cases of concentric location. A brief discussion will be given with each example. The simple parts used in these examples have no unnecessary details which might confuse the real issues involved.

When Chip Clearance is Required.— In the design examples to be shown, we will consider, for the sake of simplicity, that the work is of cast iron. In drilling cast iron, it is seldom necessary to maintain chip clearance between the drill bushings and the work. The bushing plate can be clamped directly against the face of the work. This, of course, forces the chips to come up through the drill bushings. Such a condition is not objectionable in drilling cast iron, because cast iron chips are a powder and will flow readily up the flutes of the drill. The chips will not ordinarily clog or pack and, therefore, the absence of chip clearance will not slow down the operation.

Another respect in which cast iron differs from other materials with regard to chip clearance is that other materials require coolants, whereas cast iron does not. With metals requiring a coolant for drilling, a liberal clearance between the drill bushings and the work allows the chips to escape from under the drill bushings and permits the coolant to flow freely through the drill bushing down to the cutting edges of the drill. In the design examples to be shown, if chip clearance is desired, it can easily be provided by machining a step on the concentric locator or inserting a bumper button into the top-plate center hole to provide space between the drill bushings and the work.

Case I—Concentric Internal Location from Top Plate.— In Fig. 8 is shown a part that requires the drilling of holes on a circle concentric with the finished bore machined in a previous operation. In Fig. 9 is shown a design of top plate and adapter for locating this work concentrically from the top plate. A hardened plug is provided for the top-plate center hole which enters the bored hole in the work.

Plane of Work: It is good practice to use this type of design only when the finished side of the work is in the "up" position. To establish the plane of work, a small-area adapter is used, as stated previously. The land on the locator plug must be quite small to prevent jamming in the work. Unless the locating plug enters all the way into the work, a true concentric position may not be established.

Chip Disposal: In the design shown, all the locating is done from the top plate. Gravity will tend to prevent chips from clinging to the locating surfaces. The dummy adapter is smaller than the bolt circle, and hence, the chips will fall clear of the adapter. In this particular case, chips on the adapter face cause no trouble, as they will affect neither the plane nor the concentricity of the work.

Locator Lead: In this type of design, as the operator cannot see the locating plug, it is necessary to provide ample "lead" on it. The length of the lead is not limited

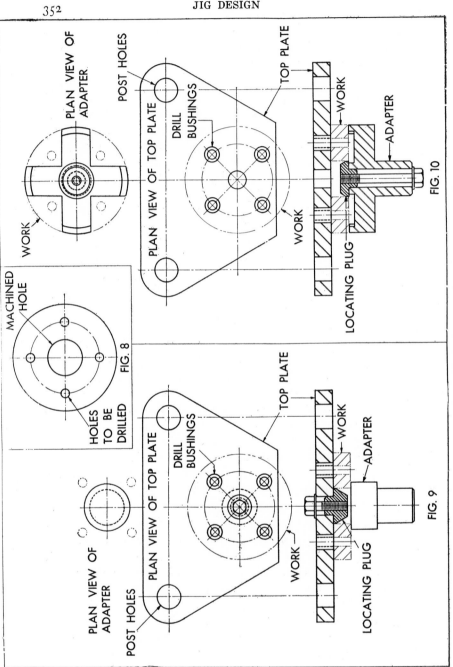

Figs. 8, 9 and 10. Methods of Locating Work in Universal Jigs.

by the thickness of the work; in the case of thin material, the dummy adapter can be counterbored to allow the locating plug to enter.

Interchangeability: This type of design allows the greatest possibilities for interchangeability. By simply removing the concentric locating plug, the top plate is left entirely free from encumbrance, so that the plate can be used for any other type of work which can be accommodated in the universal jig. This type of design also allows maximum interchangeability of the adapter. The adapter required can be a dummy, and might be considered part of the universal jig itself. This adapter need not be stored in the tool-crib with the top plate, but can be kept at the drilling station with the universal jig, as an auxiliary piece of equipment.

Case II — Concentric Internal Location from Adapter. — In Fig. 10 is shown a design of top plate and adapter for concentrically locating the work shown in Fig. 8 from the adapter.

Plane of Work: It is good practice to use this type of design only when the finished side of the work is in the "down" position. A large-area adapter is used to insure the establishment of the plane on the adapter face.

Chip Disposal: Since the adapter is below the drill bushings, it is in the path of the falling chips. There are several things that can be done to help solve the problem of chip disposal: (1) the locating plug support can be made of a smaller diameter than the plug, so that a corner is not formed where chips will gather; (2) the adapter can be cut away below the bushings, so that the chips will fall clear; and (3) the contact edges of the adapter can be made with a small total area. This will minimize the possibility of stray chips gathering on this surface.

Locator Lead: In this type of design, the operator can see the concentric locator when the jig is in the open position. It is only necessary for him to place the work so that the locating plug enters the hole in the work. The closing of the jig will force the work into a true concentric position. It is a disadvantage to have too long a lead on the plug, as the work must be slipped over the locator.

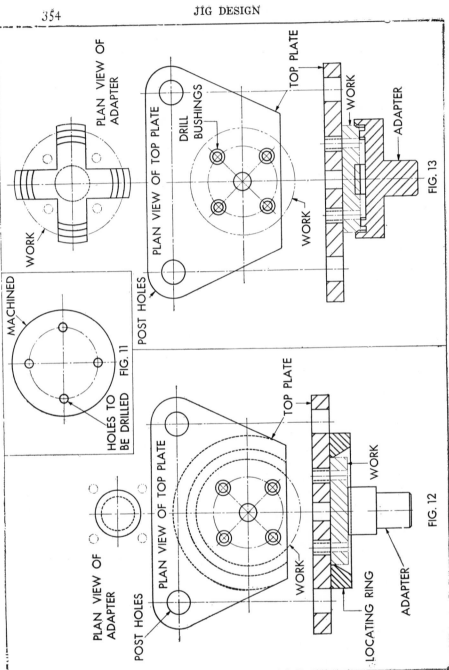

Figs. 11, 12 and 13. Methods of Locating Work.

Interchangeability: In this type of design, the top plate is entirely free from encumbrances, and consequently has the greatest possible degree of interchangeability. The adapter is interchangeable to the extent that the locating plug can be changed to suit any other diameter of hole. It is more advantageous to decrease the interchangeability of the adapter than to interfere with the efficiency of the top plate.

Case III—Concentric External Location from Top Plate.— In Fig. 11 is shown a part that will require the drilling of holes concentric with the finished outside of the work. In Fig. 12 is shown a design of top plate and adapter for locating this work from the top plate. The concentric locator is a ring machined on the inside to fit over the outside of the work. This ring is screwed and doweled to the top plate and becomes an integral part of it.

Plane of Work: It is advisable to use this type of design only when the finished side of the work is in an "up" position, with a small face area adapter. Unless the work comes "home" against the top plate, it will not be in a true horizontal or concentric position.

Chip Disposal: Since the work is located from the top plate, the chips will fall free of the locator.

Locator Lead: In this type of design, the operator cannot see the locating ring, so an ample lead must be provided on the locator. The length of the lead on the locator is not limited by the thickness of the work, as the locator can be allowed to overhang, as shown in the illustration.

Interchangeability: The interchangeability of the top plate is limited, because the locating ring is really an integral part of it; but the top plate can be turned over and the other side used, which is entirely free from encumbrances. The adapter used in this case is a simple dummy adapter.

Case IV—Concentric External Location from Adapter.— In Fig. 13 is shown a design of top plate and adapter for locating the work in Fig. 11 from the adapter. As shown in the illustration, the adapter is machined to fit over the outside of the work.

Plane of Work: This type of design should be used only when the finished side of the work is in a "down" position. Unless the work comes home against the face of the adapter, the work will be in a tilted position and also will not be concentric with the bushings.

Chip Disposal: Precautions must be taken to provide for chip disposal, because the locators are below the drill bushings and consequently in line with the falling chips. Should any chips settle on the locating surfaces of the adapter, they will affect both the plane and the concentricity of the work. As shown in the illustration, the adapter can be cut away below the drill bushings to allow the chips to fall clear. A trough should be cut between the edge used for concentric locating and the surface used for horizontal support of the work. The cutting of this trough will eliminate a corner where chips can settle. The total area of the horizontal supports should be kept to a minimum, to reduce the possibility of chip trouble.

Locator Lead: In this type of design, the operator places the work in exact position before closing the jig. A lead is provided on the sides of the concentric location face; this need not be very long. The relative amount of lead shown in the illustration will be found satisfactory.

Interchangeability: In the design being considered, the top plate retains its property of interchangeability; but the adapter is, in reality, a single-purpose tool, and has practically no possibility of interchangeability. Since the adapter cost is only a fraction of the top plate cost, it is good practice to limit the interchangeability of the adapter rather than that of the top plate.

From the examples shown, some conclusions can be drawn. However, these are, in no sense of the word, hard and fast rules. The three following rules should serve as a starting point in design procedure, and should only be used when they seem to suit the peculiarity of the work. (1) Concentric location should be from the member used to establish the horizontal plane; (2) concentric internal location should be from the top plate, where possible; (3) concentric external location should be from the adapter, where possible.

The use of these three simple rules should produce a line of tools that are most practical from the standpoint of speed of operation, accuracy of work, interchangeability, and tool cost.

In the various designs shown, it will be noted that in every case the work projects in front of the top plate. (See plan views.) This enables the operator to grasp the work and eliminates the possibility of pinching his fingers in the jig. It also greatly facilitates the operation of the jig. In the cases where the concentric location is from the top plate, projection of the work is necessary, as there is a tendency for the work to cling to the concentric locator. Unless the work projects in front of the top plate, the operator is forced to reach up under the top plate and pry the work loose.

There are occasional jobs that have both an internal and an external finished surface, thus giving the tool designer a choice for using either in concentric locating. It will be found that locating the work internally will generally produce the best results.

Radial Location in Universal Jigs.—By radial location is meant the position of the work in the horizontal plane with relation to the drill bushings. In drilling work that is entirely concentric, the radial location is, of course, immaterial. However, in drilling work that is not entirely concentric, the relation of the contour of the work and the drill bushings must be established. An example of work that is not entirely concentric is shown in Fig. 14. It is more difficult to get accurate radial location than concentric location of holes. The reason for this is that the finished hole in the work used for concentric location will vary with relation to the contour of the work because (1) the casting itself will vary; and (2) there will be a certain amount of chucking variation in the machining of the work.

Since radial locators must not bind the work on the concentric locator, the radial locators must provide a minimum clearance over the maximum casting and chucking variation. In the radial location of work, there are only two fundamental methods that can be used: (1) The radial loca-

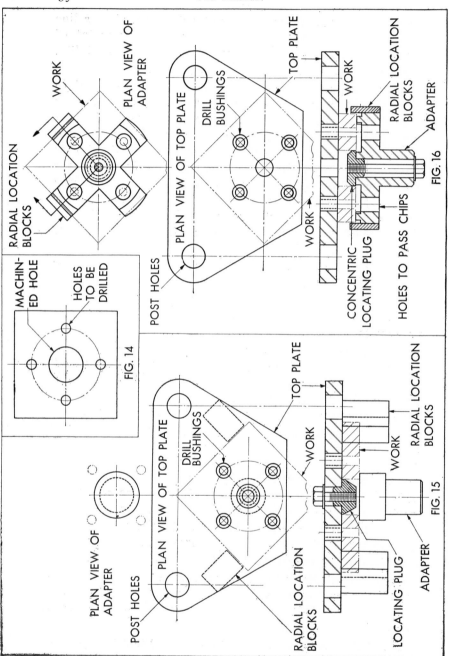

Figs. 14, 15 and 16.   Methods of Locating Work.

tion will be accomplished from the top plate; or (2) it will be done from the adapter. Examples are given to illustrate both methods of radial location.

Radial Location from Top Plate.— In Fig. 15 is shown a design of top plate and adapter to locate the work in Fig. 14 from the top plate. The work is located concentrically by a plug in the top plate center hole. The radial locating is done by screwing and doweling blocks of steel to the top plate. Clearance must be provided between the locating blocks and the work, as already explained. It will be noted that the radial locators extend an appreciable distance below the top plate. They should be made long enough so that the work can contact the locators when the top plate is in an "up" position. In this way, they help to locate the work when it is placed in the jig. At first glance, this may hardly seem necessary, but in operation, it will be found a great convenience. Since the radial location blocks are secured to the top plate, there is no problem as to chip disposal. Radial location from the top plate will reduce interchangeability, because the blocks are an integral part of the top plate. Interchangeability is practically limited to turning the top plate over and using the other side.

Radial Location from the Adapter.—In Fig. 16 is shown a design of top plate and adapter for locating the same work from the adapter. The work is located concentrically by a plug locator. Blocks of steel secured to the ends of the adapter arms locate the work radially. Suitable clearance should be provided between the radial locators and the work. The radial locators should not be higher than the thickness of the work, as this would prevent the top plate from clamping the work in place. A trough should be cut at the end of the adapter arms, so that there will be no corner into which chips can gather.

This type of design leaves the top plate free of any encumbrances so that there is perfect interchangeability of the top plate; but the adapter is essentially a single-purpose tool, with little possibility of interchangeability, obviously the lesser of two evils.

From the two examples shown, the conclusion can be

drawn that it is best practice, for radial location, to locate from the adapter, principally because of the fact that this results in greater interchangeability for the top plate. It should be kept in mind that the radial locating need not be done from the same member as the concentric locating; for example, the concentric locating can be done from the top plate and the radial locating blocks may be secured to the adapter.

Another method of radial location, which is sometimes necessary due to extreme casting and chucking variation, is to use spring-actuated movable blocks. In addition to the increased initial cost, the disadvantage of spring-actuated blocks is that they have a tendency to jam the work on the concentric locator.

Coolant Reservoir.—When a coolant is to be used during a single-spindle drilling operation, it is satisfactory to direct the coolant nozzle against the drill body. However, in the case of a multiple-drilling operation, a coolant nozzle for each drill would make a rather awkward set-up.

A more satisfactory method of directing the coolant is to provide a ring, flame-cut from 1/2-inch boiler plate. The inside diameter of this ring should be large enough to encompass all the drills in the set-up. If this boiler-plate ring is laid on top of the top plate, it forms a reservoir which will feed all the drill bushings. The coolant fluid can be poured into the reservoir with just one coolant nozzle.

The coolant ring should not be screwed to the top plate, because this would interfere with the interchangeability of the plate. Another disadvantage of securing the coolant ring to the top plate is that this would make it rather difficult to remove chips from the coolant ring. If the coolant ring is not fastened to the top plate, the chips can be swept off the jig by occasionally sliding the coolant ring. (Note that headless drill bushings were suggested earlier in this chapter.)

The coolant ring described is not intended to be a single-purpose tool, but rather a universal auxiliary piece of equipment to be kept at the drilling station.

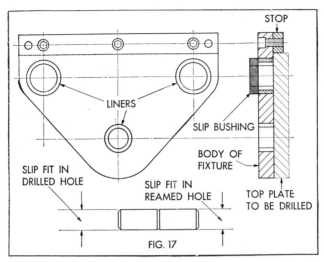

Fig. 17. Jig for Drilling Post Holes and Center
Indicating Hole in Top-plate Blanks.

Tools for Making Top Plates.—All top plates have many
points in common. It is possible to take advantage of this
similarity by making simple tools which will greatly facilitate the manufacture of top plates. The drill plate and boring fixture to be described have been designed primarily to
facilitate the making of individual top plates and to shorten
the set-up time required in carrying through this work.
Because of the simplicity of the plate and fixture, the initial
cost of these tools should be justified, even though they will
be used only occasionally.

It will be noted that all the top plates have one outstand-
ing point of similarity. They all require the boring of two
holes to fit over the posts of the universal jig, and the boring of a third hole which will serve as a center for locating
the drill bushings. A top plate with these three holes bored
is shown in Fig. 2. These holes must be accurate as to size
and relation to one another.

Simple Drill Plate.—A simple plate jig is shown in Fig. 17
for drilling and reaming these three holes. The drill plate
should be equipped with liners and two sets of bushings, so
that both the drilling and reaming operations can be done

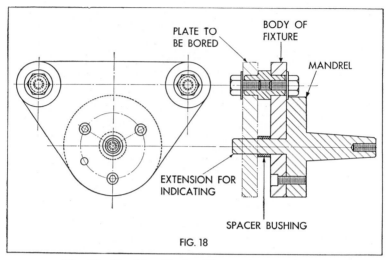

FIG. 18

Fig. 18. Precision Boring Fixture for Top Plates.

through bushings. The illustration also shows one of the pins that should be provided for slipping through the bushings and the work to prevent the drill plate from shifting during the drilling and reaming operations.

Dividing-Head Fixture.—An analysis of the cost of producing small drill jigs will generally show that the greatest item of cost is in the precision-boring of the holes for the drill bushings. In conventional shop practice, such holes are most efficiently bored in a jig-boring machine; but the average manufacturer does not have the large volume of tool work necessary to justify the purchase of such equipment. However, the accurate boring and positioning of bushing holes can be efficiently done in a milling machine by taking advantage of the fact that the dividing head can be indexed very accurately. If a top plate were mounted in the dividing head so that the center hole of the top plate coincided with the center line of the dividing head, it can be easily seen that by indexing the dividing head, the top plate could be positioned, relative to the boring tool, so as to produce holes accurately spaced on any desired bolt circle. The table of the milling machine would remain in a fixed position throughout the entire operation.

Fig. 19. Milling Machine Set-up for Precision-boring of Bushing Holes.

A very simple top-plate holding fixture can be made for the dividing head that will make it possible to secure the top plate quickly and accurately to the dividing head, so that the center hole in the top plate and the center line of the head will coincide. Such a fixture is shown in Fig. 18. One end of a steel mandrel is machined to fit the tapered hole in the dividing head. The other end is machined for a snug fit in the drilled and reamed center hole of the top plate. The mandrel is then secured to the body of the fixture with socket-head cap-screws and a dowel. The three holes required in the body are drilled and reamed with the plate jig previously described, thus eliminating an expensive precision boring operation. Two machine steel plugs are provided to fit the corner holes of the fixture body. These plugs act as spacers and also serve to secure the top plate to the fixture body.

In order to produce a complete top plate, the following procedure is suggested: (1) The top-plate blank is drilled and reamed with the plate jig to provide the two post holes and the center hole; (2) the top plate is blued and the proposed bushing holes laid out and scribed; (3) holes are drilled through the top plate in the proper position for the bushings, using a drill size considerably smaller than the full size of the bushing holes; (4) the top plate is mounted in the dividing head, using the top-plate holding fixture; (5) a fly cutter is inserted in the spindle of the milling machine and positioned in relation to one of the proposed bushing holes; (6) a light trial cut through the top plate is taken; a plug is wrung into the hole bored; a micrometer measurement is taken across the plug and shaft extension of the fixture mandrel. Then the table is repositioned so that the exact radius desired is established. When the radius is once established, the table is locked in place and the set-up is complete. The proposed bushing holes can then be accurately positioned in relation to the fly cutter by indexing the dividing head.

A typical boring set-up, using the work-holding fixture, is shown in Fig. 19. The operator is shown measuring across the bushings which have been wrung into the bored holes.

CHAPTER XVIII

PLASTIC JIGS AND THEIR APPLICATION

Plastic materials are now being used to expedite the production of drill jigs, routing forms and templets employed in airplane manufacture. This patented development (originated by engineers of one of the large airplane manufacturers) has made it possible to reduce greatly the production time for certain jigs, forms, etc.

Advantages of Plastic Jigs.—In the airplane plants where the use of plastic jigs and other plastic tools was developed, many such tools are now employed. Some of these tools required as much as 38 gallons of plastic material and in finished form weighed as much as 380 pounds. These heavy plastic tools are forms for use in sheet-metal stretching operations and they replaced zinc-alloy forms. Plastic tools are light in weight, and so they can be handled more conveniently than metal or wooden jigs. Zinc forms or dies, for example, weigh seven times as much as similar tools made of plastic. If a plastic jig or form should be broken accidentally, it can be replaced with little loss of time and with negligible cost. The plastic materials can be ground up as tools become obsolete and used over and over again.

Production of Plastic Drill Jigs.—The application of plastic materials for jigs, etc., resulted from an investigation conducted to find a substitute for the wooden drill jigs that are in wide use throughout the aircraft industry. The Basolo patent for plastic tools is based on the production of plastic jigs by employing a master part (an actual piece of work) to which drill bushings are secured wherever holes have been drilled. This master part is placed in a wooden form and the plastic material is poured into the cavity. When the plastic material has solidified in conformity to the contour of the part, either by natural or by artificial means such as baking, the bolts which hold the bushings in position on the master part are removed. The jig is then practically ready for use.

The simplicity of this method of drill jig production will be apparent from the diagrams in Fig. 1, which show a mold constructed of wood and the duralumin stamping for

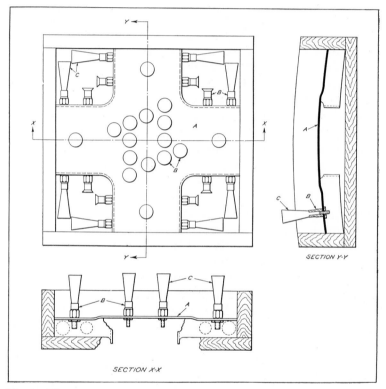

Fig. 1. Diagram Showing the Construction of a Mold for Casting a Drill Plate with the Drill Bushings Fastened to the Work-piece.

which the jig is intended. The piece of work *A* will form the bottom of the drill plate that is to be cast, with the drill bushings accurately held in their required locations. The opposite side of the work-piece will form the cavity in the nest block of the jig. It will be seen that the drill bushings *B* are fastened to the work-piece by means of special

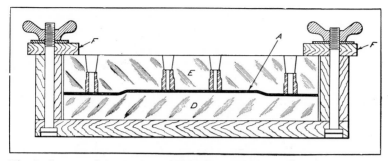

Fig. 2. Construction of a Simple Drill Jig, in which the Plastic Nest Block and Drill Plate are Assembled in a Wooden Box.

screw plugs C, which can readily be withdrawn through the plastic drill plate after the plastic material has solidified. The mold was built up with thirty-two bushings.

The construction of the complete jig is shown in Fig. 2 which is a cross-section. The jig consists of a wooden box in which the plastic nest block D, which was also poured in the mold shown in Fig. 1, is permanently secured. Drill plate E is removed for loading successive pieces of work A. The drill plate is clamped on top by means of wood blocks F, which are fastened through the use of bolts and wing-nuts.

An alternate method from that shown in Fig. 1 of fastening drill bushings to the piece of work in casting the plastic mold, is to use a loose tapered plug on top of the drill bushing and attach it to the bushing by means of a flat-head bolt. The bolt is used with the head on the bottom or inner side of the bushing and the nut is on top of the tapered plug.

Another method of casting drill jigs differs substantially in that the bushings are never cast directly in the plastic. The practice is to cast the bushing plate blank and then drill holes in the bushing plate in the correct locations as determined from the work-piece, locate the drill bushings accurately in these holes, and then set them in Cerromatrix. In pouring Cerromatrix, the user must make certain that it is not too hot or it will expand and crack the plastic. A temperature of approximately 300 degrees F. is the proper one for pouring operations.

In making a plastic tool, the greatest saving in time is

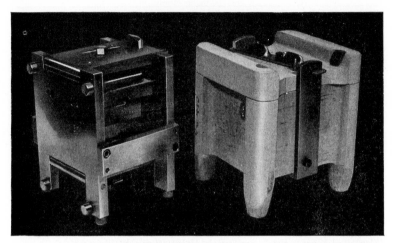

Fig. 3. Plastic Drill Jig, at the Right, and the Steel Jig, at the left,
which it has Replaced.

due to the fact that an actual piece of work, as it comes
from the drop-hammer or hydraulic press, can be used as
part of the mold to form the depression in the plastic material in which the piece of work will be seated when the
tool is placed in use.

Examples of Plastic Jig Construction.— At the left in
Fig. 3 is shown a jig of steel construction which took ninety
hours to make in the tool-room, and at the right, a plastic
jig that replaced the steel jig. The total time involved in
making the necessary mold, pouring the plastic material,
and baking the plastic required only two days. One of the
incidental advantages of this jig, in addition to economy
and speed of production, is that it can be loaded in half the
time that was required with the steel jig.

In Fig. 4 is shown a combination drill jig and routing
templet that is used in the performance of operations on
formed angles for supercharger pans, such as seen above
and below the jig. The drill bushings were assembled in
Cerromatrix in "overpressed" sheet-metal templets which
were made over pieces of work in hydro-press dies. These
sheet-metal templets were drilled to diameters larger than
the normal holes, so as to enable larger bushings of Cer-

romatrix to be cast around the drill bushings for holding them securely in place. The construction of this combined drill jig and routing templet consists of a large plastic form mounted on wood built up in sections to the required shape.

Experiments with Different Materials.— Before the selection of a plastic material suitable for the production of drill jigs, experiments were conducted with plaster and some of

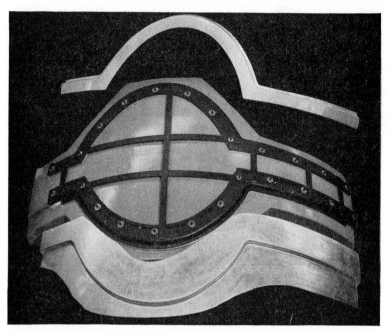

Fig. 4. Combination Drill Jig and Routing Templet in which the Drill Bushings are Held in Metal Strips Mounted on a Plastic Form of the Required Contour.

the white metals of low melting point. It was finally concluded that the ideal material for this process would be a plastic that could be poured at between 225 and 325 degrees F. and which would have a minimum softening point of 200 degrees F. These requirements make it possible to pour a plastic jig or other plastic tool in an aluminum-alloy part without damage to the latter and insure that the plastic material will not soften due to the heat generated in drilling or other operations. This is one method; the other is to use a plastic composition that is poured cold and then baked.

Other desirable characteristics which have been found attainable were that the plastic materials to be used for this purpose should be easily reclaimable, that it should be possible to machine the plastic tools with woodworking tools, that the plastic materials should have sufficient impact strength to withstand ordinary shop handling, that they should not become brittle at low temperatures or after aging, and that they should be resistant to oil and metal chips.

The result of the investigation was the adoption of (1) a thermoplastic phenol-acetone resin and (2) an acid-setting phenol formaldehyde. The phenol acetone is used without a filler and has an ultimate compressive strength of 6000 pounds per square inch. It is fairly tough and with the addition of 1/2 per cent Maracaibo wax shows satisfactory resistance to soluble oil. Walnut shell flour, fine maple wood, and ground Masonite are used as a filler with the phenol formaldehyde resin. This material has an ultimate compressive strength of over 8000 pounds per square inch and, therefore, can be satisfactorily applied in deep drawing operations on hydro-presses. It is resistant to soluble oil without any special treatment. It is, however, fairly brittle.

At first Maracaibo wax to the extent of 3 per cent was used in making the phenol-acetone material resistant to oil, but undesirable aging soon became apparent. The aging, however, appeared to be due to crystallization of the excess Maracaibo wax and so the problem was solved by reducing the quantity of wax used for oil resisting purposes. This has not adversely affected the resistance of plastic drill jigs to soluble oil.

The phenol-acetone plastic was developed for aircraft tooling. It is a phenol-ketone condensation product, which means that phenol and acetone react in the presence of an acid catalyst under heat and pressure to polymerize into a fusible thermoplastic resin that will remain thermoplastic regardless of the temperatures to which it is submitted. For use in aircraft tooling applications the plastic is modified with certain compounds of plasticizers and waxes to give the desired properties.

This composition has a cold flow point of 170 degrees F. if held for two hours at that temperature and, therefore, a shop temperature of 100 degrees F. has no tendency to make the material cold-flow. A desirable property of the material is very low heat conductivity.

The advantage of the cast phenolic resin is that it is a thermosetting compound with an acid catalyst or accelerator which hastens the reaction in polymerization. This means that the liquid resin is inhibited with an amount of acid which, through the application of heat, will set it up within approximately two hours. The less acid that is used to set up a resin, the less crystalline formation there will be in the finished product and therefore the stronger the plastic tool.

If the baking process is performed at a temperature of approximately 175 degrees F., it is possible to use a resin with less acid and obtain relatively less crystalline structure in the finished product. From 25 to 30 per cent filler material is mixed in the resin, which materially reduces the tool costs.

Plastic tools are broken readily if dropped. For this reason some of the plastic tools, such as routing blocks, are mounted on Masonite sheets. Such bases can be applied to the plastic form by using the same resin, but with additional acid supplied to quicken the reaction.

Regardless of whether the mold is constructed of wood, plaster, or metal, it should be sprayed with lacquer to protect it from the acid used in the resin. Likewise, all metal inserts in the mold, such as bushings or pins, should be lacquer sprayed. If sanding is necessary after a plastic tool has been made, the sanded sections should also be sprayed. There is a plastic lacquer available for this purpose which has a high tensile strength and which will not scratch under normal usage. If Barbary wax is later applied on the lacquer, a hard high-gloss finish is obtained, which will stand compressive loads and light oils can be used as lubricants in the drawing operations.

CHAPTER XIX

SPECIAL LOCATING AND CLAMPING ARRANGEMENTS

In the design of jig and fixtures it may happen that the size or shape of the work-piece makes it difficult, if not impossible, to locate or clamp it securely in place using "conventional arrangements." Such cases, and those involving accurate location of the fixture itself, may require the designer either to originate a new type of jig or fixture or to improvise on an existing one. The jigs and fixtures described in this chapter illustrate some of the methods that have been used by designers to overcome difficulties in locating and clamping work-pieces and fixtures, and may be used as a guide in the design of similar jigs and fixtures.

Self-Centralizing Devices for Jigs. — Automatic self-centralizing provisions whereby the work-piece can be accurately located with relation to the drill guide bushing are generally required when drilling flat plates and covers, which are not usually machined at the sides but have to be gripped or located in a jig from their rough cast edges. Similarly, such self-centralizing features will be found advantageous, time-saving, and economical in drilling parts having a similar shape, but whose over-all dimensions differ.

One of the simplest forms of self-centralizing drill jigs is shown in Fig. 1. This jig contains a rectangular cast-iron body *A,* which is flanged at the bottom for hold-down purposes. A swinging arm *B* is pivoted on a pin *C* that is pressed into both side walls of a slotted boss on top of the body. Arm *B* carries the drill bushing *D.*

Pressed into the under side of the arm, each side of the bushing, are two bearing pads *E.* When the arm is in the horizontal position, as shown, these pads will press equally on the work-piece *X,* holding it firmly to the top of the jig body. The right-hand end of arm

B has an open-end slot for the cylindrical shank of clamping stud F. A knurled nut G, threaded on the upper end of this stud, enables the arm to be clamped to the work. The stud can be swung about a pivot pin H pressed into the body.

The centralizing action on the work-piece is obtained from identically shaped spring-loaded slides J, which are mounted in a guide hole K drilled completely through the body. Springs L are held in pockets in these slides by stop-plates M, which are fastened to the sides of the jig body by screws. Each slide has a vertical projection at the inner end, with the hardened end faces of these projections inclined at an angle of approximately 10 degrees. The projections slide in slots which extend from the top edge of the jig body into

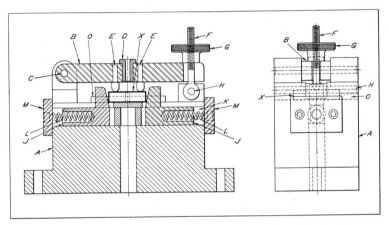

Fig. 1. Centralization of the Work-piece in this Drill Jig is Obtained from Spring-loaded Slides (J) Mounted in Guide Hole (K).

the bearing holes K. The springs force the slides inward, toward each other, and the extent of this movement is limited by either the end faces of the slots or the work-piece, as shown.

A large-diameter vertical hole extends down through the body, directly below the hole to be drilled in the work-piece, for chips to fall out of the jig. A short cylindrical plug, cross-drilled as shown, is tightly pressed into hole K to lie midway between slides J. This plug prevents chips from entering the hole K.

To mount a work-piece in the jig, arm B is swung upward. The two opposed slides J will be in their innermost positions, in contact with the end faces of the slots, and the work-piece is placed between the inclined faces of the slides. Transverse location of the work-piece is obtained by abutting it against a plate O fastened to the top face of the jig body. Arm B is then lowered into the horizontal position, and clamping stud F is swung into its vertical position, as shown. As nut G is tightened, pads E bear down on the work-piece and press it into contact with the top of the jig body. This action will cause the slides to move apart an equal amount, and the work-piece X will become located centrally with relation to bushing D. Parts differing considerably in width can be accommodated without difficulty in such a jig, because the slides can be arranged with an appreciable amount of opening and closing. Also, the jig may easily be adapted to increase these facilities merely by altering the angle of taper on the slides.

A rather unusual yet simple self-centralizing jig, which may be successfully employed in drilling parts having considerable variation in width or length, is seen in Fig. 2. The construction of this jig permits a more accurate location of the work-piece than is possible with the design illustrated in Fig. 1. As with the jig previously described, a swinging arm B is pivoted on a pin C which is pressed into jig body A. A drill bushing D is carried in the arm, and located on each side of this bushing are the identical bearing pads E. The right-hand end of arm B is slotted to admit clamping stud F, which is fitted with a knurled nut G and pivoted on pin H.

The bellcrank locating and clamping levers J are a sliding fit within a narrow slot in the jig body, and pivoted on pins K pressed into the body. Permanently fitted into a transverse slot in the body is a platform L for supporting the work-piece X. Vertical clearance holes are provided in this platform and in the jig body for the chips to fall through.

The upper inner edges of levers J, which contact the sides of the work-piece, are rounded and hardened, and can be serrated to provide a better grip. The lower ends of the levers are reduced to half their total thickness so that they overlap, and the left-hand lever is slotted to fit over a pin M pressed into the tail of the right-hand lever. When the lower halves of the levers are in a horizontal position, the center of pin M is aligned with the vertical center lines of the jig body and drill bushing. This arrangement insures that the levers will be swiveled equally.

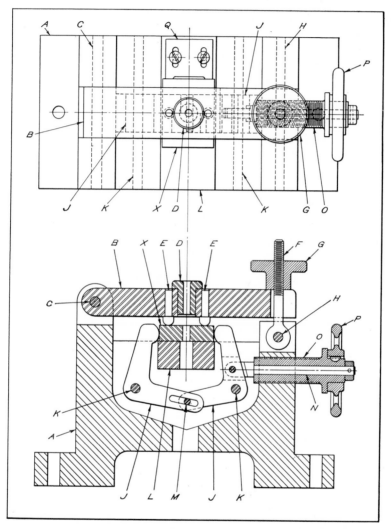

Fig. 2. Bellcrank Locating and Clamping Levers (J) are Actuated by Rod (N) when Handwheel (P) is Rotated, thus Centralizing Work-piece (X).

Actuation of the levers is obtained by means of rod N, the slotted shackle end of which is pinned to the right-hand lever. The cylindrical shank of rod N is a running fit within an externally threaded sleeve O which is screwed into the right-hand wall of body A. When handwheel P is rotated, levers J will be swiveled, due to the force of sleeve O, against the shoulder on rod N or the collar pinned to the rod.

The manner of loading and using this jig is similar to the one previously described. With arm B raised, work-piece X is placed on platform L. The contact surfaces of levers J will have been moved apart by rotating handwheel P. Transverse location of the work-piece is obtained by abutting it against an adjustably mounted stop-plate Q. The handwheel is then rotated in the opposite direction until the work is firmly gripped and centralized by the contact surfaces of the levers. Arm B is then returned to the horizontal position shown, and clamped by tightening nut G. Additional clamping pressure is thus exerted on the work by pads E.

Another type of self-centralizing jig that has been proved economical and accurate in drilling uniformly central holes through thin cover plates and similar parts having variations in width is seen in Fig. 3. In this jig, a swinging arm B is again pivoted on a pin C which is pressed into the jig body A. The arm carries a drill bushing D, and its right-hand end is slotted for a ring-head clamping bolt E that carries nut F and is pivoted on pin G.

A spring-loaded cylindrical plug H is a sliding fit in the vertical bore of the jig body. Rotation of the plug is prevented by a key N. The lower threaded end of the plug is screwed through a handwheel K which is carried in a horizontal slot in the jig body. The upper head of the plug, on which the work-piece X rests, has two diametrically opposite slots into which are fitted the triangular-shaped locator pads J. These pads pivot on pins L pressed into the side walls of the slots. The lower, outer corner of each locator pad rests on the tapered bottom surfaces of slots cut in the side walls of the jig body.

In operation, arm B is raised, and a work-piece is placed on top of plug H, being located against a fixed pin or plate, not shown. Then, by turning handwheel K, plug H is drawn downward — against the action of spring M — and pads J are pivoted toward each other, thus centralizing and gripping the work-piece. Arm B

is then lowered into the horizontal position shown and clamped by tightening nut F.

Wear can be minimized in this jig by screwing a hardened head set-screw into the tapered bottom surfaces of the slots cut in the side walls of the jig body. The rounded contact points of pads J would then bear on the hardened heads, and slight adjustments could be made by tightening or lossening the set-screws.

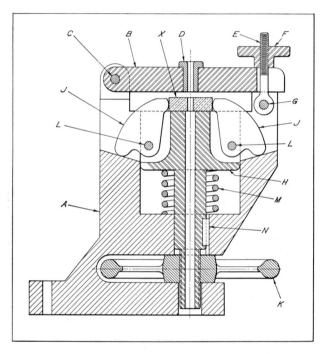

Fig. 3. In this Drill Jig, Work-piece (**X**) is Centralized by Locator pads (**J**), which are Pivoted about pins (**L**) when Handwheel (**K**) is Turned.

Another effective method of obtaining centralization of the work is illustrated in the drill jig seen in Fig. 4. Secured to the top, near the rear edge of jig body A, is a slotted bracket B. A swinging arm C, pivoted about a pin pressed into the uprights of bracket B, carries drill bushing D. The forward end of this arm is slotted to admit the shank of a ring-head clamping bolt E that carries a knurled clamping nut F. The ring head of the clamping bolt is a close fit in

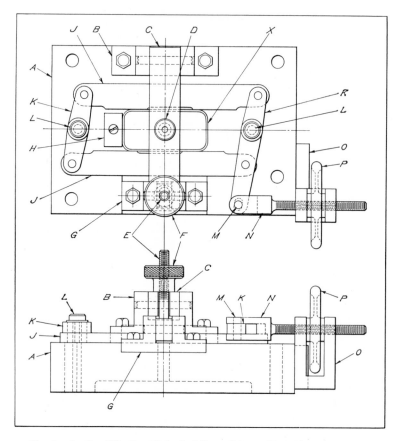

Fig. 4.   Another Effective Method of Centralizing a Work-piece Makes Use
of a Pantograph Mechanism — Bars (J) and Levers (K).

a slot on a bracket G secured to the front of the body, and pivots
about a pin pressed into the uprights of this bracket.

Work-piece X is placed on the top surface of jig body A, bearing
against a stop-plate H secured to the body for lengthwise location.
The part is centralized transversely and gripped by means of two
bars J which rest on the smooth top surface of the jig body. The
inner contacting surfaces of these bars are relieved slightly to reduce the frictional pressure on the work-piece. The ends of both
bars are pinned to levers K, thus forming a pantograph mechanism.
Levers K can be pivoted about the two headed studs L.

The front end of the extended right-hand lever K has an elongated slot to fit around a pin M pressed into the slotted end of rod N. The threaded shank of rod N passes through plain holes in both walls of a slotted bracket O secured to the right-hand edge of the jig body, and is screwed in the internally threaded handwheel P. Thus, when the handwheel is rotated, the pantograph lever system is swiveled about studs L — moving bars J either together to clamp the work or apart to permit loading and unloading. Arm C is handled the same as the arms on the jigs previously described, being swung upward while unloading and reloading, and down into the position shown when the work-piece is in place.

Simple Clamp for Accurately Locating Fixtures on a Machine Table. — In using tongues, T-nuts, or T-bolts, clearance must be provided between their faces and the surfaces of the T-slot in the machine table, so that the fixture can be slid along the table readily. This initial clearance becomes greater with repeated use of the fixture, due to wear. Setting-up difficulties or errors in the finish-machined parts often result from variations in the clearance of individual nuts or bolts and the consequent difference in the settings of respective fixtures.

By means of the simple clamp shown in Fig. 5, setting-up time can be appreciably reduced and closer accuracies maintained. In clamping with two or more of such devices, the fixture will always be drawn against one side of the T-slot, regardless of the amount of clearance. Thus, every fixture will be correctly aligned with other fixtures on the same table, as each one is located from the same side of the T-slot. Wear will be reduced to a minimum, affording prolonged accuracy, with ease of operation.

The construction of the clamping device is as follows: Fitting into the conventional T-slot in the machine table is a hardened and tempered cast-steel locating T-block. The T-block is of rectangular cross-section, as shown in the view at the lower left, with one edge of its tongue machined to provide a flat positioning ledge. The polished face of the ledge is inclined at an angle of 60 degrees from the horizontal plane. The block should be a snug sliding fit within the T-slot, clearance being kept as small as possible. A standard square-headed clamping bolt is inserted through a hole in the center of the T-block, with the head of the bolt fitting closely into a slot machined across the under side of the T-block.

A cylindrical cam-sleeve, which is a sliding fit in a hole bored through the lug of the fixture, is drilled to provide a clearance of at least $\frac{1}{32}$ inch for the clamping bolt. Two flats are machined on the lower end of this sleeve, the flat on the left being machined so that it will be in vertical alignment with the left-hand edge of the T-block. The lower portion of the flat on the opposite side of the

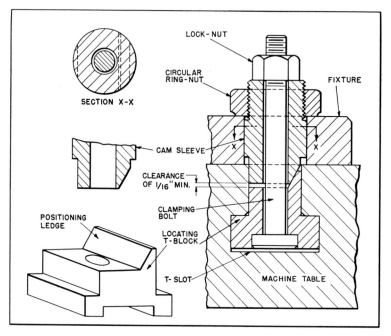

Fig. 5. Simple Clamp for Reducing Set-up Time and Insuring Accurate Alignment when Several Fixtures are to be Clamped on One Machine Table.

sleeve is inclined at an angle of 60 degrees, as shown, to mate with the positioning ledge on the T-block. Both the left-hand flat and the right-hand inclined surfaces should be hardened and polished, since they are the parts most subject to friction and wear. A clearance of $\frac{1}{16}$ inch should be provided between the lower face of the sleeve and the top surface of the T-block, as indicated.

The upper end of the cam-sleeve, which projects beyond the top face of the fixture lug, is provided with a fine-pitch external thread to accommodate the circular ring-nut. The periphery of the ring-nut is knurled to facilitate rotating it by hand. A standard hexagonal lock-nut is screwed on the upper threaded end of the clamping bolt.

In the illustration, the fixture and parts of the clamp are shown in their correct relative positions when the fixture has been properly located and clamped to the machine table. The cam-sleeve has been moved downward by simply tightening the lock-nut. This movement causes the inclined flat on the right-hand side of the sleeve to contact the positioning ledge on the T-block, thus pressing the fixture toward the left until it is stopped by the flat on the left-hand edge of the sleeve coming into contact with the side of the T-slot in the machine table. When tightening the lock-nut, the ring-nut should be backed off slightly to clear the top surface of the fixture lug and allow the sleeve to pass through the hole in the lug.

When the fixture has been thus aligned, the ring-nut is tightened — by hand pressure only — and the lock-nut is then given a final, partial turn to insure rigid clamping and positive alignment of the fixture with relation to one side of the T-slot. The ring-nut prevents the cam-sleeve from being pressed too forcibly against the positioning ledge on the T-block.

Jig for Drilling and Counterboring Unevenly Spaced Holes. — Frequently a set of holes has to be drilled and counterbored in a part with uneven spacing between the holes, which may be at different angles, and with odd spacing of the counterbores. This problem generally requires complicated tooling, and may slow up machining operations. To minimize these difficulties, equipment consisting essentially of two jigs as shown in Fig. 6 can be used.

In operation, the wedge-shaped work is first placed in jig No. 1, and drilled and reamed through bushing liner B on a drill press. Locating and clamping of the work is simple, and requires no description. The jig is then removed from the drill press and placed in jig No. 2 on a second drill press for drilling and counterboring the four holes C in the required locations.

Two pins D in jig No. 2 contact template E, which is doweled and screwed to the cast-iron fixture block *F*. A top plate *G* holds the principal liner for slip bushings. A bridge *H* is provided for lock-screw *J*. Jig No. 1 is brought into position for counterboring by sliding it along template *E*, so that index-pin *L*, passing through two axially aligned bushings *K*, enters the four bushings *M* in consecutive order.

Pins *D*, in contact with the template, together with the index-pin, provide three locating points that place jig No. 1 at the exact angle required for drilling and position it correctly for counterboring to the specified depth. When the index-pin is in position,

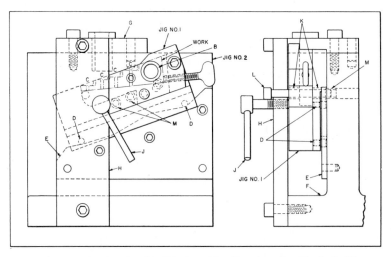

Fig. 6.   Two Jigs Used in Combination with a Template Simplify the Drilling and Counterboring of Unevenly Spaced Holes.

lock-screw *J* is applied, after which the work is drilled and counterbored. To perform this operation at the next position, the screw is unlocked and the index-pin is moved from one bushing *M* to the next one.

Adjustable Bushing Plate for Casting Variations. — The jig in Fig. 7 is employed for drilling and tapping four radial holes in the periphery of rotary valve-seats for air-brakes. To compensate for variations in the diameter of the castings to be machined, it is provided with an adjustable bushing plate. The inner radius of the plate is the same as that specified for the periphery of the rough-cast valve-seat. Since the plate can be adjusted radially, over-size as well as under-size castings can be correctly positioned to maintain the required spacing between the holes to be drilled.

The jig contains a vertical locating plate, in the bore of which the centrally cast hub on the work-piece is a sliding fit. A pin driven into this plate enters a hole in the casting to locate the work radially. Another positioning pin in the locating plate enters a cored hole in the casting, thus preventing the work from being placed on the jig in the wrong position.

The adjustable bushing plate slides in a groove in the locating plate. It is held to the locating plate by means of a socket-head cap-

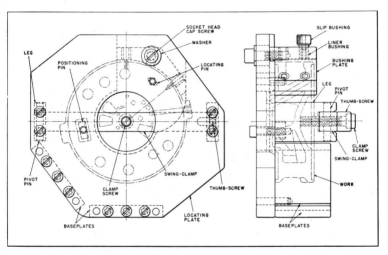

Fig. 7. Jig Used for Drilling and Tapping Four Radial Holes in the Periphery of Rotary Valve-Seats. An Adjustable Bushing Plate Compensates for Variations in the Diameter of the Cast Work-Piece.

screw and washer. A slot in the bushing plate allows it to be moved into contact with the periphery of the casting, in which position it is locked by tightening the screw. Liner bushings are pressed into holes in the bushing plate, and slip bushings of the correct sizes are provided for guiding the drills.

Two diametrically opposed legs are secured near the edges of the locating plate. A pivot-pin, driven through one of the legs, serves as the fulcrum for a hinged swing-clamp. When the casting has been located in the jig, the swing-clamp is fastened in place by means of a thumb-screw that is provided in the end of the other leg. A screw in the center of the swing-clamp is then turned until the work is secured tightly against the locating plate. Two base-plates, on each of which the jig rests while two of the four holes are being drilled and tapped, are screwed and doweled to the locating plate, diametrically opposite the bushings.

Toggle-Action Drill Jig to Clamp Casting at Four Points. — The location of drilled hold-down bolt holes through the steam cylinder heads for duplex piston pumps was often inaccurate when flat bushing plates of the same shape of the casting were used as jigs. These bushing plates were equipped with vertical pads around their peripheries to form nests for the castings. However, due to variations in the size of the castings, many of the work-pieces would be a loose fit in the jigs, thus resulting in inaccurate location of the drilled holes. To overcome this difficulty, the drill jig seen in Fig. 8 was designed to accurately clamp the work at four points by means of a single toggle action.

The two clamping arms A are slidably mounted on bushing plate B by means of studs C, the central portions of these studs passing through large holes in the arms to permit their free movement. Pins D are a loose fit in the centrally located projections on the clamping arms, and their lower, enlarged diameter ends are provided with flats to fit slots milled in the bushing plate. This permits the arms to pivot about these pins and to slide along the slots when operating handle E is rotated.

Cam F, which is rotated by handle E about stud G, is connected to clamping arms A by links H. These links can pivot about the loose-fitting studs J joining them to the clamping arms and cam. A spring-loaded latch K holds the cam, levers, and arms in the work-clamping position shown, or in the loading position when the cam is rotated counter-clockwise.

As the cam is rotated counter-clockwise, latch K will be rotated clockwise and links H will become aligned with each other. This forces clamping arms A outward, away from each other, so that the jig can be placed over work-piece X. The cam is then turned clockwise to the position shown, and arms A are pulled together firmly to clamp the work for drilling. Ten holes $\frac{3}{4}$ inch in diameter, are drilled through the cylinder head castings in this operation.

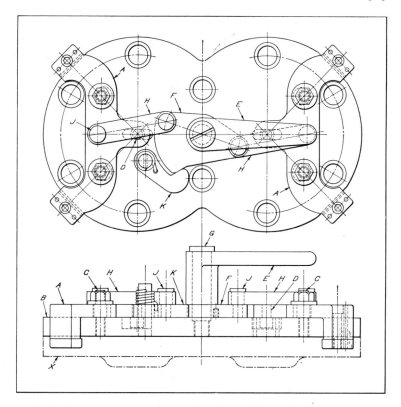

Fig. 8. Work-piece (X), which is a Cast Steam Cylinder Head for a Duplex Piston Pump, is Rigidly Clamped at Four Points in this Toggle Action Drill Jig.

Work-Holding Fixtures for Special Lathe Operations. —

For lathe operations where conventional work-holding means cannot be employed, special fixtures are often employed. Generally, these fixtures, after having been removed from the lathe, must be rechucked and checked for concentricity when they are replaced. This is a time-consuming operation, subject to inaccuracies, and the fixtures may be distorted from the chucking.

These disadvantages are eliminated by using an arbor such as the one illustrated in Fig. 9 to support the fixtures. With this arbor, when it is desired to replace a fixture in the lathe, it is merely reassembled on the arbor, which is provided with a holding taper to match one in the fixture. The assembly can then be inserted in the lathe headstock with the assurance that it will run concentrically.

A No. 4 Morse taper shank is shown on the arbor in Fig. 9, but this, of course, may be made to suit any lathe or other machine being used. The fixtures can be made without special tools. For example, a 1-inch standard pipe reamer is employed for finishing the tapered hole (¾ inch taper per foot), because this reamer is easily obtained from supply houses and is much cheaper than those made especially for the job. The taper obtained provides the self-holding properties required. A pin in the flange of the arbor supplies the driving force for the jig and prevents slipping.

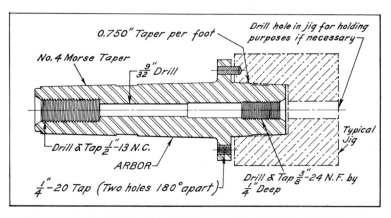

Fig. 9. Arbor for Holding Special Fixtures in Lathes. With this Arbor, a Fixture Can Be Removed from a Lathe and Replaced So That it Will Run Concentrically without Being Checked.

In addition to the holding taper, other methods may be employed for holding the fixture on the arbor. For example, a socket-head cap-screw can be inserted in the Morse taper end of the arbor so that the bottom of the head of the screw rests against the shoulder at the end of the ½–13 tapped hole in the arbor. With the fixture tapped to suit, the screw can be used as a draw-bolt. Another method is to insert a screw through the hole in the fixture to engage the ⅜–24 tapped hole in the arbor.

It will be noted that the tapped hole in the Morse taper end of the arbor can be used for engagement with a draw-bar to secure the arbor in the lathe. Tapped holes are provided in the flange for jack-screws that may be employed to remove the fixture from the arbor. With ingenuity, many different fixtures and arbor arrangements can be devised and applied to speed up short-run production and to facilitate special lathe operations.

Chucks for Holding Work-Pieces by Threaded Portions. — It is sometimes desirable to chuck a work-piece on a threaded portion of the part. If such a work-piece has a hexagonal or some other flat-sided surface, it can easily be unscrewed with a wrench at the conclusion of the operation. A wrench is generally necessary to break the seal formed between the work and the chuck face by the pressure of the cutting tools. If the part to be machined is

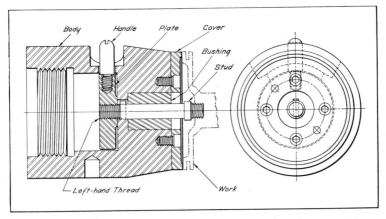

Fig. 10. Seal Formed Between the Work and Cover by the Pressure of the Cutting Tools is Broken by Moving the Handle on This Special Chuck.

round, with no flat surfaces, or if the surfaces of the work-piece should not be marked or damaged, the chuck must be designed so that this seal can be broken without using a wrench.

The chuck illustrated in Fig. 10 is used for holding a symmetrical-shaped piston by means of an internal thread while machining the opposite end of the part. The chuck seen in Fig. 11 is employed for holding a bushing by means of an external thread while finish-boring the work. An entirely different approach is necessary in designing chucks to hold work-pieces by external threads than that required for chucking on internal threads.

The male chuck, Fig. 10, consists of a body which is internally threaded to fit the spindle nose of a screw machine. A stud is threaded on one end to fit the work-piece, and has a left-hand thread on the opposite end to fit a plate. The stud is a slip fit in a hardened bushing, which is pressed into the chuck body, and is also keyed to the body by means of a pin which slides in a keyway in the body.

For additional accuracy in locating the work, a hardened cover, which is screwed and doweled to the chuck body, is machined to fit the bead on the face of the piston. A handle, screwed into the plate, can be moved through an angle of 60 degrees in a clearance slot provided for it in the chuck body. The handle is pushed against

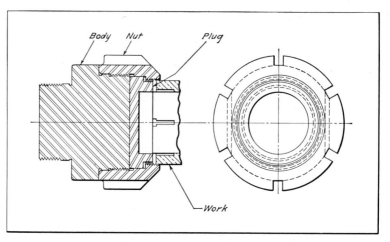

Fig. 11.   When the Work-piece has been Bored, the Nut is Rotated Slightly to Break the Seal between the Work and Chuck Face Produced by the Cutting Pressure.

one side of the clearance slot before a piece is screwed on the chuck. After the machining operation is finished, the handle is moved to the opposite side of the slot. This rotates the plate on the stud, thereby breaking the seal between the piston and the cover. A hole drilled radially in the periphery of the chuck body provides a means for mounting the chuck and removing it from the spindle nose of the machine with a spanner wrench.

The female chuck, Fig. 11, consists of a body which is threaded to fit a master chuck adapter. A nut, screwed on the chuck body, is internally threaded to fit the work. The outside of the nut is slotted to permit using a spanner wrench. The loose plug is made a slip fit in the nut, and rests against the face of the body. A recess is provided in the center of the plug to clear the boring tool.

In chucking, the work is screwed against this plug. After the work-piece has been machined, a slight turn of the nut will break the seal formed between the work and the plug. Flats are provided on the chuck body for mounting and removing the chuck from the adapter.

As can be readily seen, these chucks can be designed to fit a large variety of work-pieces and can be used on many different types of machines. They are economical to make, and yet provide a quick and accurate way to hold work during machining.

Vise with Hydraulic Jaw for Clamping Irregular-Shaped Castings. — Multiple clamping of various sizes of irregular-shaped castings can be simplified by means of a vise equipped with a hydraulic jaw, as shown in Fig. 12. With this arrangement, a uniform pressure is exerted on all of the castings, regardless of variations in dimensions or irregularities in the surface such as are produced by part numbers or names cast on the work. In the set-up shown, six lever castings A are clamped simultaneously for machining both sides and the top with the straddle milling cutters B.

Hydraulic vise jaw C is drilled to provide oil reservoirs D, two rows of six pistons E fitting into the reservoirs. The oil reservoirs are sealed by means of pipe plugs F, and the connecting oil passage G is sealed by welding plug H to the jaw after drilling. Snug fitting rubber washers J are placed in the groove of each piston to prevent the leakage of oil. Plate K, machined to fit the tapered sides of the castings, is screwed to the stationary vise jaw L.

In preparing the hydraulic vise jaw for operation, the reservoirs are filled with oil to within ¾ inch of the face of the jaw. The pistons are then carefully inserted in the jaw, and the assembly is clamped against some parallel surface to align the tops of all pistons. While clamped, one of the pipe plugs is loosened to permit air and excess oil to "bleed" from the system. This plug is then secured tightly, the assembly is unclamped, and the hydraulic vise jaw is ready for service.

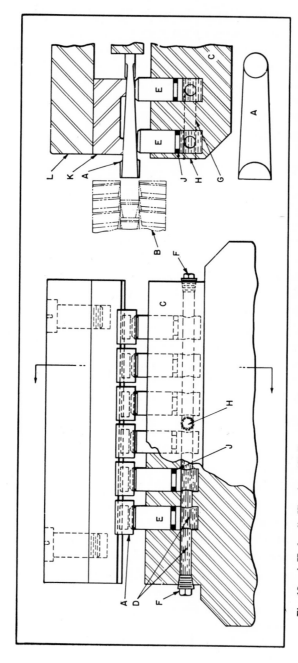

Fig. 12.   A Hydraulic Vise-jaw (C) Permits Uniform Pressure to be Exerted on all Castings (A), Regardless of Variations in Dimensions or Irregularities in the Surface.

Jig Designed for Rapid Drilling. — The drill jig shown in Fig. 13 is a good example of the simplicity of design that can be attained by using the so-called "bayonet lock" type of clamp. A clamp of this type also keeps the loading time down to the minimum required for economical production.

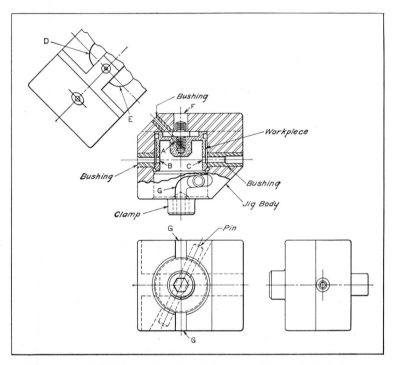

Fig. 13. Jig with Quick-acting Bayonet Clamp for Drilling Holes in Three Sides of a Sensitive Air-valve Part. Design is Simplified and Loading Time Kept to a Minimum by the Use of This Type Clamp.

The jig is composed of only six pieces — the body, clamp, pin, and three bushings. The side of the body opposite the drill bushing for the angular hole in the work-piece is machined at an angle of 90 degrees to the axis of the bushing hole to serve as a base while drilling the hole. This arrangement eliminates the necessity for providing a separate angle-block.

The jig is designed for drilling the angular hole at *A* and the two holes *B* and *C* at opposite sides of the work. The work-piece comprises a sub-assembly of a high-pressure valve and stud for a sensitive air control valve. This valve is part of a modern air brake.

The body of the jig is bored to a slip fit for the work-piece. The opposite end of the jig is flatted on both sides of the center to meet the bottom of this bore. This provides openings at D and E for the escape of chips. A clearance hole F is also drilled through this end to clear the stud in the work-piece.

The three drill bushings are pressed into holes that are accurately positioned in the jig body. The clamp is a slip fit for the hole in the body, which is made larger than the locating bore for the work, so that the jig will be easier to load. The top of the hole in the body and the end of the clamp are chamfered to facilitate inserting the clamp.

Bayonet slots G on the sides of the body are made a slip fit for the pin pressed into the clamp. These slots have a radius bend and a lateral section which permit the pin to be given a clockwise turn. These lateral ends of the slots are machined at an angle of about 95 degrees to form cam surfaces which give the bayonet lock its clamping action against the work-piece. The lateral slot on one side extends in the opposite direction from the one on the other side. The work should be clamped when the pin is at about the middle of the lateral part of the slots.

The length and diameter of the hub on the end of the clamp are such that the hub clears the plane of the flat on the side of the body on which the jig rests when drilling the angular hole. This flat provides sufficient surface beyond the center line of the bushings to premit drilling one side hole and the angular hole without causing the jig to tip. Because it is necessary to have a small hub at the end of the clamp, a hexagon socket is machined in it to fit an Allen wrench, so that the clamp can be easily tightened or loosened.

Drill Chuck Adapted as Work-Holding Device. — A conventional drill chuck may be adapted to hold small work-pieces that might otherwise be distorted if clamped directly in a vise. An example in which a drill chuck is employed for just such a purpose may be seen in Fig. 14. The chuck is mounted on a movable joint so that it can be swung through an arc of 180 degrees, or 90 degrees to each side of the perpendicular axis, as shown.

Machined on the upper end of steel shackle *A* is a tapered shaft that fits within the mounting hole in drill chuck *B*. The fork at the opposite end of the shackle slips over plug *C*. A set-screw *D*, fitting within an annular groove at the lower end of the plug, secures it in a hole drilled through T-shaped block *E*. With this arrangement, the plug and chuck can be revolved to any desired position in a horizontal plane by merely loosening the set-screw.

The shackle pivots around headed pin *F* and may be locked by means of a standard hexagon nut. Stop-pin *G* passes through the

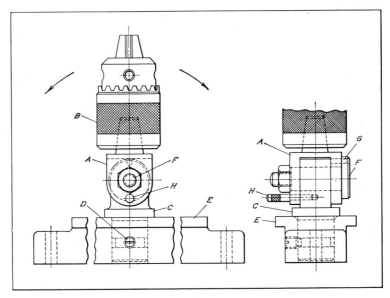

Fig. 14. Work-holding Device, Constructed Around an Ordinary Drill Chuck, May Be Clamped in a Vise or Mounted on a Machine Table.

head of pin *F* and into one cheek of the shackle, thus preventing any relative movement between the two parts. The shackle and chuck are accurately positioned in a perpendicular setting by means of a hardened steel locating pin *H*. It is situated in a hole drilled and reamed through the front cheek of the shackle and engages an in-line hole in the adjacent side of the plug *C*. The head of the pin is knurled for ease of gripping.

The T-shaped block *E* may be gripped between vise jaws, the overhanging ledges of the block resting on the top surface of the

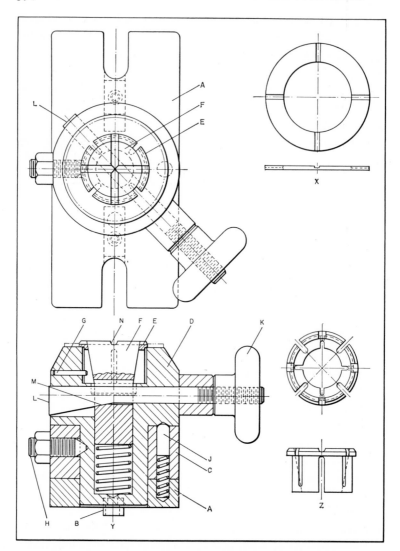

Fig. 15.   Indexing Type Milling Fixture Firmly Holds the Thrust Washer Shown at X without Distorting it.   Loading and Unloading are Rapid.

jaws. It may also be clamped to a machine table by means of strap clamps on the stepped-down ends, or by hold-down bolts passing through holes provided for that purpose in the ends of the block as shown in the figure.

Indexing Fixture for Milling Thrust Type Washers. — A bronze thrust washer, used extensively in the production of transmissions for farm tractors, is shown at X in Fig. 15. Because of the thin cross-section of the washer, clamping is difficult if springing is to be avoided and ample clearance for the cutter is to be provided when milling the oil-grooves. The indexing fixture seen at Y surmounts these obstacles.

Base A of the fixture is slotted at both ends for clamping to the machine table. Beneath the base, and in line with the slots, are two keys B, their purpose being to align the base with the table. To the top surface of the base is welded a vertical cylindrical member C. This upright member is ground on its upper face and reamed to a slip fit with adapter D.

The adapter is counterbored and reamed to receive collet jaws E and spring-loaded draw-pin F. A detailed drawing of the collet jaws may be seen at Z. Dowel-pin G prevents the jaws from turning.

A cone-point set-screw H is threaded through the wall of cylinder C. The point of the screw extends into a groove that is machined around the adapter shank for a distance equal to a 90-degree arc. A lock-nut retains the screw in position. The rounded end of spring-loaded index-pin J, which is housed within the upright cylindrical member, clicks into either of two notches located in the under side of the adapter flange. These notches are located 90 degrees apart and serve as the indexing points for the adapter assembly.

In use, the fixture is first bolted to the machine table, following which a thrust washer is slipped over the collet jaws. Approximately one-half turn of knob K will pull draw-stud L a distance sufficient to force draw-pin F in a downward direction against a spring. This is accomplished through the action of the mating tapers at M.

The first pass may then be made, using grooves N as a guide for the cutter. When this initial cut is completed, the adapter is indexed 90 degrees, or until index-pin J clicks into the second notch in the adapter flange. A second pass may now be made to complete the work-piece.

Unloading the fixture is extremely simple. By backing off knob *K,* draw-stud *L* will move to the left, relieving the pressure on draw-pin *F.* When this happens, the spring beneath the draw-pin will force it up, thereby allowing the collet jaws to spring together to their original position. The thrust washer may then be lifted from the fixture.

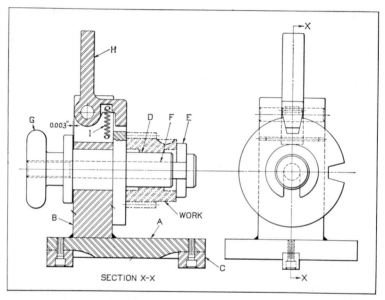

Fig. 16. Low-cost Milling Fixture Designed for Machining Two Woodruff keyways, 90 Degrees Apart, in Transmission Sliding Gears.

Quick-Acting Milling Fixture. — The milling fixture illustrated in Fig. 16 is an example of low-cost construction; yet it is fast acting and will turn out accurate interchangeable pieces. In addition, it is rigid and positive. The work to be milled is a transmission sliding gear used in self-propelled harvesting machinery. It is made of SAE 1020 steel, and two Woodruff keyslots are to be milled in it, 90 degrees apart.

Base *A* and upright *B* are welded together. Two slots are milled in base *A* to receive keys *C,* which align the fixture on the milling machine table. Arbor *D* is made in one piece and serves as an indexing plate as well as the work locator. In operation, a *C-*

washer E is slipped between the work and the draw-bolt F. By tightening hand-knob G, the work is clamped securely in place, but this does not prevent it from rotating. A slot is milled through upright B for a slip fit with an indexing handle H, which is pinned in place and held in position by a tension spring I. Arbor D has two notches 90 degrees apart in it for locating handle H when milling either keyway. The back end of arbor D is made about 0.003 inch longer than the thickness of upright B. This allows the work to revolve freely when handle H is pushed back. Arbor D and handle H are hardened to prevent wear.

It can readily be seen that while the fixture is not complicated in design, it has the advantages of a high-production tool at minimum cost.

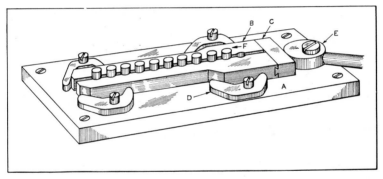

Fig. 17. Flexible Device for Securely Holding Small Parts of Uniform Shape for Milling, Grinding, Forming, or Slotting Operations.

Fixture for Holding Small Parts in Series. — Small parts of uniform size and cross-section can be held in series by the fixture illustrated in Fig. 17 for surface-grinding the ends, either square or obliquely, or for straddle-milling, slotting, or forming the ends. The base A may be fastened to a secondary base so that the fixture can be easily attached to the machine table. The work-holding members of the fixture consist of two pieces B, right- and left-hand, and a piece C, which is dovetailed to match a corresponding dovetail in parts B.

Four swinging clamp members D are mounted on body A and are arranged so that one end of each bears against a tapered portion of pieces *B*. As a result, when the work-holding unit is forced in the direction indicated by arrow *F* through the action of the eccentric clamp *E*, clamps *D* will pivot on their bearing pins and exert a force against the sides of pieces *B*, moving them slightly on the dovetail on part *C* and clamping them tightly on the work-pieces. When the clamp is first being lined up for holding a given type of work, clamp *E* is tightened very slightly. An attempt is then made to pull the work-pieces at the two extreme ends from the holder with the fingers. This is done to permit adjusting the clamping members *D* so that the two pairs will have equal clamping force.

If it is easier to pull the work-piece from one end than from the other, the clamping pressure is not equal. Then one of the two clamping members *D* at the tight end of the holder is removed, and just a small amount is ground from one of its pressure areas, after which it is replaced and another try is made. By this means, repeating the test process until it takes a sharp tug with the fingers to remove either of the end pieces when *E* is lightly set, the device is correctly adjusted, assuming the work-pieces to be uniform in size.

In most cases, operations performed on work held in a fixture of the type described will include only cuts so light that there will be little danger of the assembly being lifted from base *A* during machining. Should such trouble be experienced, however, it is only necessary to mill vees in the edges of pieces *B* where the clamping members *D* take their bearing, and grind the engaging ends of members *D* for a good line bearing in the vees.

In the design shown, the two pieces *B* were originally one, the holes being drilled first and the piece cut in two afterward. Because of the way parts *B* are mounted on piece *C*, it is possible to separate them for milling any desired shape of work seats in these parts. Thus when the cross-section of the work is not symmetrical, a work seat of a certain shape can be milled in one member *B*, and a different shaped work seat in the opposite member. If required, it is also possible to have two or more sets of pieces *B* for different types of work-pieces, which can be used with the same retainer piece *C* and the same base *A*.

A device such as described can be made without any recesses for work-pieces and used for holding a number of strips of material in a gang for surface grinding or milling their edges, machining first one edge and then the other. Other variations in the design are also possible. For example, both pieces B can be drilled with two pairs of registering holes in their inner edges to receive compression springs, so that the clamping action will take place against the resistance of these springs. The device will then automatically open, permitting the work to be easily unloaded and new parts inserted when the clamping pressure has been removed.

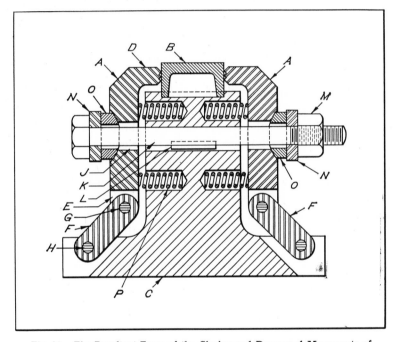

Fig. 18. The Resultant Force of the Closing and Downward Movements of the Jaws of This Vise-Type Fixture acts to Automatically Bed the Work.

Fixture Jaws Combining Downward Pull with Closing Action. — The design of a vise type fixture that assures rapid, proper, and automatic bedding of work-pieces is illustrated in Fig. 18. This feature is inherent in the movement of the two jaws A. As they close against the side of the work-piece B, which is nested in the top of the fixture body C, they also exert a slight downward movement.

The upper section of each jaw has a serrated lip D in contact with the work-piece, and the lower section is slotted centrally at E to receive the end of a steel link F, the two members being hinged together by a pin G. The body of the fixture is T-shaped at its base, which, like the lower section of the jaws, is slotted and receives the lower ends of the links. Pins H hinge the links to the base.

The central section of each jaw has a vertical slot accommodating the bolt K. This bolt is a close fit in a hole running through the fixture. A key L in the bolt, engaging a keyway in the hole, prevents the bolt from turning when the nut M is tightened or loosened. Between the bolt head and the nut are flat washers N and bushings O. These bushings are a free fit on the bolt, and also have a convex face which bears in a concave area milled into the outer sides of the jaws.

In the closing action of the fixture, as the bolt is drawn up by tightening the nut, the jaws move centrally. At the same time, the two links fulcrum on the pins H and cause the jaws and bushings to slide downward slightly as a unit. The elongated slots in the jaws and the free fit of the bushings on the bolt permit this downward movement to be made, since the bolt itself remains in a fixed horizontal plane by reason of its fit in the hole through the fixture body.

The closing action is carried out against the resistance of four compression springs P contained in holes in the fixture body. Thus, when the nut is loosened to open the fixture, the jaws will automatically move outward.

INDEX